The Best of
COUNTRY COOKING
2007

Editor: Michelle Bretl
Art Directors: Gretchen Trautman, Kathy Crawford
Vice President, Executive Editor/Books: Heidi Reuter Lloyd
Senior Editor/Books: Mark Hagen
Associate Editor: Jean Steiner
Layout Designers: Nancy Novak, Julie Stone, Emma Acevedo
Proofreader: Linne Bruskewitz
Editorial Assistant: Barb Czysz

Food Director: Diane Werner RD
Test Kitchen Manager: Karen Scales
Recipe Editors: Sue A. Jurack (Senior), Mary King, Christine Rukavena
Recipe Asset System Manager: Coleen Martin

Photographers: Rob Hagen (Senior), Dan Roberts, Jim Wieland, Lori Foy
Senior Set Stylist: Jennifer Bradley Vent
Food Stylists: Sarah Thompson (Senior), Joylyn Trickel (Senior), Kate Baumann (Assistant)
Photo Studio Coordinator: Suzanne Kern

Creative Director: Ardyth Cope
Senior Vice President, Editor in Chief: Catherine Cassidy
President: Barbara Newton
Founder: Roy Reiman

For additional copies of this book or information on other books, write *Taste of Home Books*, P.O. Box 992, Greendale WI 53129, call toll-free 1-800/344-2560 to order with a credit card or visit our Web site at *www.reimanpub.com*.

PICTURED ABOVE AND ON FRONT COVER. From top: Fluted Lemon Cake (p. 111), Italian Tossed Salad (p. 22) and Mostaccioli Casserole (p. 43).

Dig Right into 345 Home-Cooked Favorites

IN THE COUNTRY, the cooking is from-scratch, prepared with wholesome ingredients and served up with lots of love. In short, it's unbeatable...and this can't-miss cookbook gives you the best of the best!

The 10th in our popular series, *The Best of Country Cooking 2007* dishes up a whopping 345 delicious, home-style recipes for you and your family. That includes hundreds of specialties featured in recent issues of our rural-life and nostalgia magazines—*Country Woman, Country, Country EXTRA, Reminisce and Reminisce EXTRA.*

Where did all of these down-home recipes come from? First, cooks from across the countryside shared the favorite recipes they fix time and again for their own families.

Next, the experienced home economists in our Test Kitchen prepared, tasted and approved every dish. You can rest assured that each one is easy to fix and a proven winner with folks just like you.

Starting out this chock-full cookbook, the "Snacks & Beverages" chapter boasts 17 scrumptious appetizers and refreshing thirst-quenchers. Whether you're hosting dinner guests or tiding over hungry children after school, you'll find something here to satisfy.

When casual comfort food is the order of the day, turn to "Soups, Salads & Sandwiches." It offers 63 heartwarming recipes, including a special section of savory main-course salads sure to please even the biggest appetites.

From flavor-packed beef entrees to mouth-watering meatless choices, 61 specialties await you in our "Main Dishes" chapter. Your family will applaud dinners such as Linda Frisk's Taco Supper in a Bowl (p. 67), Pizza Casserole (p. 55) from Judie Heiderscheit and Individual Chicken Potpies (p. 48) shared by Vickie Wicks. See pages 62 and 63 for a sunny selection of breakfast and brunch options, too.

Need to round out your meal? Any of our 33 "Side Dishes & Condiments" will do it deliciously. You'll come to rely on them for countless occasions year-round—Christmas dinner,

weeknight suppers, special luncheons, etc.

It's impossible to resist golden baked goods fresh from the oven...and the 19 delights in "Breads & Rolls" are no exception! Lillian Davis shares New York State Apple Muffins (p. 89), moist and spicy bites that'll be snatched up before you know it. And Cherry Cream Cheese Coffee Cake (p. 95) from Linda Guiles will get any day off to a sensational start.

If your meal just isn't complete without something sweet, turn to the "Sweet Treats" chapter for a luscious lineup of 49 cakes, pies, cookies, bars, candy and other tempting goodies. Don't miss the yummy "Fun with Food" section on pages 118 and 119 for playful creations guaranteed to thrill kids of all ages.

That's not all! You'll discover more than a dozen complete menus and additional recipes in three special chapters:

Cooking for Two—A separate collection of entire meals and additional dishes (a total of 67 recipes) that are sized to feed two people without leaving lots of leftovers.

Meals in Minutes—Four full dinners (12 recipes in all) that are prepared and ready to eat in just 30 minutes or less.

Our Most Memorable Meals—Six complete menus featuring 24 unforgettable, long-time favorites from home cooks.

Want more? *The Best of Country Cooking 2007* offers handy kitchen hints and tips scattered throughout the book, from convenient recipe ideas to helpful how-to's.

As you page through *The Best of Country Cooking 2007*, watch for the blue ribbon symbol at right. It signifies a prize-winning recipe—a dish that earned high honors in a coast-to-coast cooking contest sponsored by one of our magazines.

Finally, throughout this colorful collection, you'll see "restricted diet" recipes marked with the check at right. These dishes use less fat, sugar or salt and include Nutrition Facts at the end of the recipe.

See why we call this cookbook "The Best?" So go ahead...savor a taste of the country!

CONTENTS

SATISFY *appetites before dinner, after school or anytime with the memorable munchies and thirst-quenchers in this chapter.*

EASY APPETIZER. Mango Salsa (p. 5).

Snacks & Beverages

MANGO SALSA
(Pictured at left)

Nancy Larkin, Maitland, Florida

I was raised in South Florida, where we enjoyed plenty of fresh tropical fruits. While this salsa is good with chips, I'll often serve it on seafood, too.

> 3 medium ripe mangoes, peeled, pitted and diced
> 1-1/2 cups diced seeded plum tomatoes
> 1 jar (6 ounces) mango *or* peach baby food
> 1 can (4 ounces) chopped green chilies
> 1/4 cup *each* diced green, sweet red and yellow peppers
> 2 tablespoons lime juice
> 3 garlic cloves, minced
> 4-1/2 teaspoons olive oil
> 4-1/2 teaspoons chopped fresh cilantro
> 1 tablespoon sugar
> 1-1/2 teaspoons grated lime peel
> 1/2 teaspoon salt
> 1/4 teaspoon pepper
> Tortilla chips

In a large bowl, combine the mangoes, tomatoes, baby food, chilies, peppers, lime juice, garlic, oil, cilantro, sugar, lime peel, salt and pepper. Cover and refrigerate for 4 hours or overnight. Serve with tortilla chips. **Yield:** 4 cups.

ROASTED PEPPER BEAN DIP

Jean Ecos, Hartland, Wisconsin

Cannellini beans give body to this festive snack without added fat. Try pairing the dip with your favorite fresh vegetables or wedges of pita bread.

☑ Uses less fat, sugar or salt. Includes Nutrition Facts and Diabetic Exchanges.

> 1 can (19 ounces) cannellini *or* white kidney beans, rinsed and drained
> 1 cup silken firm tofu
> 1/2 cup roasted sweet red peppers
> 1/3 cup minced fresh parsley
> 2 tablespoons lime juice

> 1/2 teaspoon garlic salt
> 1/2 teaspoon seasoned pepper
> 1/4 teaspoon salt

Place all ingredients in a food processor or blender; cover and process until smooth. Transfer dip to a bowl. Refrigerate until serving. **Yield:** 2-1/3 cups.

Nutrition Facts: 2 tablespoons dip equals 32 calories, trace fat (trace saturated fat), 0 cholesterol, 147 mg sodium, 5 g carbohydrate, 1 g fiber, 2 g protein. **Diabetic Exchange:** 1 vegetable.

THREE-FRUIT SLUSHIES

Patti Lamb, Addison, Michigan

Bananas, pineapple and orange flavors combine in this summery sensation. Wonderful on a warm day, it's a treat your gang will ask for time and again.

> 2 cups sugar
> 3 cups boiling water
> 1 can (12 ounces) frozen orange juice concentrate, thawed
> 7 medium firm bananas, sliced
> 1 can (20 ounces) crushed pineapple, undrained
> 1 bottle (20 ounces) lemon-lime soda, chilled

Dissolve the sugar in boiling water. Add the orange juice concentrate, bananas and pineapple; stir until combined.

Stir in the lemon-lime soda; pour into a large container or several small containers; freeze. Remove from the freezer about 1 hour before serving. **Yield:** 14 servings.

TOFU TIPS

Plan on making Roasted Pepper Bean Dip? You'll find tofu on supermarket shelves or in the refrigerated produce section. Silken firm tofu should be stored in an airtight container and used within 2 to 3 days after opening.

another use). Pipe or spoon the salmon mixture into the potatoes. Garnish with the fresh dill sprigs. **Yield:** 3 dozen.

Nutrition Facts: 2 stuffed potatoes equals 70 calories, 3 g fat (2 g saturated fat), 11 mg cholesterol, 261 mg sodium, 7 g carbohydrate, 1 g fiber, 4 g protein. **Diabetic Exchanges:** 1/2 starch, 1/2 lean meat.

HOT ARTICHOKE-SPINACH DIP

Michelle Krzmarzick, Redondo Beach, California

One taste of this incredibly delicious dip, and your guests will not stop eating it until it's gone. The savory blend of artichokes, spinach and Parmesan cheese is positively addictive!

  1 package (8 ounces) cream cheese, softened
1/2 cup grated Parmesan cheese
1/4 cup mayonnaise
  1 garlic clove, minced
  1 teaspoon dried basil
1/4 teaspoon garlic salt
1/4 teaspoon pepper
  1 can (14 ounces) water-packed artichoke hearts, rinsed, drained and chopped
1/2 cup frozen chopped spinach, thawed and squeezed dry
1/4 cup shredded part-skim mozzarella cheese
Assorted crackers

In a large mixing bowl, combine the cream cheese, Parmesan cheese, mayonnaise, garlic, basil, garlic salt and pepper; mix well. Stir in the artichokes and spinach. Transfer to a greased 9-in. pie plate. Sprinkle with mozzarella cheese.

Bake, uncovered, at 350° for 20-25 minutes or until bubbly and edges are lightly browned. Serve with crackers. **Yield:** 3 cups.

Editor's Note: Reduced-fat or fat-free mayonnaise is not recommended for this recipe.

SMOKED SALMON NEW POTATOES
(Pictured above)

You're bound to hear rave reviews when guests discover these baby stuffed potatoes from the Taste of Home Test Kitchen. If you're in a hurry, serve the cream cheese mixture in a bowl as a spread alongside whole wheat crackers.

☑ Uses less fat, sugar or salt. Includes Nutrition Facts and Diabetic Exchanges.

 36 small red potatoes (about 1-1/2 pounds)
  1 package (8 ounces) reduced-fat cream cheese, cubed
  2 packages (3 ounces *each*) smoked cooked salmon
  2 tablespoons chopped green onion
  2 teaspoons dill weed
  2 teaspoons lemon juice
1/8 teaspoon salt
1/8 teaspoon pepper
Fresh dill sprigs

Place the potatoes in a large saucepan and cover with water. Bring to a boil. Reduce heat; simmer, uncovered, for 20-22 minutes or until tender.

Meanwhile, in a food processor or blender, combine the cream cheese, salmon, onion, dill, lemon juice, salt and pepper. Cover and process until smooth; set aside.

Drain the potatoes and immediately place in ice water. Drain and pat dry with paper towels. Cut a thin slice off the bottom of each potato to allow it to sit flat. With a melon baller, scoop out a small amount of potato (discard or save for

CREAMY STRAWBERRY PUNCH

Marcia Hostetter, Canton, New York

I grew up on a dairy farm, and we were always on the lookout for new ways to use milk. This fun and refreshing punch is well received every time.

  4 cups cold milk
  1 pint strawberry ice cream, softened
  1 can (6 ounces) frozen lemonade concentrate, thawed
  4 cups ginger ale, chilled

In a large pitcher or punch bowl, combine the milk, ice cream and lemonade concentrate until smooth. Stir in ginger ale; serve immediately. **Yield:** 12-14 servings.

BACON-WRAPPED STUFFED JALAPENOS
(Pictured below)

Therese Pollard, Hurst, Texas

Sunday is grill-out day for my husband, and these zesty peppers are some of his specialties. We usually feature them at our annual Daytona 500 party. They disappear from the table in a flash.

- 24 medium jalapeno peppers
- 1 pound uncooked chorizo *or* bulk spicy pork sausage
- 2 cups (8 ounces) shredded cheddar cheese
- 12 bacon strips, cut in half

Make a lengthwise cut in each jalapeno, about 1/8 in. deep; remove seeds. Combine the sausage and cheese; stuff into jalapenos. Wrap each with a piece of bacon; secure with toothpicks.

Prepare grill for indirect heat, using a drip pan. Place jalapenos over pan; grill, covered, over indirect medium heat for 17-20 minutes on each side or until a meat thermometer inserted into fill-ing reads 160°. Grill, covered, over direct heat 1-2 minutes longer or until bacon is crisp. **Yield:** 2 dozen.

Editor's Note: When cutting or seeding hot peppers, use rubber or plastic gloves to protect your hands. Avoid touching your face.

EGG PENGUINS
(Pictured above)

Darline Michaelis, New Auburn, Wisconsin

These cute little appetizers are so adorable, they're likely to steal the spotlight at your next wintertime gathering or kids' party. No one believes how easily these whimsical bites come together.

- 9 large ripe olives
- 6 hard-cooked eggs
- 12 small baby carrots

For the penguin heads, attach one olive to the top of each egg with a toothpick. For beaks, cut six carrots 1/2 in. from the pointed end; attach the flat side of a pointed piece to the center of each head with half a toothpick.

For the feet, make a lengthwise cut through the remaining carrots; place flat side down in pairs (trim carrots if necessary). Place a toothpick in each carrot; press an egg on top of each pair.

For flippers, cut the remaining olives length-wise into quarters; attach one olive quarter to each side of eggs with half a toothpick. Cover; refrigerate until serving. **Yield:** 6 penguins.

Swiss Walnut Cracker Snack
(Pictured below)

Geraldine Muth, Black River Falls, Wisconsin

This spread is simple to prepare and makes an excellent snack for holiday and family gatherings. It features "Dairy State" products and has a nice crunch from the walnuts.

> 1 package (8 ounces) cream cheese, softened
> 1-1/2 cups (6 ounces) shredded Swiss cheese
> 1/2 cup sour cream
> 2 tablespoons Dijon mustard
> 1/3 cup chopped walnuts
> 1/3 cup minced fresh parsley
> 1/4 cup chopped green onions

Crackers *and/or* bagel chips

In a mixing bowl, beat cream cheese until smooth. Add the Swiss cheese, sour cream and mustard; mix well. Stir in the walnuts, parsley and onions. Refrigerate for at least 1 hour before serving. Serve with crackers and/or bagel chips. **Yield:** 2 cups.

Pink Grapefruit Punch
(Pictured above)

Terry Taylor-Heskett, Goliad, Texas

Everyone who samples this slightly sweet punch asks for a second glass...and the recipe. It's great with breakfast or brunch, but we also like it all by itself as a thirst-quencher.

> 4 cups water, *divided*
> 2 tablespoons confectioners' sugar
> 2 cups pink grapefruit juice
> 1 can (12 ounces) frozen pink lemonade concentrate, thawed
> 3 tablespoons maraschino cherry juice

Orange *or* lemon slices and maraschino cherries, optional

Combine 1/4 cup water and sugar in a small microwave-safe bowl. Microwave on high for 30 seconds or until the sugar dissolves; cool.

In a large pitcher, combine the grapefruit juice, lemonade concentrate, maraschino cherry juice, sugar mixture and remaining water. Chill. Serve over ice. Garnish with the orange or lemon slices and maraschino cherries if desired. **Yield:** 8-10 servings (1-3/4 quarts).

Extra Special

Have some leftover Swiss Walnut Cracker Snack from a party? Spread the tasty cheese mixture on the bread of your sandwich the next day for a fast flavor boost.

Snacks & Beverages

CRAB PUFFS
(Pictured below)

Nadia Miheyev, Richmond Hill, New York

If you're looking for a scrumptious way to get a party started, bring out a plate of cheesy Crab Puffs. They bake up golden brown and taste wonderful right out of the oven. Try them in place of crackers when you're having soup.

- 1 cup plus 1 tablespoon water
- 1/2 cup butter
- 1 tablespoon ground mustard
- 1 teaspoon salt
- 1 teaspoon ground cumin
- 1/8 teaspoon hot pepper sauce
- 1 cup all-purpose flour
- 4 eggs
- 2 cups (8 ounces) shredded Swiss cheese
- 1 can (6 ounces) crabmeat, drained, flaked and cartilage removed

In a large saucepan, bring the water, butter, mustard, salt, cumin and hot pepper sauce to a boil. Add flour all at once and stir until a smooth ball forms. Remove from the heat; let stand for 5 minutes.

Add eggs, one at a time, beating well after each addition. Continue beating until smooth and shiny. Stir in the cheese and crab.

Drop by rounded teaspoonfuls 2 in. apart onto greased baking sheets. Bake at 400° for 23-26 minutes or until golden brown. Remove to wire racks. Serve warm. **Yield:** about 4 dozen.

HEARTY HAM BALLS
(Pictured above)

Eulala Schwabac, Stanberry, Missouri

A very special lady shared this recipe with me. She asked me to make the ham balls when I cooked at her nursing home. Everyone there enjoyed them—and my family does, too.

- 2 pounds ground fully cooked ham
- 1 pound ground beef
- 1 pound ground pork
- 2 cups graham cracker crumbs
- 2 eggs, beaten
- 2/3 cup milk
- 1 can (10-3/4 ounces) condensed tomato soup, undiluted
- 1/2 cup packed brown sugar
- 2 to 4 tablespoons honey
- 2 tablespoons white vinegar
- 1 to 2 tablespoons ground mustard

In a large bowl, combine the ham, beef, pork, cracker crumbs, eggs and milk; mix well. Shape into 18 balls. Place in two greased 13-in. x 9-in. x 2-in. baking dishes.

Combine the remaining ingredients; pour over ham balls. Bake, uncovered, at 350° for 45-50 minutes or until browned, basting several times. **Yield:** 4 dozen.

 ## CHOCOLATE FRUIT DIP
(Pictured at right)

Sarah Maury Swan, Granite, Maryland

I've been told I'm not allowed to come to neighborhood parties unless I bring this dip! I usually serve it with strawberries and pineapple, but it's also good with other fruit, such as apples and melon.

> 1 package (8 ounces) cream cheese, softened
> 1/3 cup sugar
> 1/3 cup baking cocoa
> 1 teaspoon vanilla extract
> 2 cups whipped topping

Assorted fruit for dipping

In a mixing bowl, beat the cream cheese and sugar until smooth. Add cocoa and vanilla; mix well. Beat in whipped topping until smooth. Serve with fruit. **Yield:** 2 cups.

 ## ASPARAGUS APPETEASER
(Pictured below)

Shirley Bartels, Peshtigo, Wisconsin

You need only a handful of ingredients to whip up these change-of-pace snacks. Fresh from the oven, the roll-ups are surefire people-pleasers.

> 12 thin slices white bread
> 8 bacon strips, cooked and crumbled
> 2 packages (3 ounces *each*) cream cheese, softened
> 12 asparagus spears, cooked

Melted butter

Trim crusts from bread; roll with rolling pin to flatten slightly. Combine bacon bits and cream cheese; spread mixture on one side of each bread slice. Lay a cold, cooked asparagus spear on each slice of bread and roll up. Place on baking sheet, seam side down. Brush roll-ups with melted butter. Broil 4 in. from the heat for 2-3 minutes or until lightly browned. **Yield:** 12 appetizers.

10-MINUTE ZESTY SALSA

Kim Morin, Lake George, Colorado

The view from our mountain home includes Pike's Peak, so we frequently relax on our wraparound porch. When friends and family visit, we often savor this zippy salsa with chips while we feast on the natural beauty all around us.

> 1 can (10 ounces) diced tomatoes and green chilies, undrained
> 1 tablespoon seeded chopped jalapeno pepper
> 1 tablespoon chopped red onion
> 1 tablespoon minced fresh cilantro
> 1 garlic clove, minced
> 1 tablespoon olive oil

Dash salt
Dash pepper
Tortilla chips

In a small bowl, combine the tomatoes, jalapeno, onion, cilantro, garlic, oil, salt and pepper. Refrigerate until serving. Serve with tortilla chips. **Yield:** 1-1/2 cups.

Editor's Note: When cutting or seeding hot peppers, use rubber or plastic gloves to protect your hands. Avoid touching your face.

━━━━━━━━━━━━

LAYERED CHEESE SPREAD
(Pictured below)

Delores Boekelheidi, Northville, South Dakota

I tried this creamy snack at bridge club and thought it was so attractive, not to mention delicious! It's nice to have a different way to serve a cheese spread.

- 2 cups (8 ounces) shredded cheddar cheese
- 1/2 cup sour cream
- 1/4 cup chopped green pepper
- 1/8 teaspoon hot pepper sauce
- 2 tablespoons minced fresh parsley
- 2 cups ground fully cooked ham
- 1 can (8 ounces) crushed pineapple, drained
- 1 package (3 ounces) cream cheese, softened
- 1 teaspoon ground ginger

Assorted crackers

Line a 9-in. x 5-in. x 3-in. loaf pan with plastic wrap. In a bowl, combine the cheddar cheese, sour cream, green pepper and hot pepper sauce. Spread

into prepared pan; sprinkle with parsley. Refrigerate for 2 hours.

In a bowl, combine the ham, pineapple, cream cheese and ginger. Spread over cheese layer in pan. Refrigerate for 2 hours. Invert onto a serving platter; serve with crackers. **Yield:** 3-1/2 cups.

━━━━━━━━━━━━

CREAMY SHRIMP SPREAD

Gerrene Musser, Ephrata, Pennsylvania

This appetizer is easy to make but so good. People always come back for more! The spread goes well with crackers or fresh vegetables, too, and it can be enjoyed at any type of party—casual or formal.

- 1 package (8 ounces) cream cheese, softened
- 2 tablespoons ketchup
- 1 tablespoon mayonnaise
- 2 teaspoons dried minced onion
- 2 teaspoons prepared mustard

Dash garlic salt
- 1 can (4-1/4 ounces) tiny shrimp, rinsed and drained

French bread baguette, sliced

In a small mixing bowl, combine the cream cheese, ketchup, mayonnaise, onion, mustard and garlic salt. Stir in the shrimp. Cover and refrigerate for at least 1 hour. Serve with baguette slices. **Yield:** 1-3/4 cups.

SIT DOWN to a steaming bowl of soup, chock-full salad or hearty sandwich and enjoy a memorable meal.

FAMILY FAVORITES. Bacon 'n' Egg Salad Sandwiches (p. 13).

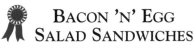

BACON 'N' EGG SALAD SANDWICHES

(Pictured at left)

Jane Ozment, Purcell, Oklahoma

My mom owns 30 chickens and keeps me supplied with farm-fresh eggs. On days I don't have much time to cook, this egg salad really hits the spot. The sandwiches are also good made with toasted bread or English muffins instead of croissants.

- 10 hard-cooked eggs, chopped
- 4 bacon strips, cooked and crumbled
- 1/2 cup shredded cheddar cheese
- 1/2 cup sour cream
- 1/3 cup mayonnaise
- 2 tablespoons snipped chives
- 1/4 teaspoon salt
- 1/4 teaspoon pepper
- 8 lettuce leaves
- 8 croissants, split

In a large bowl, combine the first eight ingredients. Cover and refrigerate for at least 2 hours. Serve the salad on lettuce-lined croissants. **Yield:** 8 servings.

FROZEN DATE SALAD

Margaret Dowdy
North Vassalboro, Maine

Our family spent 15 years in Vermont, which is famous for its maple syrup, and that's where I found this recipe. With cream cheese, dates and walnuts, the salad complements many meals.

- 1 package (8 ounces) cream cheese, softened
- 1 cup maple syrup
- 1 can (20 ounces) unsweetened crushed pineapple, drained
- 1 cup chopped dates
- 1 cup chopped walnuts
- 1 carton (8 ounces) frozen whipped topping, thawed

Line a 9-in. x 5-in. x 3-in. loaf pan with plastic wrap. In a small mixing bowl, beat cream cheese and syrup until smooth. Fold in the pineapple, dates, walnuts and whipped topping. Spoon into prepared pan; cover with foil. Freeze for at least 8 hours or overnight.

May be frozen for up to 3 months. Remove from the freezer 20 minutes before serving. Invert onto a serving plate; cut into slices. **Yield:** 8 servings.

ITALIAN WEDDING SOUP

Sherri Perfett, Moon Township, Pennsylvania

My husband and children love the combination of chicken broth, seasoned meatballs and spinach in this soup. Because it freezes so well, I often make extra to be sure I always have some on hand.

- 10 cups chicken broth
- 2 bone-in chicken breast halves (8 ounces *each*), skin removed
- 1 egg, lightly beaten
- 1/4 cup dry bread crumbs
- 4 tablespoons grated Parmesan cheese, *divided*
- 1-1/2 teaspoons Italian seasoning, *divided*
- 1 pound ground beef
- 1/2 cup uncooked orzo pasta
- 1/4 teaspoon pepper
- 1 package (10 ounces) frozen chopped spinach, thawed and drained

In a large saucepan, bring broth and chicken to a boil. Reduce heat; simmer, uncovered, for 15-20 minutes or until chicken juices run clear. Remove chicken; set aside.

In a large bowl, combine the egg, bread crumbs, 2 tablespoons Parmesan cheese and 1 teaspoon Italian seasoning. Crumble beef over mixture and mix well. Shape into 1-in. balls; add to broth. Bring to a boil. Reduce heat; simmer, uncovered, for 10 minutes or until meatballs are no longer pink. Skim fat and discard.

Remove chicken from bones; discard bones and shred meat. Add chicken, pasta, pepper and remaining Italian seasoning to soup. Bring to a boil. Reduce heat; simmer, uncovered, for 12-15 minutes or until pasta is tender. Add spinach and remaining Parmesan cheese; heat through. **Yield:** 8-10 servings.

CAJUN POTATO SALAD
(Pictured below)

Rita Futral, Ocean Spring, Mississippi

I created this recipe in my kitchen, and people tell me it's the most unique potato salad they've ever tasted. With the addition of shrimp, it seems hearty enough to be a main dish.

        5 medium red potatoes
        6 cups water
        3 tablespoons seafood seasoning
        1 tablespoon salt
        1 pound medium uncooked shrimp
    1/4 cup chopped green onions
        1 jar (2 ounces) diced pimientos, drained
    1/2 cup mayonnaise
        1 teaspoon cider vinegar
    1/2 teaspoon sugar
Additional salt to taste

Place the potatoes in a large saucepan or Dutch oven; add the water, seafood seasoning and salt. Bring to a boil. Reduce heat; cover and simmer for 25 minutes.

Add the shrimp; cover and cook for 5 minutes or until shrimp turn pink and potatoes are tender. Drain. Peel and dice the potatoes. Peel and devein the shrimp; cut into pieces.

In a large bowl, combine the potatoes, shrimp, onions and pimientos. In a small bowl, combine the mayonnaise, vinegar and sugar. Add to the potato mixture and gently toss to coat. Season with additional salt. Cover and refrigerate for at least 1 hour before serving. **Yield:** 8-10 servings.

SHREDDED PORK BARBECUE

Joan Iwasko, Rio Grande, New Jersey

This flavor-packed pork mixture is convenient because it can be baked ahead of time and reheated before serving. A big hit at baby showers and wedding receptions, it truly is a family favorite.

    1-1/2 cups water
    1-1/4 cups ketchup
      1/2 cup chopped onion
      1/4 cup lemon juice
        6 teaspoons chili powder
        3 teaspoons spicy brown mustard
    1-1/2 teaspoons salt
    1-1/2 teaspoons Worcestershire sauce
        3 to 5 drops hot pepper sauce
    3-1/2 pounds boneless pork, cut into 1-inch cubes
       12 to 14 hamburger buns, split

In a Dutch oven, combine the first nine ingredients; bring to a boil. Remove from the heat; stir in pork. Cover and bake at 350° for 3 hours or until meat is tender. Shred pork with two forks; serve on buns. **Yield:** 12-14 servings.

NUTTY WILD RICE SALAD

Mary McLeod, Monticello, Florida

Wild rice is sensational in this chilled salad. I often serve it in lettuce cups for a pretty presentation, and sometimes I stir in diced ham and asparagus to turn it into a main course.

    1-1/2 cups beef *or* chicken broth
      1/2 cup uncooked wild rice
        1 cup frozen peas, thawed
        2 celery ribs, sliced
        4 green onions, thinly sliced
      1/4 cup slivered almonds, toasted
DRESSING:
      1/4 cup vegetable oil
        2 tablespoons red wine vinegar
        1 tablespoon soy sauce
        2 teaspoons sesame oil
        1 teaspoon sugar

In a large saucepan, bring the broth to a boil. Stir in the wild rice. Reduce the heat; cover and simmer for 1 hour or until the rice is tender. Drain; fluff with a fork. Stir in the peas, celery, green onions and almonds.

In a small jar with a tight-fitting lid, combine the dressing ingredients; shake well. Pour over salad and toss to coat. Cover and refrigerate for 1 hour before serving. **Yield:** 4 servings.

HAM 'N' SAUSAGE STROMBOLI
(Pictured above)

Lee Gregory, Ashland, Ohio

Warm slices of this hearty stromboli are delicious. Because the recipe makes a lot, it's a great choice when you're serving a group.

    1 package (16 ounces) hot roll mix
1-1/4 cups warm water (120° to 130°)
    3 tablespoons olive oil, *divided*
  1/3 pound sliced deli ham
  1/3 pound sliced salami
    4 slices process American cheese, cut into thin strips
    1 cup (4 ounces) shredded part-skim mozzarella *or* provolone cheese
  1/4 pound bulk Italian sausage, cooked and crumbled
    2 tablespoons grated Parmesan cheese
    1 teaspoon dried oregano
  1/2 teaspoon garlic powder
  1/4 teaspoon coarsely ground pepper

In a bowl, combine the contents of hot roll mix and yeast. Stir in warm water and 2 tablespoons oil until dough pulls away from sides of bowl. Turn onto a floured surface; knead until smooth and elastic, about 5 minutes. Cover and let rest for 5 minutes. Press into a lightly greased 15-in. x 10-in. x 1-in. baking pan.

Layer ham, salami, American cheese, mozzarella cheese and Italian sausage over dough. Roll up jelly-roll style, starting with a long side; pinch seam to seal. Place diagonally in pan. Brush dough with remaining oil; sprinkle with Parmesan cheese, oregano, garlic powder and pepper.

Bake at 375° for 35-40 minutes or until golden brown. Let stand for 10 minutes before slicing. **Yield:** 16-18 servings.

MUSHROOM POTATO SOUP
(Pictured below)

Clare Wallace, Lynchburg, Virginia

Potatoes, leeks, carrots and a buttery mushroom flavor make this soup hearty and warming. Waxy red potatoes and all-purpose Yukon Golds hold together well in the boiling water.

    2 medium leeks, sliced
    2 large carrots, sliced
    6 tablespoons butter, *divided*
    6 cups chicken broth
    5 cups diced peeled potatoes
    1 tablespoon minced fresh dill
    1 teaspoon salt
  1/8 teaspoon pepper
    1 bay leaf
    1 pound sliced fresh mushrooms
  1/4 cup all-purpose flour
    1 cup heavy whipping cream

In a Dutch oven or soup kettle, saute the leeks and carrots in 3 tablespoons butter for 5 minutes or until tender. Stir in the broth, potatoes, dill, salt, pepper and bay leaf. Bring to a boil. Reduce heat; cover and simmer for 15-20 minutes or until potatoes are tender.

Meanwhile, in a large skillet, saute the mushrooms in remaining butter for 4-6 minutes or until tender. Discard the bay leaf from soup. Stir in the mushroom mixture. In a small bowl, combine the flour and heavy whipping cream until smooth; gradually stir into soup. Bring to a boil; cook and stir for 2 minutes or until thickened. **Yield:** 12 servings (3 quarts).

CHEESY CRAB ENGLISH MUFFINS

Mary Lou Crouch, Granite Falls, Washington

These hot-from-the-oven sandwiches are so good on a cool afternoon or as a quick dinner. Chopped pecans give the crab salad extra crunch.

>   2 packages (8 ounces *each*) imitation
>   crabmeat, chopped
>   1 cup chopped celery
>   1 cup mayonnaise
>   1 jar (2 ounces) diced pimientos, drained
>   1/4 cup chopped pecans
>   2 tablespoons finely chopped onion
>   6 English muffins, split and toasted
>   12 slices cheddar cheese

In a large bowl, combine the crab, celery, mayonnaise, pimientos, pecans and onion. Spread over English muffin halves. Broil 3-4 in. from the heat for 5 minutes or until bubbly. Top with cheese slices; broil 1-2 minutes longer or until cheese is melted. **Yield:** 6 servings.

SPICY SLOW-COOKED CHILI
(Pictured above)

Sabrina Corrigan, Williamsburg, Pennsylvania

I love that I can put the ingredients for this recipe in the slow cooker and forget about it for a few hours. If you like your chili thick, you'll love this version.

>   2 pounds ground beef
>   2 to 3 hot chili peppers of your choice
>   3 cans (16 ounces *each*) kidney beans,
>   rinsed and drained
>   1 can (6 ounces) tomato paste
>   1 medium onion, chopped
>   1 medium green pepper, seeded and
>   chopped
>   2 teaspoons chili powder
>   2 teaspoons cider vinegar
>   1 teaspoon garlic powder
>   1 teaspoon dried oregano
>   1/4 to 1/2 teaspoon ground cinnamon
>   1/4 teaspoon pepper
>   2 to 4 cups tomato juice

In a large skillet, cook beef over medium heat until no longer pink; drain. Transfer to a 5-qt. slow cooker. Remove seeds from the chili peppers if desired; chop peppers. Add to the slow cooker. Stir in the beans, tomato paste, onion, green pepper, seasonings and 2 cups tomato juice.

Cover and cook on low for 4-6 hours or until heated through, adding more tomato juice if needed to achieve desired thickness. **Yield:** 8 servings.

Editor's Note: When cutting or seeding hot peppers, use rubber or plastic gloves to protect your hands. Avoid touching your face.

TUNA PASTA SALAD

Sue Gronholz, Beaver Dam, Wisconsin

Pasta shells, tuna and veggies make this a satisfying lunch salad or even a light supper. It's convenient to prepare ahead of time and store in the refrigerator.

> ✓ Uses less fat, sugar or salt. Includes Nutrition Facts and Diabetic Exchanges.

>   1 package (7 ounces) small pasta shells
>   1-1/2 cups chopped celery
>   1 can (6 ounces) light water-packed tuna,
>   drained and flaked
>   1/2 cup chopped green pepper
>   1/2 cup frozen peas, thawed
>   1 jar (4 ounces) diced pimientos, drained
>   1 tablespoon chopped onion
>   1 cup fat-free mayonnaise
>   1 teaspoon salt

Cook the pasta shells according to the package directions; drain and rinse in cold water. In a large bowl, combine the pasta shells, celery, tuna, green pepper, peas, pimientos and onion. Combine the mayonnaise and salt; fold into the salad. Cover and refrigerate for at least 2 hours or until chilled. **Yield:** 6 servings.

Nutrition Facts: 1 cup equals 225 calories, 1 g fat (trace saturated fat), 10 mg cholesterol, 800 mg sodium, 38 g carbohydrate, 3 g fiber, 14 g protein. **Diabetic Exchanges:** 2 starch, 1 very lean meat, 1 vegetable.

POLYNESIAN SHRIMP SALAD
(Pictured below)

Elaine Carncross, Hilo, Hawaii

Pineapple is one of our state's best-known products. It's delicious paired with shrimp and pasta in this crowd-pleasing salad.

  1 can (20 ounces) pineapple chunks
  2 teaspoons cornstarch
  1/2 to 1 teaspoon curry powder
  1/8 teaspoon salt
  1/8 teaspoon pepper
  1/3 cup mayonnaise
  1/3 cup sour cream
  1 pound cooked medium shrimp, peeled
    and deveined
  2 cups cooked medium pasta shells
  1 can (8 ounces) sliced water chestnuts,
    drained
  1/4 cup chopped sweet red pepper

Drain pineapple, reserving 3/4 cup juice. Set the pineapple aside. In a small saucepan, combine the cornstarch, curry powder, salt, pepper and reserved pineapple juice until smooth. Bring to a boil; cook and stir for 1 minute or until thickened. Remove from the heat; cool to room temperature. Stir in mayonnaise and sour cream.

In a large bowl, combine the shrimp, pasta, water chestnuts, red pepper and reserved pineapple. Add the dressing and toss to coat. Cover and refrigerate for at least 2 hours before serving. **Yield:** 6-8 servings.

VEGGIE GRILLED CHEESE
(Pictured above)

Tracy Hayes, Mount Olive, North Carolina

Fast-to-fix coleslaw makes a fun and colorful addition to these toasted sandwiches. Using Havarti or Swiss cheese gives them a delightfully different flavor.

  3 tablespoons butter, softened
  8 slices sourdough bread
  3 to 4 tablespoons honey mustard
1-1/2 cups broccoli coleslaw mix
  6 ounces dill Havarti *or* Swiss cheese,
    sliced

Spread butter over one side of each slice of bread; turn bread butter side down. Generously spread mustard over four slices of bread. Layer each with a fourth of the broccoli coleslaw mix and a fourth of the cheese; top with remaining bread, butter side up.

Heat a griddle or large skillet over medium heat. Toast sandwiches until the bread is lightly browned on each side and the cheese is melted. **Yield:** 4 sandwiches.

NO-MESS GRILLED CHEESE

When I need to turn the bread for grilled cheese sandwiches so that the buttered side is down, I turn the bread onto waxed paper. It keeps my countertop nice and clean.
—*Sharon Crider, Lebanon, Missouri*

Sensational Main-Dish Salads

THINK a salad won't satisfy your hungry family? You'll change your mind when you try these hearty medleys chock-full of filling ingredients.

■▪■▪■▪■▪■▪■

GRILLED STEAK SALAD

Mildred Sherrer, Roanoke, Texas

With plenty of sliced steak and veggies, this main-dish salad will please even the biggest appetites. It's a terrific dinner on hot summer days or any time you feel like grilling.

✓ Uses less fat, sugar or salt. Includes Nutrition Facts and Diabetic Exchanges.

  1/2 teaspoon salt
  1/2 teaspoon garlic powder
  1/2 teaspoon pepper
   1 beef flank steak (1 pound)
   1 large sweet onion, sliced
   1 package (5 ounces) spring mix salad greens
   1 can (16 ounces) kidney beans, rinsed and drained
   1 jar (7 ounces) roasted sweet red peppers, drained and sliced
  1/3 cup balsamic vinegar
   2 tablespoons minced fresh basil *or* 2 teaspoons dried basil
   2 tablespoons olive oil
   1 teaspoon Dijon mustard

Combine the salt, garlic powder and pepper; rub over steak. Place onion slices on a double thickness of heavy-duty foil (about 12 in. square). Fold foil around onion and seal tightly. Cut about six 1-in. slits in top of packet; set aside.

Coat the grill rack with nonstick cooking spray before starting the grill. Grill the steak, covered, over medium heat for 6-8 minutes on each side or until the meat reaches desired doneness (for medium-rare, a meat thermometer should read 145°; medium, 160°; well-done, 170°). Grill the onion packet for 8-10 minutes or until the onions are crisp-tender, turning the packet once. Let

the steak stand for 5 minutes.

Meanwhile, in a large bowl, combine the greens, beans, red peppers and grilled onion. In a small bowl, whisk the vinegar, basil, oil and mustard. Pour 1/4 cup over salad; toss to coat. Divide among serving plates. Slice flank steak across the grain; arrange over salads. Drizzle with remaining dressing. **Yield:** 4 servings.

Nutrition Facts: 1 serving equals 367 calories, 15 g fat (4 g saturated fat), 54 mg cholesterol, 688 mg sodium, 28 g carbohydrate, 6 g fiber, 30 g protein. **Diabetic Exchanges:** 3 lean meat, 2 vegetable, 2 fat, 1 starch.

■▪■▪■▪■▪■▪■

SHRIMP AND RICE SALAD

Beulah Lewis, Seattle, Washington

This tasty salad is a popular one in our community, where seafood of all kinds is readily available. The shrimp, rice, ripe olives, celery and hard-cooked eggs are a great combination.

   3 cups hot cooked long grain rice
   3 tablespoons vegetable oil
   2 tablespoons cider vinegar
   1 tablespoon prepared mustard
  1-1/2 teaspoons salt
  1/8 teaspoon pepper
   2 cups chopped celery
  1-1/2 cups cooked small shrimp
   1 cup sliced ripe olives
  1/2 cup mayonnaise
  1/4 cup chopped dill pickle
  1/4 cup diced pimientos
   2 tablespoons finely chopped onion
   2 hard-cooked eggs, sliced

Place hot rice in a large bowl. In a jar with a tight-fitting lid, combine the oil, vinegar, mustard, salt and pepper; shake well. Pour over rice; cool to room temperature.

Add the celery, shrimp, olives, mayonnaise, pickle, pimientos and onion; toss gently. Cover and refrigerate for 1 hour or until chilled. Garnish with egg slices. **Yield:** 6 servings.

▪▪▪▪▪▪▪▪▪▪▪▪▪

HEARTY STIR-FRY SALAD
(Pictured above)

Michelle Smith, Running Springs, California

I tossed together this savory salad for some business friends a few years ago. The meat has to marinate first, but it's well worth the wait.

3/4 cup sherry *or* chicken broth
1/3 cup soy sauce
1 small onion, sliced
2 garlic cloves, minced
1-1/2 teaspoons ground ginger
1-1/2 teaspoons chili powder
1/2 teaspoon pepper
1 pound boneless beef top round steak, cut into 2-inch strips
3/4 pound boneless skinless chicken breasts, cut into 1/2-inch cubes
4 teaspoons vegetable oil, *divided*
3 medium carrots, julienned
1 cup fresh broccoli florets
1 medium green pepper, julienned
1 medium onion, thinly sliced
1 cup sliced fresh mushrooms
1/2 cup minced fresh cilantro
12 cups torn mixed salad greens
3 medium navel oranges, peeled and cut into 1/2-inch pieces

In a bowl, combine the first seven ingredients. Pour 2/3 cup marinade into a large resealable plastic bag; add beef. Pour 1/3 cup marinade into another plastic bag; add chicken. Seal bags and turn to coat; refrigerate for up to 2 hours. Cover and refrigerate remaining marinade.

Drain and discard marinade from beef and chicken. In a large skillet or wok, heat 1-1/2 teaspoons oil; stir-fry beef until no longer pink. Remove and keep warm. In the same pan, stir-fry chicken in 1-1/2 teaspoons oil until juices run clear. Remove and keep warm. Stir-fry carrots and broccoli in remaining oil for 5 minutes. Add the green pepper, onion and mushrooms; stir-fry for 5-6 minutes or until vegetables are crisp-tender. Stir in cilantro and reserved marinade.

Toss salad greens and oranges; place on a large serving plate. Top with the stir-fried beef, chicken and vegetables. **Yield:** 6-8 servings.

PEAR-LIME GELATIN SALAD
(Pictured below)
Bernice Miller, Bonner Springs, Kansas

This easy, make-ahead gelatin is a "must" at our family reunions. The green color is nice for holidays, too. For extra flair, decorate the top with maraschino cherries in addition to the pecans.

  1 can (15 ounces) pear halves
  1 package (3 ounces) lime gelatin
  1 package (8 ounces) cream cheese, cubed
  1 can (20 ounces) unsweetened crushed pineapple, well drained
  1 cup chopped pecans, toasted, *divided*
  1 carton (8 ounces) frozen whipped topping, thawed

Drain pears, reserving juice; set pears aside. In a small saucepan, bring juice to a boil. Stir in gelatin until dissolved. Remove from the heat; cool slightly.

In a food processor, combine pears and cream cheese; cover and process until smooth. Transfer to a large bowl; stir in gelatin mixture until blended. Stir in the pineapple and 3/4 cup pecans. Fold in whipped topping.

Pour into an ungreased 11-in. x 7-in. x 2-in. dish. Refrigerate until set. Sprinkle with remaining pecans. Cut into squares. **Yield:** 8 servings.

PRETZEL-CRUSTED BURGERS
Shirley Zembsch, Cherokee, Iowa

Add some excitement to your next backyard barbecue with these deliciously different burgers. After one bite of the beef patties coated with pretzel crumbs, your guests will be asking for the recipe.

    2 eggs, lightly beaten
    1 can (8 ounces) tomato sauce
1-1/2 cups crushed pretzels, *divided*
    1 small onion, chopped
    1 teaspoon salt
  1/2 teaspoon pepper
  1/4 teaspoon garlic powder
    2 pounds ground beef
    8 hamburger buns, split

In a large bowl, combine the eggs, tomato sauce, 1 cup pretzel crumbs, onion, salt, pepper and garlic powder. Crumble beef over mixture and mix well. Shape into eight 3/4-in.-thick patties. Coat with remaining pretzel crumbs.

Grill the beef patties, uncovered, over medium heat for 7-8 minutes on each side or until a meat thermometer reads 160°. Serve on hamburger buns. **Yield:** 8 servings.

NUTTY PEAR SPINACH SALAD
Laurie LaClair, North Richland Hills, Texas

This elegant, savory salad with a homemade dressing draws oohs and aahs every time I put it on the table. Guests always think I've fussed, so I keep it my little secret that I can prepare this dish from start to finish in only 15 minutes!

    6 cups fresh baby spinach
    1 large pear, thinly sliced
  2/3 cup coarsely chopped pecans, toasted
  1/2 cup dried cherries
  1/2 cup crumbled blue cheese
    2 tablespoons balsamic vinegar
    1 tablespoon soy sauce
    1 tablespoon honey
1-1/2 teaspoons stone-ground mustard
    1 garlic clove, minced
  1/4 teaspoon salt
  1/8 teaspoon pepper
  1/2 cup olive oil

In a large bowl, combine the spinach, pear, pecans, cherries and blue cheese. In a small bowl, whisk the vinegar, soy sauce, honey, mustard, garlic, salt and pepper. Gradually whisk in oil. Pour over salad and toss to coat. Serve immediately. **Yield:** 4 servings.

CURRIED CHICKEN SALAD SANDWICHES
(Pictured below)

Carole Martin, Coffeeville, Mississippi

When you want to "show off" a little, turn to this tasty sandwich. It features an interesting combination of chicken, nuts, cranberries, curry and other ingredients. I mix it up the night before so the flavors blend.

    2 cups cubed cooked chicken breast
  3/4 cup chopped apple
  3/4 cup dried cranberries
  3/4 cup mayonnaise
  1/2 cup chopped walnuts
  1/2 cup chopped celery
    2 teaspoons lemon juice
    1 tablespoon chopped green onion
    1 teaspoon curry powder
    6 lettuce leaves
    6 croissants, split

In a large bowl, combine the chicken, apple, dried cranberries, mayonnaise, walnuts, celery, lemon juice, green onion and curry powder. Place the lettuce on the croissants. Top with the chicken salad mixture. **Yield:** 6 servings.

GARLIC SOUP
(Pictured above)

Iola Egle, Bella Vista, Arkansas

While this soup simmers, the great aroma of garlic will fill your kitchen. We love the toasted bread floating on top of each rich and creamy bowlful. It's terrific as a first course or all by itself.

    6 garlic cloves, minced
    1 tablespoon olive oil
    8 cups chicken broth
  1/2 teaspoon salt
  1/8 teaspoon pepper
  1/8 teaspoon dried thyme
  1/8 teaspoon dried rosemary, crushed
    3 egg yolks
  1/2 cup half-and-half cream
    8 slices frozen garlic bread, thawed and toasted
Grated Parmesan cheese

In a large saucepan, cook and stir the garlic in oil over low heat for 5 minutes or until lightly browned. Add the broth, salt, pepper, thyme and rosemary; simmer, uncovered, for 1 hour.

Strain broth and return to the pan. In a small bowl, whisk egg yolks and cream. Stir in 1/2 cup hot broth. Return all to the pan, stirring constantly. Cook and stir over medium heat until soup reaches 160° (do not boil). Top each serving with a slice of garlic bread; sprinkle with Parmesan cheese. **Yield:** 8 servings.

ture and ham. Replace the bread top. Cut into wedges. **Yield:** 8-10 servings.

Editor's Note: Giardiniera is a vegetable mixture available in mild and hot varieties. Look for it in the Italian or pickle section of your local grocery store.

ITALIAN TOSSED SALAD
(Pictured on front cover)

Mary Elizabeth Costello, Venice, Florida

Here's a great way to complement lasagna, spaghetti or any other Italian entree. The four-ingredient dressing is a breeze to prepare.

- 4 cups torn iceberg lettuce
- 4 cups torn romaine
- 1 cup water-packed artichoke hearts, rinsed, drained and quartered
- 1 jar (2 ounces) sliced pimientos, drained
- 1 small red onion, thinly sliced
- 1/3 cup olive oil
- 2 tablespoons red wine vinegar
- 1/2 teaspoon salt
- 1/4 teaspoon pepper
- 1/3 cup grated Parmesan cheese

In a large salad bowl, combine the lettuce, romaine, artichokes, pimientos and onion. Cover and refrigerate until serving.

In a jar with a tight-fitting lid, combine the oil, vinegar, salt and pepper; shake well. Just before serving, shake dressing and pour over salad; toss gently to coat. Sprinkle with Parmesan cheese; toss again. **Yield:** 6 servings.

DILLY SWEET ONIONS

Peggy Potts, Lima, Ohio

As soon as Vidalia or other sweet onions are available each year, I make this tangy salad. Everyone loves it, and I've received many recipe requests.

- 1 pound sweet onion, thinly sliced
- 1/2 cup sugar
- 1/2 cup cider vinegar
- 1/4 cup vegetable oil
- 2 teaspoons dill weed
- 1 teaspoon salt

Place the onions in a large bowl. In a small saucepan, combine the sugar, vinegar, oil, dill and salt; bring to a boil, stirring constantly. Pour over onions and toss to coat. Cover and refrigerate for at least 5 hours. Serve with a slotted spoon. **Yield:** 4 servings.

HEARTY MUFFULETTA
(Pictured above)

Ruth Hayward, Lake Charles, Louisiana

Famous in my home state, muffulettas are cold cuts, olive salad and cheese layered in an Italian bread shell. I was thrilled when a friend and co-worker gave me this recipe so I could make them myself.

- 1/2 cup finely chopped celery
- 1/2 cup sliced stuffed olives, drained
- 1/2 cup sliced ripe olives, drained
- 1/2 cup giardiniera
- 1/3 cup finely chopped onion
- 1/3 cup olive oil
- 1/4 cup finely chopped green onions
- 1/4 cup minced fresh parsley
- 3 tablespoons lemon juice
- 1 teaspoon dried oregano
- 1 garlic clove, minced
- 1/8 teaspoon pepper
- 1 round loaf (24 ounces) unsliced Italian bread
- 1/4 pound thinly sliced hard salami
- 1/4 pound provolone cheese
- 1/4 pound thinly sliced deli ham

In a large bowl, combine the first 12 ingredients. Cover and refrigerate for at least 8 hours. Drain, reserving 2 tablespoons liquid.

Cut the loaf of bread in half; hollow out the top and bottom, leaving a 1-in. shell (discard removed bread or save for another use). Brush the cut sides of bread with the reserved liquid. Layer the bottom of bread shell with the salami, half of the olive mixture, provolone cheese, remaining olive mix-

CHERRY WILD RICE SALAD
(Pictured below)

Yvonne Gorges, New London, Wisconsin

While visiting Door County in my home state, I sampled this unique salad. As soon as I got home, I wrote a letter asking the lady who'd made it for the recipe. The mix of wild rice, vegetables and orchard-fresh fruit is a tasty way to remember Wisconsin's premier cherry-growing area.

  2 cups fresh snow peas, halved
  2 cups cooked wild rice
  1 cup cooked long grain rice
  1 can (8 ounces) sliced water chestnuts, drained
  1 cup dried cherries
1/2 cup thinly sliced celery
1/4 cup chopped green onions
DRESSING:
  6 tablespoons sugar
  6 tablespoons vegetable oil
  3 tablespoons cider vinegar
4-1/2 teaspoons soy sauce
  1 to 2 garlic cloves, peeled
3/4 teaspoon minced fresh gingerroot
3/4 cup cashew halves, toasted

In a large bowl, combine the first seven ingredients. For dressing, in a blender, combine the sugar, oil, vinegar, soy sauce, garlic and ginger; cover and process until blended. Pour over rice mixture and toss to coat. Cover and refrigerate until serving. Just before serving, stir in the cashews. **Yield:** 6-8 servings.

SHRIMP CHOWDER
(Pictured above)

E. B. Twitchell, Turner, Maine

Hands-down, this is my family's favorite chowder. It's not only delicious, but it's simple to make and doesn't need to simmer for long.

  3 medium potatoes, peeled and diced
  2 medium onions, sliced
  2 cups water
3/4 teaspoon salt
Dash seafood seasoning, optional
1-1/2 cups milk
  1 can (5 ounces) evaporated milk
  4 ounces process cheese (Velveeta), cubed
  1 can (6 ounces) small shrimp, drained
  2 tablespoons butter
  1 tablespoon minced fresh parsley

In a large saucepan or soup kettle, combine the potatoes, onions, water, salt and seafood seasoning if desired; bring to a boil. Reduce heat; cover and simmer until potatoes are tender.

Stir in the milk, evaporated milk and cheese; heat until cheese is melted. Add the shrimp, butter and parsley; heat through. **Yield:** 6 servings.

"BERRY" GOOD SALAD

Crazy about cranberries? Feel free to substitute an equal amount of dried cranberries for the dried cherries in Cherry Wild Rice Salad. Or use a combination of the two.

boil over medium heat; cook and stir for 2 minutes or until thickened. Remove from the heat. Stir a small amount into egg; return all to the pan, stirring constantly. Cook and stir until a thermometer reads 160° and mixture is thickened. Remove from the heat; stir in butter. Cool to room temperature.

In a mixing bowl, beat heavy whipping cream on high speed until stiff peaks form. Gently fold into custard. Spread over gelatin; sprinkle with cheddar cheese. Refrigerate 1 hour or until chilled. **Yield:** 12-16 servings.

TOMATO-PESTO CHEDDAR MELTS

Lil Morris, Emerald Park, Saskatchewan

Give ordinary grilled cheese sandwiches a boost with this tasty recipe. Prepared pesto and sliced tomato add an interesting and delicious twist.

     1 tablespoon prepared pesto
     2 slices white bread
     1 small tomato, sliced
   1/2 cup shredded cheddar cheese
   1/8 teaspoon salt
   1/8 teaspoon pepper
     1 tablespoon butter

Spread pesto over one side of each slice of bread. Top with tomato and cheese; sprinkle with salt and pepper. In a large skillet over medium-low heat, melt butter; add sandwiches. Cover and cook until bread is lightly toasted and cheese is melted. **Yield:** 2 servings.

CRANBERRY BROCCOLI SALAD

Cheryl Urban, Wisconsin Rapids, Wisconsin

Since our home state is a top producer of cranberries, I've nicknamed this recipe Wisconsin Salad. It features sweetened dried cranberries, which our family produces from the crop we harvest every fall.

     4 cups fresh broccoli florets
   1/2 to 3/4 cup thinly sliced red onion
     1 cup dried cranberries
   1/3 cup crumbled cooked bacon
   1/2 cup mayonnaise
   1/2 cup half-and-half cream
     3 tablespoons sugar

In a large salad bowl, combine the broccoli, onion, cranberries and bacon. In a small bowl, combine the mayonnaise, cream and sugar until smooth. Pour over broccoli mixture and toss to coat. Refrigerate until serving. **Yield:** 6 servings.

FRUITED GELATIN SALAD
(Pictured above)

Norma Warner, Hot Springs Village, Arkansas

This dressed-up gelatin is perfect for potlucks and special occasions. It cuts nicely into squares and can be served on lettuce leaves if you like.

     2 packages (3 ounces *each*) orange gelatin
     2 cups boiling water
     1 cup apricot nectar
     1 cup pineapple juice
     1 can (15 ounces) apricot halves, drained and mashed
     1 can (8 ounces) crushed pineapple, drained
     4 cups miniature marshmallows
TOPPING:
   1/2 cup sugar
     2 tablespoons all-purpose flour
   1/2 cup apricot nectar
   1/2 cup pineapple juice
     1 egg, lightly beaten
     2 tablespoons butter
     1 cup heavy whipping cream
     1 cup (4 ounces) shredded cheddar cheese

In a bowl, dissolve the gelatin in boiling water. Stir in the juices, apricots and pineapple. Transfer to a 13-in. x 9-in. x 2-in. dish coated with nonstick cooking spray. Refrigerate for 30 minutes or until partially set. Sprinkle with the marshmallows; refrigerate.

For the topping, combine the sugar and flour in a saucepan. Gradually whisk in juices. Bring to a

BEEF GYROS
(Pictured below)

Sheri Scheerhorn, Hills, Minnesota

Going out to restaurants for gyros got to be expensive for our family, so I came up with this homemade version. Usually, I set out the fixings so everyone can assemble their own. My husband and our two busy teens request them often.

- 1 cup ranch salad dressing
- 1/2 cup chopped seeded peeled cucumber
- 1 pound boneless beef sirloin steak, cut into thin strips
- 2 tablespoons olive oil
- 5 whole gyro-style pitas (6 inches)
- 1 medium tomato, chopped
- 1 can (2-1/4 ounces) sliced ripe olives, drained
- 1/2 small onion, thinly sliced
- 1 carton (4 ounces) crumbled feta cheese
- 2-1/2 cups shredded lettuce

In a small bowl, combine the salad dressing and cucumber; set aside. In a large skillet, brown beef in oil over medium heat. Layer half of each pita with steak, tomato, olives, onion, feta cheese, lettuce and dressing mixture. Bring edges of each pita over filling and secure with a toothpick. **Yield:** 5 servings.

TANGERINE TOSSED SALAD
(Pictured above)

Helen Musenbrock, O'Fallon, Missouri

I learned to cook from my mother when I was a young girl. I love the combination of sweet tangerines and crunchy caramelized almonds in this recipe.

- 1/2 cup sliced almonds
- 3 tablespoons sugar, *divided*
- 2 medium tangerines *or* navel orange
- 6 cups torn lettuce
- 3 green onions, chopped
- 2 tablespoons cider vinegar
- 2 tablespoons olive oil
- 1/4 teaspoon salt
- 1/4 teaspoon pepper

In a skillet, cook and stir the almonds and 2 tablespoons sugar over medium-low heat for 25-30 minutes or until sugar is melted and almonds are toasted. Remove from heat. Peel and section tangerines, reserving 1 tablespoon juice.

In a large bowl, combine the lettuce, onions, tangerines and almonds. In a small bowl, whisk the vinegar, oil, salt, pepper, reserved juice and remaining sugar. Drizzle over salad and toss to coat. **Yield:** 6 servings.

ALL DRESSED UP

Ranch salad dressing is great not only in gyros, but also in tuna sandwiches. I use it in place of mayonnaise, and my family really loves the extra flavor.
—*Ingrid Mello*
Gustine, California

LEMONY FRUIT SALAD

Rochelle Greenway, Cambridge, Idaho

When I was a teenager, I did all of the cooking for my family of 10. I created this recipe when I was halfway through making a different salad—and discovered that I didn't have all the ingredients!

    1/4 cup sugar
    1/4 cup lemon juice
      2 teaspoons grated lemon peel
  1-1/2 teaspoons poppy seeds
      4 medium apples, diced
      1 can (11 ounces) mandarin oranges,
        drained
      1 large carrot, grated
    1/2 cup raisins
Lettuce leaves, optional

For dressing, combine sugar, lemon juice, peel and seeds in a small saucepan. Cook over medium heat for 5-6 minutes or until sugar is dissolved, stirring occasionally. Remove from heat; cool.

In a large bowl, combine the apples, oranges, carrot and raisins. Add dressing and toss to coat. Cover and refrigerate for 4 hours. Serve in a lettuce-lined bowl if desired. **Yield:** 8 servings.

SEASHELL SALAD

Renee Durell, Fairy Glen, Saskatchewan

I frequently rely on this easy, crowd-pleasing pasta salad. With plenty of colorful veggies, it goes over big every time I serve it.

      2 cups uncooked medium pasta shells
      2 medium tomatoes, seeded and chopped
    1/2 medium green pepper, diced
    1/4 cup chopped cucumber
      1 green onion, sliced
    1/4 cup sugar
    1/4 cup vegetable oil
      2 tablespoons plus 1-1/2 teaspoons
        ketchup
      2 tablespoons cider vinegar
    1/4 teaspoon salt
    1/4 teaspoon paprika
    1/8 teaspoon pepper

Cook pasta according to package directions; drain and rinse in cold water. In a large serving bowl, combine the pasta, tomatoes, green pepper, cucumber and onion.

In a small bowl, whisk the sugar, oil, ketchup, vinegar, salt, paprika and pepper until smooth. Pour over salad and toss to coat. Cover and refrigerate until chilled. **Yield:** 4-6 servings.

CHEDDAR POTATO SOUP
(Pictured above)

Susan Peck, Republic, Missouri

I came up with this recipe as an alternative to plain potato soup. Hearty and comforting, it disappears quickly when I serve it to my family on chilly evenings. Team it with bread and a green salad, and you have a complete meal.

      1 large onion, chopped
    3/4 cup chopped celery
    1/4 cup butter
      5 cups cubed peeled potatoes
      3 cups water
      3 cups milk, *divided*
      4 teaspoons chicken bouillon granules
    1/2 teaspoon salt
    1/2 teaspoon pepper
    1/4 cup all-purpose flour
      4 cups (16 ounces) shredded cheddar
        cheese
    1/2 pound sliced bacon, cooked and
        crumbled

In a large Dutch oven or soup kettle, saute the onion and celery in butter for 5 minutes. Add the potatoes and water. Bring to a boil. Reduce heat; cover and simmer for 15 minutes or until the potatoes are tender.

Stir in 2 cups milk, bouillon, salt and pepper. Combine flour and remaining milk until smooth; gradually stir into soup. Bring to a boil; cook and stir for 2 minutes or until thickened. Reduce heat. Add cheese and bacon; stir until cheese is melted. **Yield:** 10-12 servings (about 2-1/2 quarts).

SUMMERTIME SLAW
(Pictured below)

Sharon Payne, Mayfield, Kentucky

When I wanted a change from mayonnaise-laden slaw, I tossed together this refreshing alternative. It uses many of the garden vegetables I grow, so it's also economical. I serve it at church socials and our family reunion each Fourth of July.

      3/4 cup sugar
      3/4 cup white vinegar
      1/3 cup vegetable oil
        1 tablespoon water
        1 teaspoon salt
        1 teaspoon pepper
      1/2 teaspoon crushed red pepper flakes,
            optional
        1 package (16 ounces) coleslaw mix
        2 medium tomatoes, peeled, seeded and
            chopped
        1 large onion, chopped
        1 small green pepper, chopped
        1 small sweet red pepper, chopped
      1/2 cup sweet pickle relish

In a large saucepan, combine the sugar, vinegar, oil, water, salt, pepper and pepper flakes if desired. Cook and stir over medium heat until mixture comes to a boil. Cook 2 minutes longer or until sugar is dissolved. Cool to room temperature, stirring several times.

In a large salad bowl, combine the coleslaw mix, tomatoes, onion, peppers and pickle relish. Add the dressing and toss to coat. Cover and refrigerate overnight. Serve with a slotted spoon. **Yield:** 10-12 servings.

 ## TUNA PUFF SANDWICHES
(Pictured above)

Stella Dobmeier, Kamloops, British Columbia

My husband and I can't get enough of this hot supper sandwich. The cheese and tomato top off the tuna salad deliciously. Sometimes I replace the tuna with canned salmon, ham, chicken or turkey.

      3/4 cup mayonnaise, *divided*
        2 tablespoons chopped green pepper
    1-1/2 teaspoons grated onion
    1-1/2 teaspoons prepared mustard
      1/4 teaspoon Worcestershire sauce
        1 can (6 ounces) tuna, drained and flaked
        3 hamburger buns, split
        6 slices tomato
      3/4 cup shredded cheddar cheese

In a small bowl, combine 1/4 cup mayonnaise, green pepper, onion, mustard and Worcestershire sauce; stir in tuna. Spread over each bun half; top each with a tomato slice. Arrange sandwiches on a baking sheet. In a small bowl, combine the cheese and remaining mayonnaise; spoon cheese mixture over tomato. Bake at 400° for 11-13 minutes or until topping is puffy and golden brown. **Yield:** 6 servings.

MISTY MELON SALAD
(Pictured below)

Rita Reifenstein, Evans City, Pennsylvania

A pleasant poppy seed dressing complements this mix of cantaloupe, honeydew, strawberries and pineapple. The refreshing salad is great for a group.

    1 medium cantaloupe, cut into cubes
    1 medium honeydew, cut into cubes
    2 cups fresh strawberries, halved
    1 can (20 ounces) pineapple chunks
  1/2 cup sugar
    1 tablespoon chopped onion
    1 teaspoon salt
    1 teaspoon ground mustard
  1/2 cup vegetable oil
    2 to 3 teaspoons poppy seeds

In a large bowl, combine the cantaloupe, honeydew and strawberries. Drain pineapple, reserving 1/3 cup juice; set juice aside. Add pineapple to fruit mixture; cover and refrigerate until chilled.

For dressing, in a blender, combine the sugar, onion, salt, mustard and reserved pineapple juice; cover and process until blended. While processing, gradually add oil in a steady stream. Stir in poppy seeds. Cover and refrigerate until chilled. Serve with fruit salad. **Yield:** 10-12 servings.

FRESH MOZZARELLA SANDWICHES
(Pictured at right)

Kristine Chayes, Smithtown, New York

As kids, my sisters and I always helped our mother make these hearty melted cheese sandwiches. Served with a robust tomato sauce for dipping, they made a quick, nutritious lunch or dinner. Nowadays, I prepare them for my husband and our two sons.

  1/4 cup chopped onion
    1 garlic clove, minced
    2 tablespoons olive oil
    1 can (28 ounces) crushed tomatoes in
      puree
    1 teaspoon grape jelly
  1/2 teaspoon dried oregano
  1/2 teaspoon dried basil
  1/2 teaspoon salt
  1/8 teaspoon pepper
SANDWICHES:
    1 pound fresh mozzarella cheese, cut into
      1/2-inch slices
    8 slices sourdough bread (3/4 inch thick)
    2 eggs, lightly beaten
  3/4 cup milk
  1/2 teaspoon salt
  1/4 teaspoon pepper
    2 tablespoons butter

In a large saucepan, saute onion and garlic in oil until tender. Stir in the tomatoes, jelly, oregano, basil, salt and pepper. Bring to a boil. Reduce heat; simmer, uncovered, for 20 minutes, stirring several times.

Meanwhile, for sandwiches, arrange cheese on four slices of bread to within 1/2 in. of edges. Top with remaining bread. In a shallow bowl, combine the eggs, milk, salt and pepper. Dip sandwiches in egg mixture.

Melt 1 tablespoon butter in a large skillet over medium heat. Add two sandwiches; toast over medium heat for 4-5 minutes on each side or until golden brown and the cheese is melted. Repeat with the remaining sandwiches and butter. Serve sandwiches with the tomato sauce for dipping. **Yield:** 4 servings.

SAUCY POSSIBILITIES

The flavorful tomato sauce that accompanies Fresh Mozzarella Sandwiches can jazz up other dippers, too. For example, try serving the sauce alongside your favorite Italian breadsticks or breaded mozzarella sticks.

Soups, Salads & Sandwiches

TURKEY SALAD CROISSANTS
(Pictured below)

Karen Jantz, New Plymouth, Idaho

I created this creamy, crunchy salad for a small tea party I was having one winter afternoon. The recipe is a great way to use up leftover holiday turkey.

    4 cups cubed cooked turkey breast
    1 can (8 ounces) sliced water chestnuts,
        drained and chopped
2/3 cup chopped pecans
    2 celery ribs, sliced
    2 green onions, sliced
    1 cup mayonnaise
    2 teaspoons prepared mustard
1/2 teaspoon garlic pepper blend
1/4 teaspoon salt
    8 lettuce leaves
    8 croissants, split

In a large bowl, combine the turkey, water chestnuts, pecans, celery and onions. Combine the mayonnaise, mustard, garlic pepper and salt; pour over turkey mixture and toss to coat. Cover and refrigerate until serving. Spoon onto lettuce-lined croissants. **Yield:** 8 servings.

GRAPE 'N' PEAR TOSSED SALAD

This sweet medley from our Test Kitchen staff will complement most any meal. Yogurt, apple juice and sugar create the quick but yummy dressing.

✓ Uses less fat, sugar or salt. Includes Nutrition Facts and Diabetic Exchanges.

1/2 cup reduced-fat plain yogurt
    2 tablespoons unsweetened apple juice
    1 tablespoon sugar
    6 cups torn mixed salad greens
1/2 cup halved seedless red grapes
    1 small pear, cubed
    2 tablespoons coarsely chopped pecans,
        toasted
    2 tablespoons sliced green onion

For dressing, combine the yogurt, apple juice and sugar in a small bowl. Cover and refrigerate for 1 hour. In a large salad bowl, combine the greens, grapes, pear, pecans and onion; add dressing and toss to coat. **Yield:** 4 servings.

Nutrition Facts: 1-1/2 cups equals 104 calories, 4 g fat (1 g saturated fat), 2 mg cholesterol, 43 mg sodium, 17 g carbohydrate, 3 g fiber, 4 g protein.
Diabetic Exchanges: 1/2 starch, 1/2 fruit, 1/2 fat.

CHILI WITH BARLEY
(Pictured at right)

Shirley McClanahan, Falmouth, Kentucky

This is one of those quick but delicious, one-dish dinner recipes you can never have too many of. It's the perfect meal for cold winter days when you need to be warmed from the inside out.

- 1 pound ground beef
- 1 medium onion, chopped
- 2 garlic cloves, minced
- 4 cups water
- 1 cup quick-cooking barley
- 1 can (15-1/2 ounces) chili beans, undrained
- 1 can (14-1/2 ounces) diced tomatoes, undrained
- 1 can (6 ounces) tomato paste
- 1 envelope chili seasoning

In a large saucepan, cook the beef, onion and garlic over medium heat until meat is no longer pink; drain. Add water; bring to a boil. Stir in the barley. Reduce heat; cover and simmer for 10 minutes or until barley is tender. Stir in the beans, tomatoes, tomato paste and chili seasoning; heat through. **Yield:** 6-8 servings.

MARINATED CHICKEN SANDWICHES

Ruth Lee, Troy, Ontario

Every bite of this grilled chicken is packed with flavor. The sweet brown sugar combines well with zesty mustard and ginger.

✓ Uses less fat, sugar or salt. Includes Nutrition Facts and Diabetic Exchanges.

- 1/2 cup reduced-sodium soy sauce
- 1/4 cup packed brown sugar
- 1/4 cup ketchup
- 1 tablespoon canola oil
- 1 tablespoon molasses
- 1 teaspoon garlic powder
- 1 teaspoon minced fresh gingerroot
- 1 teaspoon prepared mustard
- 6 boneless skinless chicken breast halves (6 ounces *each*)
- 3 tablespoons reduced-fat mayonnaise
- 6 kaiser rolls, split and toasted
- 6 lettuce leaves
- 6 slices (1/2 ounce *each*) reduced-fat Swiss cheese

In a large resealable plastic bag, combine the first eight ingredients; add the chicken. Seal bag and turn to coat; refrigerate for at least 1 hour.

Coat grill rack with nonstick cooking spray before starting the grill. Drain and discard marinade. Grill chicken, covered, over medium heat for 4-6 minutes on each side or until juices run clear. Spread mayonnaise over bottom of rolls; top with chicken, lettuce and cheese. Replace roll tops. **Yield:** 6 servings.

Nutrition Facts: 1 sandwich equals 430 calories, 12 g fat (3 g saturated fat), 103 mg cholesterol, 595 mg sodium, 34 g carbohydrate, 2 g fiber, 45 g protein. **Diabetic Exchanges:** 5 lean meat, 2 starch.

HOMEMADE COLESLAW DRESSING

Jewel Kiswer, Cartersville, Georgia

Some cooked dressings can be heavy and overly sweet, especially if they contain cream, but this one isn't. The family-favorite recipe dates back to 1942.

- 2 tablespoons sugar
- 1/2 teaspoon salt
- 1/4 teaspoon ground mustard
- 1/4 teaspoon paprika
- 4 egg yolks
- 1/2 cup water
- 1/3 cup white vinegar
- 2 cups shredded green cabbage
- 2 cups shredded red cabbage

In a heavy saucepan, whisk the sugar, salt, mustard, paprika and egg yolks until smooth. Gradually whisk in water and vinegar. Cook and stir over medium heat until a thermometer reads 160° and mixture is thickened. Remove from the heat; cool to room temperature.

Place the shredded cabbage in a bowl; add the dressing and toss to coat. Refrigerate until serving. **Yield:** 6-8 servings.

FROZEN GRAPEFRUIT-AVOCADO SALAD

(Pictured below)

Daphne York, Alford, Florida

You might wonder about this unusual combination of grapefruit, avocado, grapes and pecans, but you'll find it's a real taste treat. The different flavors and textures go together beautifully.

    1 package (8 ounces) cream cheese,
      softened
    1 cup (8 ounces) sour cream
  1/2 cup sugar
  1/4 teaspoon salt
    1 can (24 ounces) grapefruit sections,
      drained
    1 medium ripe avocado, peeled and diced
    1 cup green grapes, halved
  1/2 cup chopped pecans

In a large mixing bowl, beat cream cheese until smooth. Add the sour cream, sugar and salt; mix well. Gently stir in the grapefruit, avocado, grapes and pecans.

Transfer the salad to a 9-in. x 5-in. x 3-in. loaf pan lightly coated with nonstick cooking spray. Cover and freeze for 4 hours or until firm. Invert onto a cutting board; cut into slices. **Yield:** 10-12 servings.

NUTTY CHICKEN ROLL-UPS

Shelly Eckholm, Wing, North Dakota

Chili powder and cumin give these chicken wraps a bit of a kick. I like that I can make them in advance and keep them in the fridge until mealtime.

    3 cups chopped cooked chicken breast
  1/2 cup finely chopped pecans, toasted
  1/4 cup finely chopped onion
    1 celery rib, finely chopped
  1/2 cup mayonnaise
  1/2 teaspoon chili powder
  1/4 teaspoon salt
  1/4 teaspoon ground cumin
  1/8 teaspoon pepper
    7 lettuce leaves
    7 flour tortillas (8 inches)

In a large bowl, combine the chicken, pecans, onion and celery. Combine mayonnaise, chili powder, salt, cumin and pepper; stir into chicken mixture.

Place lettuce on tortillas. Top each with about 1/2 cup chicken mixture; roll up tightly. Serve immediately, or wrap in plastic wrap and refrigerate until serving. **Yield:** 7 servings.

HEARTY COUNTRY BURGERS

Gladys Gibbs, Brush Creek, Tennessee

When I plan a casual cookout, I invite these dressed-up burgers to the table. Bacon, onion, tomato and cheese toppings really boost the flavor, and the mildly seasoned meat turns out nice and juicy.

    2 garlic cloves, minced
    1 tablespoon olive oil
  1/3 cup plus 1 teaspoon lime juice, *divided*
    2 tablespoons cola, *divided*
    1 tablespoon orange juice
    1 tablespoon soy sauce
    1 pound ground beef
  1/2 teaspoon garlic powder
    4 slices provolone cheese
    4 bacon strips, halved and cooked
    4 hamburger buns, split and toasted
    4 lettuce leaves
    4 slices tomato
    1 slice onion, separated into rings

In a small skillet, saute the garlic in oil for 1-2 minutes or until golden. Stir in 1/3 cup lime juice, 1 tablespoon cola, orange juice and soy sauce. Bring to a boil; cook and stir for 5-6 minutes or until slightly thickened. Set aside for basting.

Crumble beef into a large bowl. Sprinkle with garlic powder and remaining lime juice and cola; mix well. Shape into four 3/4-in.-thick patties.

Grill, covered, over medium heat for 8-9 minutes on each side or until a meat thermometer reads 160°, basting occasionally with sauce. During the last 2 minutes, top burgers with cheese and bacon. Serve on buns with lettuce, tomato and onion. **Yield:** 4 servings.

GENOA SANDWICH LOAF
(Pictured below)

Melita Doyle, Milton Freewater, Oregon

I'm an Italian American, and I love this open-faced meat-and-cheese sandwich because it reminds me of "home." My Irish husband enjoys it just as much as my relatives do when I fix it for family gatherings.

    1/3 cup olive oil
1-1/4 cups packed minced fresh parsley
      1 cup minced fresh basil
    1/2 cup shredded Parmesan cheese, *divided*
      4 garlic cloves, peeled
    1/4 teaspoon ground nutmeg
      1 package (8 ounces) cream cheese, softened
      1 loaf (1 pound) French bread, halved lengthwise
      1 pound thinly sliced hard salami
      2 large tomatoes, thinly sliced

For pesto, in a blender, combine the oil, parsley, basil, 1/4 cup Parmesan cheese, garlic and nutmeg. Cover and process on high until blended.

Spread cream cheese over cut sides of bread; spread with pesto. Layer the salami and tomatoes over pesto; sprinkle with the remaining Parmesan cheese. Place on an ungreased baking sheet. Bake at 350° for 15-20 minutes or until cheese is melted. Let stand for 10 minutes before cutting. **Yield:** 8-10 servings.

HERBED POTATO SOUP
(Pictured above)

Jo Crouch, East Alton, Illinois

This creamy potato soup is almost as easy to make as canned soup...and tastes so much better. Rosemary and thyme add just the right amount of seasoning.

      3 medium potatoes, peeled and diced
      2 cups water
      1 large onion, chopped
    1/4 cup butter, cubed
    1/4 cup all-purpose flour
      1 teaspoon salt
    1/2 teaspoon dried thyme
    1/4 teaspoon dried rosemary, crushed
    1/4 teaspoon pepper
1-1/2 cups milk

Place potatoes and water in a large saucepan; cook over medium heat until tender. Meanwhile, in another saucepan, saute onion in butter until tender. Stir in the flour, salt, thyme, rosemary and pepper. Gradually add milk. Bring to a boil; cook and stir for 2 minutes. Add potatoes with cooking liquid; heat through. **Yield:** 5 servings.

GREAT GARNISHING

Craving a crunchy garnish for Herbed Potato Soup? Top each steaming bowlful with your favorite seasoned salad croutons. Or, add some cooked and crumbled bacon.

3/4 teaspoon salt
1 teaspoon pepper
1/2 cup vegetable oil
1/4 cup chopped fresh parsley
3/4 cup finely chopped fully cooked ham
1 cup (4 ounces) finely shredded Swiss cheese

3/4 teaspoon salt
1 teaspoon pepper
1/2 cup vegetable oil
1/4 cup chopped fresh parsley
3/4 cup finely chopped fully cooked ham
1 cup (4 ounces) finely shredded Swiss cheese

Place potatoes in a saucepan; cover with water. Boil until tender. Drain; cool and peel. Cut into 1/2-in. cubes; set aside.

Combine vinegar, wine or water, onion, mustard, salt, pepper, oil and parsley in a jar with a tight-fitting lid. Shake well. Add ham and cheese to the potatoes; pour two-thirds of dressing over potato mixture. Mix until blended. Cover; chill thoroughly. Before serving, stir remaining dressing and add more if desired. **Yield:** 4 servings.

★★★★★★★★★★★★

OPEN-FACED REUBENS
(Pictured at right)

Mary Ann Dell, Phoenixville, Pennsylvania

Anyone who likes the distinctive taste of reuben sandwiches is sure to love these. Using coleslaw mix speeds up the preparation.

2-1/2 cups coleslaw mix
8 green onions, sliced
1/2 cup mayonnaise, *divided*
2 tablespoons cider vinegar
1/2 teaspoon salt
1/2 teaspoon pepper
1/4 cup Dijon mustard
8 slices rye bread, lightly toasted
16 slices Swiss cheese
1 pound thinly sliced deli corned beef

In a large bowl, combine the coleslaw mix, onions, 1/4 cup mayonnaise, vinegar, salt and pepper. Cover and refrigerate until chilled.

Meanwhile, combine the mustard and remaining mayonnaise. Spread over one side of each slice of toast; top with a cheese slice, corned beef and another cheese slice. Place on foil-lined baking sheets. Bake at 450° for 5-6 minutes or until cheese is melted. Top each with 1/4 cup coleslaw. **Yield:** 8 servings.

★★★★★★★★★★

MARINATED TOMATO SALAD
(Pictured above)

Jean Stever, Clearwater, Kansas

I purchased this terrific recipe at our church auction from the minister's wife. It was definitely worth the price because it's always the talk of the table, no matter what I serve with it!

5 to 6 medium fresh tomatoes, sliced
1/4 pound fresh mushrooms, sliced
3/4 cup vegetable oil
1/4 cup red wine vinegar
3 garlic cloves, minced
1 tablespoon minced fresh parsley
1/2 teaspoon salt

In a large shallow dish, layer the tomatoes and mushrooms. In a bowl, whisk the oil, vinegar, garlic, parsley and salt. Pour over vegetables. Cover and refrigerate for at least 4 hours, turning occasionally. Serve salad with a slotted spoon. **Yield:** 8 servings.

★★★★★★★★★★★★

 HAM, SWISS CHEESE AND POTATO SALAD

Ruth Swift, Portland, Oregon

If you prefer potato salad that's on the heartier side, you'll enjoy this version. With chopped ham and shredded Swiss, it's almost a meal in itself.

1-1/2 pounds red potatoes
3 tablespoons white wine vinegar
4-1/2 tablespoons white wine *or* 3-1/2 teaspoons water plus 1 tablespoon more white wine vinegar
1/4 cup chopped green onion
3 tablespoons Dijon mustard

NICE SLICING

When making baked or broiled sandwiches that have cheese in them, I like to use my vegetable peeler to slice the cheese. It results in thin and uniform slices. *—Sarah Schartz Prineville, Oregon*

MANDARIN BARLEY SALAD
(Pictured below)

Jean Thomsen, Melfort, Saskatchewan

Think barley is boring? You won't after you've tried this salad. Any leftovers you may have are still delicious the second day.

- 1 cup uncooked quick-cooking barley
- 1 can (8 ounces) mushroom stems and pieces, drained
- 1 cup diced celery
- 1/4 cup sliced green onion
- 1/2 cup vegetable oil
- 2 tablespoons cider vinegar
- 2 tablespoons soy sauce
- 1/2 teaspoon salt
- 1 can (11 ounces) mandarin oranges, drained
- 1/2 cup slivered almonds

Cook barley according to package directions; drain and cool. In a bowl, combine the barley, mushrooms, celery and onion.

In a jar with a tight-fitting lid, combine oil, vinegar, soy sauce and salt; shake well. Pour over barley mixture and stir to coat. Gently stir in oranges and almonds. Cover and refrigerate for 4 hours or overnight. **Yield:** 6-8 servings.

MONTE CRISTOS

Debbie Brunssen, Randolph, Nebraska

These classic creations are bound to please even the biggest sandwich fan. Plus, they come together quickly with deli meats, packaged sliced cheese and bottled salad dressing.

- 1/4 cup mayonnaise
- 2 teaspoons Thousand Island salad dressing
- 1 teaspoon Dijon mustard
- 8 slices white bread
- 1/4 pound thinly sliced deli turkey
- 1/4 pound thinly sliced deli ham
- 4 slices Swiss cheese
- 2 eggs, beaten
- 1 cup half-and-half cream
- 1/4 teaspoon ground mustard
- 2 tablespoons butter
- 1/4 cup strawberry preserves

In a small bowl, combine the mayonnaise, Thousand Island dressing and Dijon mustard; spread over one side of each slice of bread. On four slices, layer the turkey, ham and Swiss cheese; top with remaining bread. In a shallow bowl, combine the eggs, cream and ground mustard. Dip the sandwiches in the egg mixture.

On a griddle or large skillet, melt butter. Toast sandwiches over medium heat for 2-3 minutes on each side or until bread is golden brown. Serve with preserves. **Yield:** 4 servings.

MELT-IN-YOUR-MOUTH SAUSAGES
(Pictured above right)

Ilean Schultheiss, Cohocton, New York

My family absolutely loves this recipe. It's such a good all-around dish, especially if you eat the sausage on buns or with spaghetti.

- 8 Italian sausage links (2 pounds)
- 1 jar (48 ounces) spaghetti sauce
- 1 can (6 ounces) tomato paste
- 1 large green pepper, thinly sliced
- 1 large onion, thinly sliced
- 1 tablespoon grated Parmesan cheese
- 1 teaspoon dried parsley flakes
- 1 cup water
- 8 brat buns, split

Additional Parmesan cheese, optional

Place sausage in a large skillet; cover with water. Simmer 10 minutes; drain.

Meanwhile, place next seven ingredients in a 5-qt. slow cooker. Add sausage. Cover and cook

on low for 4 hours. Increase temperature to high; cook 1 hour longer.

Serve in buns. Sprinkle with additional Parmesan cheese if desired. **Yield:** 8 servings.

CREAMY SHELL PASTA SALAD

Rose Friesen, Bonners Ferry, Idaho

When I brought this to a ladies' salad luncheon, the bowl was completely cleaned out! The from-scratch dressing adds unbeatable homemade flavor.

  1 cup uncooked small pasta shells
3/4 cup fresh broccoli florets
  1 small carrot, thinly sliced
1/3 cup cubed American cheese
1/4 cup chopped cucumber
1/4 cup diced celery
1/4 cup sunflower kernels
  1 hard-cooked egg, peeled and chopped
DRESSING:
1/2 cup mayonnaise
1/4 cup prepared ranch salad dressing
  3 tablespoons milk
  2 tablespoons red wine vinegar
  1 tablespoon dried minced onion
1/2 teaspoon seasoned salt
1/4 teaspoon garlic powder
1/4 teaspoon dried parsley flakes
1/4 teaspoon pepper
1/4 teaspoon prepared mustard

Cook pasta according to package directions; drain and rinse in cold water. In a large bowl, combine the pasta, broccoli, carrot, cheese, cucumber, celery, sunflower kernels and egg. In a small bowl,

combine the dressing ingredients. Pour over the salad and toss to coat. Serve immediately. **Yield:** 6-8 servings.

STRAWBERRY-TURKEY SPINACH SALAD
(Pictured below)

This light, refreshing salad from our Test Kitchen is the perfect change of pace after heavy holiday meals. Plus, it puts leftover turkey to great use.

✓ Uses less fat, sugar or salt. Includes Nutrition Facts and Diabetic Exchanges.

  6 cups fresh baby spinach
  2 cups julienned cooked turkey breast
  2 cups sliced fresh strawberries
1/2 large sweet yellow pepper, julienned
  4 green onions, sliced
1/4 cup red wine vinegar
  3 tablespoons olive oil
  2 tablespoons water
  4 tcaspoons honey
1/2 teaspoon dried minced onion
1/2 teaspoon salt
1/4 teaspoon pepper

In a large salad bowl, toss the spinach, turkey, strawberries, yellow pepper and onions. In a jar with a tight-fitting lid, combine the remaining ingredients; shake well. Drizzle over salad and toss to coat. **Yield:** 4 servings.

Nutrition Facts: 1-3/4 cups equals 260 calories, 11 g fat (2 g saturated fat), 60 mg cholesterol, 374 mg sodium, 17 g carbohydrate, 4 g fiber, 23 g protein. **Diabetic Exchanges:** 3 lean meat, 1 fruit, 1 fat.

SPINACH SALAD
(Pictured below)

Linda McCoy, Greensburg, Indiana

Many people don't care for spinach, but not one person who's tried this dressed-up salad has said they didn't like it. And it's so nutritious, too.

> 1 pound fresh spinach, torn
> 1 can (14 ounces) bean sprouts, drained
> 1 can (8 ounces) sliced water chestnuts, drained
> 4 hard-cooked eggs, sliced
> 1/4 cup green onions with tops, sliced
> 1/2 pound bacon, cooked and crumbled
> 1 cup fresh mushrooms, sliced

DRESSING:
> 3/4 cup sugar
> 1/4 cup white vinegar
> 1/4 cup vegetable oil
> 1/3 cup ketchup
> 2 teaspoons salt
> 1 teaspoon Worcestershire sauce

In a large serving bowl, combine the first seven ingredients. In a jar with a tight-fitting lid, combine all the dressing ingredients; cover and shake well. Just before serving, drizzle dressing over salad; toss until well coated. Serve immediately. **Yield:** 8 cups.

SPINACH PO'BOYS
(Pictured above)

Darlyne Plaisance, Poplarville, Mississippi

I discovered this recipe when I lived in New Orleans, where po'boys are very popular. This meatless version featuring spinach and cheese can be served as an appetizer or sandwich. Or, try it as a side dish with your favorite pasta casserole.

> 2 loaves (8 ounces *each*) French bread
> 1 cup butter, softened, *divided*
> 3/4 cup chopped green onions
> 1 package (10 ounces) fresh spinach, trimmed and coarsely chopped
> 1 teaspoon garlic powder
> 1/4 teaspoon hot pepper sauce
> 1 cup (4 ounces) shredded sharp cheddar cheese
> 1 cup (4 ounces) shredded part-skim mozzarella cheese

Cut each loaf of bread in half lengthwise. Spread cut sides with 1/2 cup butter; set aside. In a large skillet, cook onions in remaining butter for 4-5 minutes or until tender. Add the spinach, garlic powder and hot pepper sauce; cook and stir for 3 minutes or until spinach is tender.

Spread spinach mixture over the bottom halves of bread. Sprinkle with cheeses; replace bread tops. Wrap each loaf in foil; place on a baking sheet. Bake at 375° for 20 minutes. Carefully open foil; bake 5 minutes longer or until cheese is melted. Cut into slices. **Yield:** 12-16 slices.

SOUTHWEST BARLEY SALAD

Lois Taylor, Russellville, Alabama

With black beans, corn, peppers and onions, this tasty barley dish is a filling accompaniment to any entree. Plus, the salad can be served warm or cold.

✓ Uses less fat, sugar or salt. Includes Nutrition Facts and Diabetic Exchanges.

   3 cups reduced-sodium chicken broth *or* vegetable broth
3/4 cup uncooked medium pearl barley
   1 cup fresh *or* frozen corn
   1 cup canned black beans, rinsed and drained
3/4 cup chopped sweet red pepper
1/2 cup chopped green pepper
1/2 cup chopped green onions
1/2 cup minced fresh cilantro
   1 garlic clove, minced
1/2 cup salsa
   3 tablespoons reduced-fat sour cream
   2 tablespoons lime *or* lemon juice

In a saucepan, bring broth to a boil. Stir in barley. Reduce heat; cover and simmer for 40-45 minutes or until tender. Drain and cool. In a large bowl, combine the corn, beans, peppers, onions, cilantro and garlic. Stir in barley.

Just before serving, combine the salsa, sour cream and lime juice; add to barley mixture. Serve warm or cold. **Yield:** 6 servings.

Nutrition Facts: 3/4 cup equals 184 calories, 2 g fat (1 g saturated fat), 3 mg cholesterol, 687 mg sodium, 36 g carbohydrate, 8 g fiber, 7 g protein. **Diabetic Exchanges:** 2 starch, 1 vegetable.

PEACH CHICKEN SALAD
(Pictured above)

Priscilla Gilbert, Indian Harbour Beach, Florida

This special medley is a great way to use leftover cooked chicken or fresh mint from your garden. Feel free to substitute nectarines for the peaches.

   3 medium fresh peaches, peeled and cubed
   2 cups cubed cooked chicken breast
   1 medium cucumber, seeded and chopped
   3 tablespoons finely chopped red onion
MINT VINAIGRETTE:
1/4 cup white wine vinegar
   1 tablespoon lemon juice
1/3 cup sugar
1/4 cup minced fresh mint
1/4 teaspoon salt
1/8 teaspoon pepper
   4 lettuce leaves

In a large bowl, combine the peaches, chicken, cucumber and onion; set aside. In a blender, combine the vinegar, lemon juice, sugar, mint, salt and pepper; cover and process until smooth. Drizzle over chicken mixture; toss to coat. Cover and refrigerate until chilled. Use a slotted spoon to serve on lettuce-lined plates. **Yield:** 4 servings.

Exciting Ideas for Avocados

A VERSATILE FRUIT, the avocado can liven up a seemingly endless variety of recipes...including the terrific dishes featured here.

■■■■■■■■■■■

GRAPEFRUIT AVOCADO SALAD
(Pictured below)

This pretty, refreshing salad from our Test Kitchen pairs well with roasted meats and poultry. The avocado, red onion, tart fruit and garlic-mustard dressing make a deliciously different blend.

    1/4 **cup olive oil**
    2 **tablespoons lemon juice**
    2 **tablespoons orange juice**
    1 **teaspoon Dijon mustard**
    1 **garlic clove, minced**
    1/2 **teaspoon salt**
Freshly ground pepper to taste
Lettuce leaves
    2 **large red grapefruit, peeled and**
      sectioned

    1 **small red onion, thinly sliced and**
      separated into rings
    1 **medium ripe avocado, peeled and sliced**

In a jar with a tight-fitting lid, combine the first seven ingredients; shake well. On four salad plates, arrange the lettuce, grapefruit, onion and avocado. Drizzle with dressing. Serve immediately. **Yield:** 4 servings.

■■■■■■■■■■■

 ### ZESTY GARLIC-AVOCADO SANDWICHES
(Pictured at right)

Tricia Farnum, Branson West, Missouri

Here's a tasty meatless sandwich I created by combining some of our family's favorite ingredients. For variation, add fresh chives or minced sun-dried tomato to the cream cheese.

    1 **package (8 ounces) cream cheese,**
      softened

1-1/2 pounds fresh green beans, trimmed
1 can (11 ounces) mandarin oranges, drained
1 medium red onion, thinly sliced
6 to 8 tablespoons olive oil
1/4 cup cider vinegar
3 to 4 teaspoons sugar
1/2 to 1 teaspoon salt
1/4 teaspoon pepper
4 cups torn mixed salad greens
1 ripe avocado, peeled and sliced
1/2 cup chopped pecans

Place the beans in a large saucepan and cover with water; bring to a boil. Cook, uncovered, for 8-10 minutes or until crisp-tender. Drain and rinse in cold water.

In a large bowl, combine the beans, mandarin oranges and red onion. In a small bowl, whisk the oil, vinegar, sugar, salt and pepper. Pour over the bean mixture and toss to coat. Cover and refrigerate for at least 2 hours. Just before serving, add the salad greens, avocado and pecans; toss gently. **Yield:** 8-9 servings.

2 medium ripe avocados, peeled
1 garlic clove, minced
1/8 teaspoon salt
6 whole grain bagels, split and toasted
6 slices tomato
1/2 cup sliced cucumber
6 slices red onion
6 sweet red pepper rings
6 lettuce leaves

In a small mixing bowl, beat the cream cheese, avocados, garlic and salt until smooth. Spread on bagels; top with tomato, cucumber, onion, pepper rings and lettuce. **Yield:** 6 servings.

 GREEN BEAN TOSSED SALAD
(Pictured at right)

Shirley Kosto, Chugiak, Alaska

To jazz up a salad that contained mandarin oranges, onion and lettuce, I decided to add some fresh green beans. This recipe is the flavorful result.

WHETHER *you're after chicken, beef, pork, seafood or meatless main courses, you'll find plenty of pleasing choices here.*

APPEALING ENTREE. Molasses-Glazed Baby Back Ribs (p. 43).

Main Dishes

MOLASSES-GLAZED BABY BACK RIBS
(Pictured at left)

Kim Braley, Dunedin, Florida

My husband grills these luscious ribs for our family at least once a month during the summer.

4-1/2 pounds pork baby back ribs
   2 liters cola
  1/2 teaspoon salt
  1/2 teaspoon pepper
  1/4 teaspoon garlic salt
  1/4 teaspoon dried oregano
  1/4 teaspoon onion powder
  1/8 teaspoon cayenne pepper
BARBECUE SAUCE:
  1/4 cup ketchup
  1/4 cup honey
  1/4 cup molasses
   1 tablespoon prepared mustard
  1/2 teaspoon cayenne pepper
  1/2 teaspoon salt

Place the ribs in large resealable plastic bags; add cola. Seal bags; turn to coat. Refrigerate for 8 hours or overnight.

Drain and discard cola. Pat ribs dry with paper towels. Combine salt, pepper, garlic salt, oregano, onion powder and cayenne; rub over ribs.

Prepare grill for indirect heat, using a drip pan. Place ribs over pan; grill, covered, over indirect medium heat for 1 hour, turning occasionally. In a small bowl, combine barbecue sauce ingredients. Brush over ribs; grill 10-20 minutes longer or until meat is tender. **Yield:** 4 servings.

BEEF 'N' CHILI BEANS

Anita Hudson, Savoy, Texas

This crowd-pleaser was a big hit when I took it to a church supper. The slow-cooker recipe is so simple.

☑ Uses less fat, sugar or salt. Includes Nutrition Facts.

   3 **pounds beef stew meat, cut into 1-inch cubes**

   2 tablespoons brown sugar
1-1/2 teaspoons ground mustard
   1 teaspoon salt
   1 teaspoon paprika
  1/2 teaspoon chili powder
  1/4 teaspoon pepper
   1 large onion, chopped
   2 cans (10 ounces *each*) diced tomatoes and green chilies
   1 can (15 ounces) ranch-style beans *or* chili beans, undrained
   1 can (15-1/4 ounces) whole kernel corn, drained

Place beef in a 3-qt. slow cooker. Combine sugar, mustard, salt, paprika, chili powder and pepper; sprinkle over beef and toss to coat. Top with remaining ingredients. Cover; cook on low for 6-8 hours or until meat is tender. **Yield:** 6-8 servings.

Nutrition Facts: 3/4 cup equals 373 calories, 14 g fat (5 g saturated fat), 106 mg cholesterol, 1,047 mg sodium, 22 g carbohydrate, 5 g fiber, 37 g protein.

MOSTACCIOLI CASSEROLE
(Pictured on front cover)

Barbara Leeds, Plymouth, Michigan

It's easy to turn ground beef into this Italian-flavored dinner. Canned soup speeds up the preparation.

   2 cups uncooked mostaccioli
   1 pound ground beef
   2 tablespoons chopped onion
   1 can (10-3/4 ounces) condensed tomato soup, undiluted
   1 can (8 ounces) tomato sauce
   1 teaspoon dried oregano
  1/2 teaspoon salt
  1/4 cup shredded Colby cheese

Cook pasta according to package directions. Meanwhile, in a large skillet, cook beef and onion over medium heat until meat is no longer pink; drain. Stir in the soup, tomato sauce, oregano and salt.

Drain pasta; stir into beef mixture. Transfer to a greased 1-1/2-qt. baking dish; top with cheese. Bake, uncovered, at 350° for 30-35 minutes or until heated through. **Yield:** 4 servings.

BRAZILIAN-STYLE TURKEY WITH HAM
(Pictured below)

Carol Marriott, Centreville, Virginia

Grilling is a different and fun way to prepare whole turkey. My mom has served this impressive main course for weddings at her home, "Christmas in July" parties and other events.

>   1 whole turkey (12 pounds)
> 4-1/2 teaspoons salt
>   2 teaspoons pepper
>   3 garlic cloves, minced
> 1-1/2 cups white vinegar
>   1 cup olive oil
>   4 medium tomatoes, seeded and chopped
>   4 medium green peppers, seeded and chopped
>   1/2 cup minced fresh parsley
>   2 pounds smoked ham, thinly sliced

Remove the giblets from the turkey and discard. Place a turkey-size oven roasting bag inside a second roasting bag; add the turkey. Place in a roasting pan. Combine the salt, pepper and garlic; rub over the turkey.

In a bowl, combine the vinegar, oil, tomatoes, peppers and parsley. Pour over turkey and into cavity. Squeeze out as much air as possible from bag; seal and turn to coat. Refrigerate for 12-24 hours, turning several times.

Drain and discard marinade. Skewer turkey openings; tie drumsticks together. Prepare grill for indirect heat, using a drip pan. Coat grill rack with nonstick cooking spray before starting grill.

Grill turkey, covered, over indirect medium heat for 2 to 2-1/2 hours or until a meat thermometer reads 180°, tenting turkey with foil after about 1 hour. Let stand for 20 minutes before slicing. Meanwhile, warm the ham. Layer turkey and ham slices on a serving platter. **Yield:** 12 servings plus leftovers.

LOUISIANA BARBECUE BRISKET

Allan Stackhouse, Jennings, Louisiana

Rely on this saucy sensation when you need a special entree for a crowd. The recipe includes many make-ahead steps, and there's no last-minute fuss because the meat grills unattended for several hours.

>   3 tablespoons paprika
>   2 teaspoons *each* salt, garlic powder and pepper
>   1 teaspoon *each* cayenne pepper, dried oregano and ground mustard
>   1/2 teaspoon chili powder
>   1 fresh beef brisket (4 to 6 pounds)
> BARBECUE SAUCE:
>   2 cups ketchup
>   1 cup packed brown sugar
>   1 cup unsweetened pineapple juice
>   2/3 cup light corn syrup
>   1/2 cup finely chopped onion
>   1/2 cup apple juice
>   1/4 cup chili powder
>   2 to 4 tablespoons hot pepper sauce
>   4 teaspoons Worcestershire sauce
>   1 to 4 teaspoons Liquid Smoke, optional

In a small bowl, combine the seasonings. Rub 2 teaspoons over brisket. (Place remaining seasoning mixture in an airtight container; save for up to 3 months for another use.)

In a bowl, combine the sauce ingredients; stir until brown sugar is dissolved. Pour 2 cups into a large resealable plastic bag; add the brisket. Seal bag and turn to coat; refrigerate for 8 hours or overnight, turning several times. Cover and refrigerate remaining sauce.

Prepare grill for indirect heat, using a drip pan. Drain and discard marinade from brisket; pat dry with paper towels. Place brisket over pan; grill, covered, over indirect low heat for 30-45 minutes on each side or until browned.

Transfer brisket to a heavy-duty disposable roasting pan. Pour 1-1/4 cups of the reserved sauce over brisket. Cover with a double layer of heavy-duty foil and seal tightly. Grill, covered, over indirect low heat for 3-4 hours or until meat is fork-tender. Slice brisket across the grain. Serve with remaining sauce. **Yield:** 12-16 servings.

HOT 'N' SOUR SHRIMP
(Pictured above)

Mary Ann Dell, Phoenixville, Pennsylvania

Looking for something quick, colorful and chock-full of wholesome ingredients? Try spooning this hearty shrimp-and-veggie dish over spaghetti. It gets a bit of a kick from red pepper flakes.

  1 tablespoon brown sugar
  2 teaspoons cornstarch
  2 tablespoons water
  2 tablespoons cider vinegar
  2 tablespoons soy sauce
  1 tablespoon vegetable oil
  1 large sweet red pepper, julienned
3/4 cup sliced fresh mushrooms
  1 pound uncooked medium shrimp, peeled and deveined
  2 garlic cloves, minced
1/4 teaspoon crushed red pepper flakes
1/2 small cucumber, seeded and sliced
Hot cooked spaghetti, optional

In a small bowl, combine the first five ingredients until smooth; set aside. In a skillet or wok, heat oil; stir-fry red pepper and mushrooms for 4 minutes. Add the shrimp, garlic and pepper flakes; stir-fry 3-4 minutes longer or until shrimp turn pink and vegetables are crisp-tender.

Stir cornstarch mixture and add to pan. Bring to a boil; cook and stir for 1 minute or until thickened. Add cucumber; cook and stir 1 minute longer or until heated through. Serve with spaghetti if desired. **Yield:** 4 servings.

CHERRY-GLAZED ROAST PORK
(Pictured below)

Beth Brandenburger, Rochester, Minnesota

This tender roast looks impressive, yet it's so easy to prepare that I use it as a main dish for holidays and other special occasions year-round. The nicely spiced cherry glaze makes a mouth-watering topping.

  1 boneless rolled pork loin roast (3 to 4 pounds)
1/2 teaspoon salt, *divided*
1/4 teaspoon pepper
  1 jar (12 ounces) cherry preserves
1/4 cup cranberry-raspberry juice
  2 tablespoons corn syrup
1/4 teaspoon ground cinnamon
1/4 teaspoon ground nutmeg
1/4 teaspoon ground cloves

Place roast fat side up on a rack in a shallow roasting pan. Sprinkle with 1/4 teaspoon salt and pepper. Bake, uncovered, at 350° for 1-1/4 hours.

In a small saucepan, combine the preserves, juice, corn syrup, spices and remaining salt. Bring to a boil. Reduce heat; simmer for 5 minutes. Pour 1/2 cup sauce over roast. Bake 30 minutes longer or until a meat thermometer reads 160°. Cover and let stand for 15 minutes before slicing.

Scrape up browned bits and pan drippings; add to remaining sauce. Cook and stir until heated through. Serve over roast. **Yield:** 10-12 servings.

mint if desired, cinnamon and pepper. Set aside.

For sauce, melt butter in a saucepan over medium heat. Stir in flour until smooth; gradually add milk. Bring to a boil; cook and stir for 2 minutes or until thickened. Remove from the heat. Stir a small amount of hot mixture into eggs; return all to the pan, stirring constantly. Add the Parmesan cheese and salt.

Place half of the potato slices in a greased shallow 3-qt. baking dish. Top with half of the meat mixture. Arrange the remaining potatoes over meat mixture; top with the remaining Parmesan sauce.

Bake, uncovered, at 350° for 1 hour or until potatoes are tender. Let stand for 10 minutes before serving. **Yield:** 8-10 servings.

BAVARIAN CASSEROLE

Barbara LaFlair, Houghton Lake, Michigan

This one-dish supper is a little different from the usual meat-and-potato casseroles. The sauerkraut and tomatoes add a nice, tangy flavor to the tender pork chops. I've also used boneless skinless chicken breasts and turkey bacon with good results.

        4 medium red potatoes
        6 bacon strips, diced
        6 bone-in pork loin chops (3/4 inch
           thick)
        1 large onion, chopped
        1 jar (32 ounces) sauerkraut, rinsed and
           well drained
        1 can (28 ounces) stewed tomatoes,
           drained
        1 teaspoon caraway seeds
    1/2 teaspoon salt
    1/4 teaspoon pepper

Place potatoes in a saucepan and cover with water. Bring to a boil. Reduce heat; cover and simmer for 25-30 minutes or until almost tender. Drain; when cool enough to handle, cut into 1/4-in. slices.

In a large skillet, cook bacon over medium heat until crisp. Using a slotted spoon, remove to paper towels. In the drippings, brown pork chops on both sides. Remove chops; drain, reserving 1 tablespoon drippings. Saute onion in drippings until tender. Stir in sauerkraut and bacon; cook for 3-4 minutes.

Spoon sauerkraut mixture into a greased 13-in. x 9-in. x 2-in. baking dish. Layer with the pork chops, potato slices and tomatoes. Sprinkle with caraway seeds, salt and pepper. Cover and bake at 350° for 40-45 minutes or until a meat thermometer reads 160°. **Yield:** 6 servings.

BEEF AND POTATO MOUSSAKA
(Pictured above)

Jean Puffer, Chilliwack, British Columbia

When my son was in grade school, he brought home this recipe for moussaka, a classic Greek entree, as part of an assignment about Greece. The tasty beef bake got high marks when we made it for his class.

        1 pound ground beef
        1 medium onion, chopped
        1 garlic clove, minced
    3/4 cup water
        1 can (6 ounces) tomato paste
        3 tablespoons minced fresh parsley
        1 teaspoon salt
    1/2 teaspoon dried mint, optional
    1/4 teaspoon ground cinnamon
    1/4 teaspoon pepper
PARMESAN SAUCE:
    1/4 cup butter
    1/4 cup all-purpose flour
        2 cups milk
        4 eggs, beaten
    1/2 cup grated Parmesan cheese
    1/2 tcaspoon salt
        5 medium potatoes, peelcd and thinly
           sliced

In a large skillet, cook the beef, onion and garlic over medium heat until meat is no longer pink; drain. Stir in water, tomato paste, parsley, salt,

▰▰▰▰▰▰▰▰▰▰▰▰
BAKED HADDOCK
(Pictured below)

Alma Troyer, Newport, Maine

A colorful topping of sliced plum tomatoes plus bread crumbs mixed with herbs and vegetables is wonderful on these flaky fillets. They were a big hit with our friends and family at a dinner party.

     1/2 cup chopped onion
     1/4 cup chopped celery
       3 tablespoons butter
     1/2 cup chopped fresh mushrooms
       2 cups soft bread crumbs
       1 teaspoon salt
     1/8 teaspoon pepper
Pinch dried tarragon
Pinch dried rosemary, optional
       2 pounds fresh *or* frozen haddock fillets, thawed
       1 tablespoon lemon juice
       4 plum tomatoes, sliced

In a skillet, saute onion and celery in butter for 3 minutes or until tender. Add the mushrooms; saute 1 minute longer or until tender. Remove from the heat; stir in the bread crumbs, salt, pepper, tarragon and rosemary if desired.

Place the fillets in a greased 11-in. x 7-in. x 2-in. baking dish. Sprinkle with lemon juice. Spoon the bread crumb mixture onto fillets; top with tomatoes. Bake, uncovered, at 375° for 25-30 minutes or until fish flakes easily with a fork. **Yield:** 6 servings.

▰▰▰▰▰▰▰▰▰▰▰▰
 ## MARINATED CHUCK ROAST
(Pictured above)

Mary Lee Baker, Enon, Ohio

Jazzed up with a marinade of orange juice, soy sauce, brown sugar and Worcestershire, this beef roast always wins raves. It's a great make-ahead recipe.

     1/2 cup orange juice
       3 tablespoons soy sauce
       3 tablespoons brown sugar
       1 teaspoon Worcestershire sauce
       1 boneless beef chuck roast (3 to 4 pounds)

In a large resealable plastic bag, combine the orange juice, soy sauce, brown sugar and Worcestershire sauce; add the roast. Seal bag and turn to coat; refrigerate for 8 hours or overnight.

Pour the marinade into a Dutch oven. Bring to a boil; boil for 2 minutes. Add roast to the pan. Cover and bake at 325° for 3 to 3-1/2 hours or until the meat is tender. Let stand for 10 minutes before slicing. Thicken juices for gravy if desired. **Yield:** 8-10 servings.

COOKING FISH FILLETS

To check fillets for doneness, insert a fork at an angle into the thickest portion of the fish and gently part the meat. When it flakes into sections, it is cooked completely.

Family-Pleasing Meat Pies

WHEN savory comfort food fills the bill, you'll want to put together one of these memorable meat pies. Pop one in the oven tonight for a supper that's sure to satisfy.

◆◆◆◆◆◆◆◆◆◆◆◆◆

INDIVIDUAL CHICKEN POTPIES
(Pictured below)

Vickie Wicks, Saint Joseph, Missouri

These little pies look so appetizing with their golden pastry crust and colorful filling. Home-style and rich, they're always well-received by guests. Sometimes I adapt the recipe to make one large casserole.

1/4 cup chopped onion
2 tablespoons chopped green pepper
1/4 cup butter
1/3 cup all-purpose flour
1 can (14-1/2 ounces) chicken broth
1 cup milk
1 cup fresh broccoli florets
1/2 cup fresh cauliflowerets
1/2 cup thinly sliced celery
1/2 cup thinly sliced carrot
1 cup (4 ounces) shredded Swiss cheese
2 cups cubed cooked chicken
PASTRY:
1-1/3 cups all-purpose flour
1/2 teaspoon salt
1/2 teaspoon paprika
1/2 cup shortening
3 to 4 tablespoons cold water

In a large saucepan, saute the onion and green pepper in butter until onion is tender. Add flour until blended. Stir in the broth, milk, broccoli, cauliflower, celery and carrot. Bring to a boil; cook and stir for 2 minutes or until thickened. Remove from the heat. Stir in cheese. Divide chicken among four ungreased 1-1/2-cup baking dishes. Top with vegetable mixture.

Combine flour, salt and paprika in a bowl; cut in shortening until crumbly. Gradually add water, tossing with a fork until dough forms a ball. Divide into four portions; roll out each to 1/8-in. thickness. Place pastry over vegetable mixture. Trim pastry to 1/2 in. beyond edge of dish; flute edges. Cut slits in top. Bake at 350° for 30-40 minutes or until golden brown. **Yield:** 4 servings.

◆◆◆◆◆◆◆◆◆◆◆◆◆

STEAK POTPIE

Kristin Shaw, Castleton, New York

This classic meat pie really hits the spot on a chilly winter night. With plenty of steak, vegetables and gravy, it's hearty and satisfying.

1-1/4 pounds boneless beef sirloin steak, cut into 1/2-inch cubes

2 tablespoons butter
1/4 teaspoon pepper
1 package (16 ounces) frozen vegetables for stew
2 tablespoons water
1/2 teaspoon dried thyme
1 jar (12 ounces) mushroom *or* beef gravy
1 tube (8 ounces) refrigerated crescent rolls

In a large ovenproof skillet, brown beef in butter. Remove beef; season with pepper and keep warm. In same skillet, combine vegetables, water and thyme. Stir in gravy. Bring to a boil. Reduce heat; simmer, uncovered, until vegetables are thawed. Stir in beef; remove from heat.

Separate crescent dough into eight triangles. Starting from the wide end of each triangle, roll up a third of the length and place over beef mixture with pointed ends toward the center. Bake, uncovered, at 375° for 16-18 minutes or until golden brown. **Yield:** 4-6 servings.

POTATO-TOPPED MEAT PIE
(Pictured above right)

Jo Crouch, East Alton, Illinois

My husband is a meat-and-potatoes guy and could eat the same thing every day, but I like variety. So I've come up with different ways to use those main ingredients. This recipe is one of our favorites.

1 pound ground beef
1 medium onion, chopped
3 garlic cloves, minced
1 egg
2 tablespoons Worcestershire sauce
1 cup dry bread crumbs
Salt and pepper to taste
1 package (10 ounces) frozen corn, thawed
1 package (10 ounces) frozen peas, thawed
1 can (10-3/4 ounces) condensed cream of mushroom soup, undiluted
1/2 cup milk
3 cups mashed potatoes (prepared with milk and butter)

In a large skillet, cook the beef, onion and garlic over medium heat until meat is no longer pink; drain. Cool for 5 minutes. In a bowl, combine the egg, Worcestershire sauce, bread crumbs, salt and pepper. Stir in meat mixture.

Transfer to a greased 13-in. x 9-in. x 2-in. baking dish. In a bowl, combine the corn, peas, cream of mushroom soup and milk. Spread over the meat mixture. Top with the mashed potatoes. Bake, uncovered, at 375° for 35 minutes or until lightly browned. **Yield:** 4 servings.

MILK IN A PINCH

I always keep powdered milk on hand in case I run out of milk. I prepare the powdered milk according to the package directions and use it in casseroles and other recipes.

Paige Alexander, Littleton, Colorado

BROCCOLI TUNA ROLL-UPS
(Pictured below)

Mary Wilhelm, Sparta, Wisconsin

For a family-pleasing main dish that's on the lighter side, consider these cheesy tortilla wraps. They're a fun and tasty alternative to the usual tuna casserole.

☑ Uses less fat, sugar or salt. Includes Nutrition Facts and Diabetic Exchanges.

   1 can (10-3/4 ounces) reduced-fat reduced-sodium condensed cream of mushroom soup, undiluted
   1 cup fat-free milk
   2 cans (6 ounces *each*) light water-packed tuna, drained and flaked
   1 package (10 ounces) frozen chopped broccoli, thawed and drained
2/3 cup shredded reduced-fat cheddar cheese, *divided*
1/3 cup sliced almonds, *divided*
   6 flour tortillas (7 inches)
   1 large tomato, seeded and chopped

In a small bowl, combine the cream of mushroom soup and milk; set aside. Combine the tuna, broccoli, 1/3 cup cheese and 3 tablespoons almonds. Stir in half of the soup mixture.

Spoon filling down the center of each tortilla; roll up. Place seam side down in an 11-in. x 7-in.

x 2-in. baking dish coated with nonstick cooking spray. Pour remaining soup mixture over top; sprinkle with tomato.

Cover and bake at 350° for 35 minutes. Uncover; sprinkle with remaining cheese and almonds. Bake 5 minutes longer or until cheese is melted. **Yield:** 6 servings.

Nutrition Facts: One roll-up equals 321 calories, 10 g fat (3 g saturated fat), 26 mg cholesterol, 696 mg sodium, 34 g carbohydrate, 4 g fiber, 25 g protein. **Diabetic Exchanges:** 3 lean meat, 2 starch.

GRILLED VEGGIE SAUSAGE PIZZA

Faith Sommers, Bangor, California

I did some experimenting to come up with this crispy, thin-crust pizza. It met with such approval, my guests were eager to try it in their own backyards.

   1 tablespoon active dry yeast
1-1/3 cups warm water (110° to 115°)
   5 teaspoons sugar
   4 teaspoons vegetable oil
1/4 teaspoon salt
1/4 teaspoon garlic salt
1/4 teaspoon dried oregano
3-1/4 to 3-1/2 cups all-purpose flour
TOPPINGS:
1/2 pound bulk Italian sausage
1-1/2 cups pizza sauce
   2 cups (8 ounces) shredded part-skim mozzarella cheese
   1 cup sliced fresh mushrooms
1/4 cup chopped sweet red pepper
1/4 cup chopped green pepper

In a large mixing bowl, dissolve yeast in water. Add the sugar, oil, salt, garlic salt, oregano and 1-1/2 cups flour. Stir in enough of the remaining flour to form a soft dough.

Turn onto a floured surface; knead until smooth and elastic, about 6-8 minutes. Place in a greased bowl, turning once to grease top. Cover and let rise in a warm place for 30 minutes.

Wrap foil over the outside bottom of two 12-in. pizza pans; grease pans and set aside. In a skillet, cook sausage over medium heat until no longer pink; drain and set aside. Divide dough in half. On a floured surface, roll each portion into a 13-in. circle. Transfer to prepared pans; build up edges slightly.

Spread pizza sauce over crusts; sprinkle with sausage, cheese, mushrooms and peppers. Grill, covered, over medium heat for 15-20 minutes or until bottom of crust is browned and cheese is melted. **Yield:** 2 pizzas (8 slices each).

 ## SPICY MEAT LOAF
(Pictured above)

Marie Hiskey, Springfield, Missouri

This is not your typical meat loaf! The green chili salsa really gives it some zip, and the pork sausage combined with the beef provides variety.

      2 eggs
  1/2 cup green *or* red chili salsa
      1 cup seasoned bread crumbs
      2 pounds ground beef
  1/2 pound bulk pork sausage
Additional salsa, optional

In a large bowl, combine the eggs, salsa and bread crumbs. Crumble beef and sausage over mixture and mix well. Press into an ungreased 9-in. x 5-in. x 3-in. loaf pan.

Bake, uncovered, at 350° for 1 hour or until meat is no longer pink and a meat thermometer reads 160°; drain. Let stand for 10 minutes before slicing. Top with additional salsa if desired. **Yield:** 8-10 servings.

DILLY HAM BALLS
(Pictured at right)

Dixie Terry, Marion, Illinois

To create a main course my grandchildren would enjoy, I shaped a ham loaf into balls and added a sauce. The kids raved about it—and so did the adults. I've handed out this recipe many times.

      1 pound ground fully cooked ham
  1/2 cup dry bread crumbs
  1/4 cup finely chopped green onions
      3 tablespoons finely chopped fresh dill *or*
      3 teaspoons dried dill, *divided*
  1/4 cup milk
      1 egg, lightly beaten
      1 teaspoon Dijon mustard
  1/2 teaspoon pepper, *divided*
      1 to 2 tablespoons butter
      1 to 2 tablespoons vegetable oil
      2 tablespoons all-purpose flour
      1 cup water
      1 cup (8 ounces) sour cream
Hot cooked noodles

In a bowl, combine ham, bread crumbs, onions, 1 tablespoon fresh dill (or 1 teaspoon dried), milk, egg, mustard and 1/4 teaspoon pepper. Shape into 1-in. balls.

In a large skillet, heat 1 tablespoon butter and 1 tablespoon oil. Brown ham balls, adding remaining butter and oil as needed. Remove ham balls to a serving dish; cover and keep warm.

Pour ham drippings into a saucepan; blend in flour. Gradually add water and stir until smooth. Bring to a boil; cook and stir for 2 minutes or until thickened. Reduce heat to low. Add sour cream and remaining dill and pepper; heat through, but do not boil. Pour over the ham balls. Serve over noodles. **Yield:** 6 servings.

★★★★★★★★★★★★★

SKILLET CHICKEN CORDON BLEU

(Pictured above)

Nancy Zimmerer, Medina, Ohio

A dear friend from my high school days shared this recipe with me. It gives you all the goodness of chicken cordon bleu without a lot of fuss.

> 4 boneless skinless chicken breast halves
> 4 thin slices fully cooked ham
> 4 thin slices Swiss cheese
> 3 tablespoons all-purpose flour
> 1 teaspoon paprika
> 1/3 cup butter
> 1/2 cup white grape juice
> 1 chicken bouillon cube
> 1 cup heavy whipping cream
> 1 tablespoon cornstarch

Flatten chicken to 1/4-in. thickness. Top each with a slice of ham and cheese; fold to fit. Roll up tightly and secure with toothpicks. In a shallow bowl, combine the flour and paprika. Coat chicken with flour mixture.

In a large skillet over medium heat, melt butter. Cook chicken for 5 minutes on each side or until browned. Add grape juice and bouillon. Reduce heat; cover and simmer for 30 minutes or until chicken is tender.

Remove chicken and keep warm. In a small bowl, combine cream and cornstarch until smooth. Gradually stir into pan juices. Bring to a boil; cook and stir for 2 minutes or until thickened. Spoon over chicken. **Yield:** 4 servings.

★★★★★★★★★★★★★

SPICED SALMON

Donna Reynolds, Innisfail, Alberta

This tongue-tingling fish comes together with spices I usually have on hand. Because the recipe is so quick to prepare, it's a great choice for parties.

> 3 tablespoons brown sugar
> 1/2 teaspoon garlic powder
> 1/2 teaspoon ground mustard
> 1/2 teaspoon paprika
> 1/2 teaspoon pepper
> 1/4 teaspoon dill weed
> Dash salt
> Dash dried tarragon
> Dash cayenne pepper
> 2 tablespoons butter, melted
> 2 tablespoons olive oil
> 2 tablespoons soy sauce
> 1 salmon fillet (2 pounds)

In a small bowl, combine the first nine ingredients. Add the butter, oil and soy sauce; brush over top of salmon. Coat grill rack with nonstick cooking spray before starting the grill. Place salmon skin side down on rack. Grill, covered, over medium heat for 10-15 minutes or until fish flakes easily with a fork. **Yield:** 6-8 servings.

★★★★★★★★★★★★★

MEXICALI CASSEROLE

Mrs. Gertrudis Miller, Evansville, Indiana

If you like Mexican food but are watching your diet, try this tasty bake. It takes advantage of ground turkey and reduced-fat cheese without sacrificing flavor.

☑ Uses less fat, sugar or salt. Includes Nutrition Facts and Diabetic Exchanges.

> 1 pound ground turkey breast
> 1-1/2 cups chopped onions
> 1/2 cup chopped green pepper
> 1 garlic clove, minced
> 1 teaspoon chili powder
> 1/2 teaspoon salt
> 1 can (16 ounces) kidney beans, rinsed and drained
> 1 can (14-1/2 ounces) diced tomatoes, undrained
> 1 cup water
> 2/3 cup uncooked long grain rice
> 1/3 cup sliced ripe olives
> 1/2 cup shredded reduced-fat cheddar cheese

In a large skillet coated with nonstick cooking spray, cook the turkey, onions, green pepper and garlic over medium heat until meat is no longer pink and vegetables are tender; drain. Sprinkle with chili powder and salt. Stir in the beans, tomatoes, water, rice and olives.

Transfer to a 2-1/2-qt. baking dish coated with nonstick cooking spray. Cover and bake at 375° for 50-55 minutes or until rice is tender. Uncover; sprinkle with cheese. Bake 5 minutes longer or until cheese is melted. **Yield:** 6 servings.

Nutrition Facts: One serving equals 348 calories, 10 g fat (3 g saturated fat), 66 mg cholesterol, 508 mg sodium, 41 g carbohydrate, 9 g fiber, 24 g protein. **Diabetic Exchanges:** 2-1/2 lean meat, 2 starch, 2 vegetable.

MUSTARD-HERB GRILLED TENDERLOIN
(Pictured below)

Phyllis Schmalz, Kansas City, Kansas

Our area is known for beef, and we enjoy this tenderloin recipe often. The marinade would also be delicious with grilled pork or chicken.

  2/3 cup olive oil
  1/2 cup beef broth
    3 tablespoons Dijon mustard
    2 tablespoons red wine vinegar
    2 tablespoons lemon juice
  1/2 teaspoon sugar
    2 garlic cloves, minced
  1/2 teaspoon salt
  1/4 teaspoon *each* dried oregano, summer savory, tarragon and thyme
  1/8 teaspoon pepper
    1 beef tenderloin (about 1-1/2 pounds)

In a bowl, combine the oil, broth, mustard, vinegar, lemon juice, sugar and seasonings. Pour 3/4 cup into a large resealable plastic bag; add the

beef. Seal bag and turn to coat; refrigerate overnight, turning bag once or twice. Cover and refrigerate remaining marinade for basting.

Drain and discard marinade from beef. Grill, covered, over medium heat for 20-25 minutes or until meat reaches desired doneness (for medium-rare, a meat thermometer should read 145°; medium, 160°; well-done, 170°). Turn once and baste with 1/4 cup reserved marinade during the last 5 minutes. Let tenderloin stand for 10 minutes before slicing. Serve with the remaining reserved marinade. **Yield:** 6 servings.

EASY ARROZ CON POLLO
(Pictured above)

Debbie Harris, Bolivar Tucson, Arizona

My children really look forward to supper when they know I'm serving this "rice with chicken." And just as the name implies, the recipe is a breeze to prepare.

1-3/4 cups uncooked instant rice
    6 boneless skinless chicken breast halves
Garlic salt and pepper to taste
    1 can (14-1/2 ounces) chicken broth
    1 cup picante sauce
    1 can (8 ounces) tomato sauce
  1/2 cup chopped onion
  1/2 cup chopped green pepper
  1/2 cup shredded Monterey Jack cheese
  1/2 cup shredded cheddar cheese

Spread the rice in a greased 13-in. x 9-in. x 2-in. baking dish. Sprinkle both sides of chicken with garlic salt and pepper; place over rice. In a bowl, combine the broth, picante sauce, tomato sauce, onion and green pepper; pour over the chicken.

Cover and bake at 350° for 55 minutes or until rice is tender and chicken juices run clear. Sprinkle with cheeses. Bake, uncovered, 5 minutes longer or until cheese is melted. **Yield:** 6 servings.

CHICKEN PIE IN A PAN
(Pictured below)

Kristine Conway, Alliance, Ohio

Hearty and filling, this potpie is the perfect way to use up chicken or turkey leftovers. It also travels well, so it's an ideal dish to take to a potluck.

> 2 celery ribs, diced
> 2 medium carrots, diced
> 1 small onion, chopped
> 3 tablespoons butter
> 1/4 cup all-purpose flour
> 1/2 teaspoon salt
> 1 cup milk
> 1 cup chicken broth
> 1 can (10-3/4 ounces) condensed cream of mushroom soup, undiluted
> 4 cups cubed cooked chicken

CRUST:

> 1-1/2 cups all-purpose flour
> 3/4 teaspoon baking powder
> 1 teaspoon salt
> 3 tablespoons cold butter
> 1/2 cup milk
> 2 cups (8 ounces) shredded cheddar cheese

In a large skillet, saute the celery, carrots and onion in butter until tender. Stir in flour and salt until blended; gradually add milk and broth. Bring to a boil; cook and stir for 2 minutes or until thickened. Stir in soup and chicken. Spoon into a greased 13-in. x 9-in. x 2-in. baking dish; set aside.

For crust, combine the flour, baking powder and salt. Cut in butter until crumbly. Add milk, tossing with a fork until mixture forms a soft dough; shape into a ball.

On a lightly floured surface, roll into a 12-in. x 10-in. rectangle. Sprinkle with cheese. Roll up jelly-roll style, starting from a long side. Cut into 12 slices. Place cut side down over chicken mixture. Bake, uncovered, at 350° for 35-40 minutes or until the crust is lightly browned. **Yield:** 6-8 servings.

SOUTHERN BARBECUED CHICKEN

Revonda Stroud, Fort Worth, Texas

Growing up in a military family, I traveled all over the U.S. and abroad. Sampling the cuisine of many different places has made me adventurous in the kitchen, but this Southern specialty remains a favorite.

> 2 cups cider vinegar
> 1 cup canola oil
> 1 egg, beaten
> 2 tablespoons hot pepper sauce
> 1 tablespoon garlic powder
> 1 tablespoon poultry seasoning
> 2 teaspoons salt
> 1 teaspoon pepper
> 1 broiler/fryer chicken (3 to 4 pounds), cut up

In a saucepan, combine the first eight ingredients. Bring to a boil, stirring constantly. Reduce the heat; simmer, uncovered, for 10 minutes, stirring often. Cool.

Pour 1-2/3 cups marinade into a large resealable plastic bag; add chicken. Seal bag; turn to coat. Refrigerate overnight, turning occasionally. Cover and refrigerate remaining marinade for basting.

Prepare grill for indirect heat, using a drip pan. Drain and discard marinade from chicken. Place skin side down over pan. Grill, covered, over indirect medium heat for 20 minutes. Turn; grill 20-30 minutes longer or until juices run clear, basting occasionally with reserved marinade. **Yield:** 4 servings.

FREEZER CONVENIENCE

Whenever I have leftover cooked chicken or turkey, I cube it and freeze it in serving-size portions. That way, I have it on hand to use in my favorite casseroles, potpies and other dishes.
—*Pauline Bondy, Grand Forks, North Dakota*

 ## BEAN AND PORK CHOP BAKE

(Pictured above)

LaRita Lang, Lincoln, Nebraska

Having grown up on a pork-producing farm, I'm always happy to include that versatile meat in my cooking. This recipe, featuring pork chops, has apple-cinnamon flavor with a hint of sweet maple.

- 4 boneless pork loin chops (1/2 inch thick)
- 1 tablespoon vegetable oil
- 1 large tart apple, peeled and chopped
- 1 small onion, chopped
- 1 can (28 ounces) baked beans
- 1/3 cup raisins
- 1/4 teaspoon ground cinnamon, *divided*
- 1 tablespoon maple pancake syrup
- 1/4 teaspoon salt

In a large skillet, brown pork chops on both sides in oil. Remove and keep warm. In same pan, saute apple and onion until tender. Stir in beans, raisins and 1/8 teaspoon cinnamon. Spoon into a greased 2-1/2-qt. baking dish; top with pork chops.

Cover and bake at 350° for 40 minutes. Brush chops with syrup; sprinkle with the salt and remaining cinnamon. Bake, uncovered for 5-10 minutes or until the meat juices run clear. **Yield:** 4 servings.

PIZZA CASSEROLE

Judie Heiderscheit, Holy Cross, Iowa

You'll get big smiles all around when you put this cheesy, beefy pasta bake on the dinner table. Kids and adults alike enjoy the fantastic pizza taste.

- 8 ounces uncooked wagon wheels *or* pasta of your choice
- 1 pound ground beef
- 1 small onion, chopped
- 1 jar (14 ounces) pizza sauce
- 1 can (4 ounces) mushroom stems and pieces, drained
- 1 can (2-1/4 ounces) sliced ripe olives, drained
- 1/2 teaspoon Italian seasoning

Salt to taste

- 1/2 to 1 cup shredded part-skim mozzarella cheese

Cook pasta according to package directions. Meanwhile, in a large skillet, cook beef and onion over medium heat until meat is no longer pink; drain. Stir in sauce, mushrooms, olives, seasoning and salt. Drain pasta; stir into beef mixture.

Transfer to a greased shallow 2-qt. baking dish; sprinkle with cheese. Bake, uncovered, at 350° for 25 minutes or until heated through and cheese is melted. **Yield:** 6 servings.

water and salt. Bring to a boil. Reduce heat; simmer, uncovered, for 1 hour.

Remove the ham bone; when cool enough to handle, remove the meat from bone and discard bone. Set meat aside. To the bean mixture, add the green onion, green pepper, parsley, tomato sauce, garlic, Worcestershire sauce, pepper, cayenne pepper, oregano, thyme and hot pepper sauce. Cook on low for 1 hour.

Add sausage and reserved ham; cook 30 minutes longer or until heated through, stirring occasionally. Serve over rice. **Yield:** 8-10 servings.

▰▰▰▰▰▰▰▰▰▰▰▰
MICROWAVE LASAGNA

Betty Ruenholl, Syracuse, Nebraska

It's almost hard to believe that this traditional, mouthwatering dish comes from the microwave. While the lasagna cooks, use your oven to bake some rolls or bread to complete the meal.

> 1 pound ground beef
> 1 jar (26 ounces) spaghetti sauce
> 1/2 teaspoon dried basil
> 1/4 teaspoon garlic powder
> 2 cups (16 ounces) cottage cheese
> 1 tablespoon minced fresh parsley
> 1 egg, beaten
> 1/4 teaspoon pepper
> 6 uncooked lasagna noodles
> 2 cups (8 ounces) shredded part-skim
>   mozzarella cheese, *divided*
> 1/2 cup water

In a microwave-safe dish, microwave beef on high for 3 minutes; stir. Cook 2 minutes longer or until no longer pink; drain well. Stir in the spaghetti sauce, basil and garlic powder; cover and microwave for 2 minutes or until heated through. Set aside. In a bowl, combine the cottage cheese, parsley, egg and pepper.

Spread 1/2 cup meat sauce in a greased microwave-safe 11-in. x 7-in. x 2-in. dish. Layer with three noodles, half the cottage cheese mixture, half the remaining meat sauce and 1 cup mozzarella cheese. Layer remaining noodles, cottage cheese mixture and meat sauce. Pour water along edges of casserole on short sides of dish.

Cover with plastic wrap; microwave on high for 20 minutes or until noodles are tender, rotating dish after 10 minutes. Sprinkle with remaining cheese. Cover and heat for 2 minutes or until cheese is melted. Let stand for 10 minutes before cutting. **Yield:** 8 servings.

Editor's Note: This recipe was tested in a 1,100-watt microwave. The noodles are not cooked before assembling the lasagna.

▰▰▰▰▰▰▰▰▰▰▰▰
CAJUN RED BEANS
(Pictured above)

Crystal Graham, Eureka Springs, Arkansas

Served over rice and loaded with sausage and ham, this dish is one of my favorites to make for guests because it serves a bunch. Warm corn bread is the perfect accompaniment.

> 1 pound dry red kidney beans
> 1 large ham bone
> 2 quarts water
> 1 tablespoon salt
> 2 cups chopped green onion
> 1 cup chopped green pepper
> 1 cup chopped fresh parsley
> 1 can (8 ounces) tomato sauce
> 2 garlic cloves, minced
> 1 tablespoon Worcestershire sauce
> 1 teaspoon pepper
> 1/2 to 1 teaspoon cayenne pepper
> 1/4 teaspoon dried oregano
> 1/4 teaspoon dried thyme
> 3 dashes hot pepper sauce
> 1 pound fully cooked smoked sausage,
>   sliced

Hot cooked rice

Place beans in a Dutch oven or soup kettle; add water to cover by 2 in. Bring to a boil; boil 2 minutes. Remove from the heat; cover and let stand for 1 hour.

Drain and rinse beans, discarding liquid. Return beans to Dutch oven. Add the ham bone,

ARTICHOKE RAVIOLI
(Pictured below)

Darlene Brenden, Salem, Oregon

This unusual ravioli tastes like you spent hours preparing it, but it's actually quick and easy to put together. I think the artichokes add a tangy, gourmet flavor. Round out the menu with a tossed green salad, and you're done with dinner!

2 packages (9 ounces *each*) refrigerated cheese ravioli
1 jar (26 ounces) meatless spaghetti sauce
1 can (14 ounces) water-packed artichoke hearts, rinsed, drained and chopped
1 jar (4-1/2 ounces) whole mushrooms, drained
1 can (2-1/2 ounces) sliced ripe olives, drained
1-1/2 cups (6 ounces) shredded part-skim mozzarella cheese

Cook the ravioli according to the package directions; drain and return to the pan. Add the spaghetti sauce, artichokes, mushrooms and ripe olives; gently toss.

Transfer to a greased 13-in. x 9-in. x 2-in. baking dish. Sprinkle with cheese. Bake, uncovered, at 400° for 15-20 minutes or until heated through and cheese is melted. **Yield:** 6 servings.

TRIPLE PORK WITH RICE
(Pictured above)

Margaret Pache, Mesa, Arizona

Any meat lovers you know are bound to enjoy this meal-in-one featuring pork, ham and bacon.

1/2 pound lean boneless pork, cut into 1/2-inch cubes
4 ounces fully cooked ham, diced
4 bacon strips, diced
1 medium onion, sliced
1 medium sweet red pepper, julienned
1/2 cup lemon juice
1 to 2 jalapeno peppers, seeded and minced
1 teaspoon ground cumin
1/2 teaspoon caraway seeds
1/2 teaspoon salt
2 tablespoons vegetable oil
1-1/2 cups uncooked long grain rice
2 cans (14-1/2 ounces *each*) beef broth
1 can (14-1/2 ounces) diced tomatoes, undrained
1 can (8 ounces) kidney beans, rinsed and drained
1 medium ripe avocado, peeled and sliced, optional

In a large resealable plastic bag, combine the first 10 ingredients. Seal bag and turn to coat. Refrigerate for 1-2 hours.

Drain and discard marinade. In a large skillet, cook pork mixture in oil over medium heat for 5-6 minutes. Stir in the rice; cook for 3 minutes. Add broth and tomatoes; bring to a boil. Reduce heat; cover and simmer for 20 minutes. Stir in the beans. Cover and simmer 5 minutes longer or until rice is tender. Garnish with avocado if desired. **Yield:** 8 servings.

Editor's Note: When cutting or seeding hot peppers, use rubber or plastic gloves to protect your hands. Avoid touching your face.

CHICKEN FRICASSEE WITH DUMPLINGS
(Pictured below)

Lena Hrynyk, Sherwood Park, Alberta

If your family is craving old-fashioned comfort food, give this recipe a try. With plenty of chicken, veggies and dumplings on top, it's a complete meal in one.

1 bay leaf
9 whole peppercorns
4 whole cloves
1/3 cup all-purpose flour
1-1/2 teaspoons salt
1 teaspoon dried marjoram
1 broiler/fryer chicken (3 to 4 pounds), cut up
2 to 4 tablespoons butter
6 large carrots, cut into 1-inch pieces
1-1/2 cups chopped onions
2 celery ribs, cut into 1-inch pieces
1 can (14-1/2 ounces) chicken broth
1 cup water

DUMPLINGS:
1-1/2 cups biscuit/baking mix
2 tablespoons minced chives
1 egg, lightly beaten
1/4 cup milk
2 tablespoons all-purpose flour
1/2 cup half-and-half cream

Place the bay leaf, peppercorns and cloves on a double thickness of cheesecloth; bring up corners of cloth and tie with string to form a bag. Set aside. In a large resealable bag, combine flour, salt and marjoram. Add chicken, a few pieces at a time, and shake to coat.

In a Dutch oven, brown chicken in batches in butter. Remove and keep warm. In the drippings, saute carrots, onions and celery for 5-6 minutes or until onions begin to brown. Add broth, water and spice bag. Bring to a boil; add chicken. Reduce heat; cover and simmer for 40 minutes. Discard spice bag.

For dumplings, combine biscuit mix and chives in a bowl. Combine egg and milk; add to biscuit mix just until moistened. Drop by heaping tablespoonfuls onto simmering chicken mixture. Cook, uncovered, for 10 minutes. Cover and cook 10 minutes longer or until a toothpick inserted into dumplings comes out clean.

Using a slotted spoon, carefully remove chicken and dumplings; keep warm. Combine flour and cream until smooth; stir into cooking juices. Bring to a boil; cook and stir for 2 minutes or until thickened. Serve with chicken and dumplings. **Yield:** 6-8 servings.

POACHED EGGS IN STEWED TOMATOES

Carol Hostetter, Manson, Washington

I discovered this meatless dish in a cookbook I bought along with some sweet onions at a farm stand. My husband often requests this for dinner.

1 large sweet onion, chopped
1 medium carrot, chopped
1 celery rib, chopped
1/2 cup chopped green pepper
1 garlic clove, minced
2 tablespoons olive oil
2 cans (14-1/2 ounces *each*) diced tomatoes, undrained
2 tablespoons honey
1 to 3 teaspoons chili powder
1/4 teaspoon salt
1/4 teaspoon pepper
1 bay leaf
8 eggs
1/2 cup shredded cheddar cheese

In a large skillet, saute the onion, carrot, celery, green pepper and garlic in oil until tender. Stir in the tomatoes, honey, chili powder, salt, pepper and bay leaf. Simmer, uncovered, for 15-20 minutes or until thickened. Discard bay leaf.

With a spoon, make eight indentations in tomato mixture. Break eggs into indentations. Cover; cook over low heat for 10 minutes or until whites are completely set and yolks begin to thicken. Sprinkle with cheese. Cover; cook until cheese is melted, about 1 minute. **Yield:** 8 servings.

TURKEY STIR-FRY
(Pictured above)

Becky Baird, Salt Lake City, Utah

Fresh ginger, soy sauce and paprika lend a tangy flavor to this colorful blend of turkey, tomatoes, mushrooms, sweet peppers and bean sprouts. It's a mainstay in our house for supper.

    1 tablespoon cornstarch
  1/2 teaspoon paprika
    1 cup chicken broth
    2 tablespoons soy sauce
    2 tablespoons vegetable oil, *divided*
    1 package (20 ounces) turkey breast
      tenderloins, cut into 1/2-inch strips
    1 large onion, halved and thinly sliced
    1 large sweet red pepper, julienned
    2 celery ribs, thinly sliced
    1 cup sliced fresh mushrooms
    1 teaspoon minced fresh gingerroot
    1 garlic clove, minced
    2 large tomatoes, sliced and seeded
    1 can (14 ounces) bean sprouts, rinsed
      and drained
Hot cooked rice, optional

In a small bowl, combine the cornstarch, paprika, chicken broth and soy sauce until smooth; set aside. In a large skillet or wok, heat 1 tablespoon oil; stir-fry the turkey until the juices run clear. Remove and keep warm.

In the same pan, stir-fry the onion, red pepper, celery and mushrooms in remaining oil for 8 minutes. Add ginger and garlic; stir-fry 2 minutes longer. Return turkey to the pan. Stir cornstarch mixture and add to the pan. Bring to a boil; cook and stir for 2 minutes or until thickened. Add tomatoes and bean sprouts; heat through. Serve with rice if desired. **Yield:** 8 servings.

THREE CHEESE ENCHILADAS
(Pictured below)

Gretchen Mellberg, Hawarden, Iowa

This easy-to-prepare main dish has proven popular with dinner guests of all ages—especially teenagers. The enchiladas are tasty but not too spicy.

  1-1/2 cups (6 ounces) shredded Monterey
        Jack cheese, *divided*
  1-1/2 cups (6 ounces) shredded cheddar
        cheese, *divided*
      1 package (3 ounces) cream cheese,
        softened
      1 cup picante sauce, *divided*
      1 medium green *or* sweet red pepper,
        diced
    1/2 cup sliced green onions
      1 teaspoon ground cumin
      8 flour tortillas (7 to 8 inches *each*)
Shredded lettuce
Chopped tomato
Sliced ripe olives
Additional picante sauce, optional

Combine 1 cup Monterey Jack cheese, 1 cup cheddar cheese, cream cheese, 1/4 cup picante sauce, the pepper, onions and cumin; mix well. Spoon 1/4 cup cheese mixture down the center of each tortilla. Roll and place, seam side down, in a 13-in. x 9-in. x 2-in. baking dish. Spoon remaining picante sauce evenly over enchiladas; cover with remaining cheeses.

Bake at 350° for 20 minutes or until heated through. Top with the lettuce, tomato and ripe olives; serve with additional picante sauce if desired. **Yield:** 4 servings.

13-in. x 9-in. x 2-in. baking dish. Spread with ricotta cheese. Top with half of the mozzarella cheese and remaining sausage mixture.

Cover and bake at 350° for 40 minutes. Uncover; sprinkle with remaining cheese. Bake 5 minutes longer or until cheese is melted. Let stand for 10 minutes before serving. **Yield:** 12 servings.

SHRIMP-STUFFED CHICKEN BREASTS

Wendy McGowan, Poulsbo, Washington

The delicious filling of shrimp, mayonnaise, onions and tarragon makes these golden chicken breasts extra special. They're great for dinner parties.

      6 boneless skinless chicken breast halves
        (6 ounces *each*)
2-1/2 cups frozen cooked salad shrimp,
        thawed
    1/2 cup chopped green onions
    1/2 cup mayonnaise
      1 tablespoon dried tarragon
      1 tablespoon lemon juice
    1/2 teaspoon Liquid Smoke, optional
      1 tablespoon vegetable oil
    1/4 teaspoon salt
    1/4 teaspoon pepper

Flatten chicken to 1/4-in. thickness. In a bowl, combine the shrimp, onions, mayonnaise, tarragon, lemon juice and Liquid Smoke if desired. Place about 1/3 cup down the center of each chicken breast half; fold chicken over filling and secure with toothpicks.

Brush chicken with oil; sprinkle with salt and pepper. Grill, covered, over medium heat for 6-8 minutes on each side or until juices run clear. Discard toothpicks before serving. **Yield:** 6 servings.

EGGPLANT SAUSAGE CASSEROLE
(Pictured above)

Carol Mieske, Red Bluff, California

If you want your kids to happily eat eggplant, serve it in this lovely layered casserole. Our whole family enjoys it, and it's popular at potlucks, too.

      1 package (1 pound) penne *or* medium
        tube pasta
      2 pounds bulk Italian sausage
      1 medium eggplant, peeled and cubed
      1 large onion, chopped
      2 garlic cloves, minced
      2 tablespoons olive oil
      1 can (28 ounces) diced tomatoes,
        undrained
      1 can (6 ounces) tomato paste
      1 teaspoon salt
      1 teaspoon dried basil
      1 teaspoon paprika
      1 carton (15 ounces) ricotta cheese
      4 cups (16 ounces) shredded part-skim
        mozzarella cheese, *divided*

Cook pasta according to package directions. Meanwhile, in a large skillet, cook sausage over medium heat until no longer pink; drain. Set sausage aside.

In the same skillet, sauté the eggplant, onion and garlic in oil. Stir in the tomatoes, tomato paste, salt, basil and paprika; simmer, partially covered, for 15 minutes. Remove from the heat. Drain pasta; stir into eggplant mixture. Add sausage.

Spread half of the sausage mixture in a greased

CHEESY BEEF CASSEROLE

Sharon Crider, Lebanon, Missouri

When it comes to family-pleasing casseroles, this dish can't miss! The taco flavor, ground beef and Mexican cheese ensure satisfied smiles.

1-1/2 pounds ground beef
      1 envelope taco seasoning
      2 cups water
      2 cups uncooked instant rice
      1 can (10-3/4 ounces) condensed cream
        of chicken soup, undiluted
      1 can (10-3/4 ounces) condensed cream
        of mushroom soup, undiluted

Main Dishes

1 can (4 ounces) chopped green chilies,
  undrained
2 cups (8 ounces) shredded Mexican
  cheese blend

In a large skillet, cook beef over medium heat until no longer pink; drain. Stir in the taco seasoning, water, rice, soups and chilies. Transfer to a greased 13-in. x 9-in. x 2-in. baking dish. Cover and bake at 350° for 25 minutes. Uncover; sprinkle with cheese. Bake 5 minutes longer or until heated through and cheese is melted. **Yield:** 6-8 servings.

SALMON STEAKS WITH VEGGIE CREAM SAUCE

(Pictured below)

Dorothy Michel, Kirkland, Washington

I'm a grandmother and have had this recipe for over 30 years. When guests stay for supper, I often prepare these tasty steaks along with a tossed green salad and my homemade rolls.

6 salmon steaks (1 inch thick)
2 tablespoons lemon juice
1/2 teaspoon salt
1-1/2 cups frozen pearl onions
3/4 cup frozen peas
1 package (8 ounces) cream cheese,
  cubed
3 tablespoons milk
1 teaspoon dill weed
1/2 cup dry bread crumbs
2 tablespoons butter

Place the salmon steaks in a greased 13-in. x 9-in. x 2-in. baking dish. Sprinkle with lemon juice and salt. Bake, uncovered, at 350° for 20-25 minutes or until fish flakes easily with a fork.

Meanwhile, in a saucepan, combine onions, peas, cream cheese, milk and dill. Cook and stir over low heat until cheese is melted and sauce is heated through. In a small skillet, saute bread crumbs in butter until lightly browned. Spoon the sauce over salmon steaks; sprinkle with toasted crumbs. **Yield:** 6 servings.

BRIEF BURRITOS

(Pictured above)

Ginger Burow, Fredericksburg, Texas

With three children in school, our weeknights are usually hectic. I can put this Southwestern dish together after school and still have time to run back out for evening activities. Best of all, the kids love it.

1 pound ground beef
1 can (16 ounces) refried beans
1 can (10 ounces) diced tomatoes and
  green chilies, drained
1/2 cup chili sauce
8 flour tortillas (10 inches), warmed
1/2 cup shredded cheddar cheese
1/2 cup sour cream

In a large skillet, cook beef over medium heat until no longer pink; drain. Stir in the refried beans, tomatoes and chili sauce; heat through. Spoon about 1/2 cup down the center of each tortilla; top with cheese and sour cream. Fold ends and sides over filling. Serve immediately. **Yield:** 8 burritos.

Sunny Breakfast Specialties

WAKE UP with these eye-opening breakfast and brunch recipes. Whether you're looking for golden pancakes or a cheesy egg bake, you'll love the daybreak dishes here.

BRUNCH LASAGNA
(Pictured below)

Judy Munger, Warren, Minnesota

Everyone can appreciate make-ahead recipes like this one. Pop it in the oven before guests arrive, add fresh fruit and muffins, and you have an instant brunch. If you like, drizzle the lasagna with a little salsa.

    8   uncooked lasagna noodles
    8   eggs
  1/2   cup milk
Butter-flavored nonstick cooking spray
    2   jars (16 ounces *each*) Alfredo sauce
    3   cups diced fully cooked ham
  1/2   cup chopped green pepper

  1/4   cup chopped green onions
    1   cup (4 ounces) shredded cheddar cheese
  1/4   cup grated Parmesan cheese

Cook the lasagna noodles according to the package directions. Meanwhile, in a large bowl, beat the eggs and milk. In a large nonstick skillet coated with butter-flavored cooking spray, cook eggs over medium-low heat until set but moist. Remove from the heat. Drain the noodles.

Spread 1/2 cup Alfredo sauce in a greased 10-in. square or 13-in. x 9-in. x 2-in. baking dish. Layer with four lasagna noodles (trim noodles if necessary to fit dish), ham, green pepper and onions.

Top with half of the remaining Alfredo sauce and the remaining noodles. Layer with scrambled eggs, cheddar cheese and remaining Alfredo sauce. Sprinkle with Parmesan cheese.

Bake, uncovered, at 375° for 45-50 minutes or until heated through and bubbly. Let stand for 10 minutes before cutting. **Yield:** 10-12 servings.

CORNMEAL PANCAKES

Betty Claycomb, Alverton, Pennsylvania

I joke that these pancakes are so light, you have to hold them down! If I have the chance, I use freshly ground cornmeal bought at local festivals.

  1-1/3   cups all-purpose flour
    2/3   cup cornmeal
      2   tablespoons sugar
      4   teaspoons baking powder
      1   teaspoon salt
      2   eggs
  1-1/3   cups milk
    1/4   cup vegetable oil
Pancake syrup

In a bowl, combine the flour, cornmeal, sugar, baking powder and salt. In another bowl, whisk the eggs, milk and oil; stir into dry ingredients just until moistened.

Pour batter by 1/4 cupfuls onto a lightly greased hot griddle. Turn when bubbles form on top; cook

until the second side is golden brown. Serve with syrup. **Yield:** 4 servings.

FETA BREAKFAST BAKE

Cheryl Rude, Winfield, Kansas

Guests at our family's bed-and-breakfast love this easy-prep brunch item. I garnish it with oregano.

      4 cups seasoned salad croutons
  1-1/2 cups (6 ounces) crumbled feta cheese
      8 eggs
      4 cups milk
      1 tablespoon minced fresh basil *or*
         1 teaspoon dried basil
      1 tablespoon minced fresh oregano *or*
         1 teaspoon dried oregano
    1/4 teaspoon pepper
  1-1/2 cups cubed fully cooked ham

In a bowl, combine the croutons and feta cheese; transfer to a greased 13-in. x 9-in. x 2-in. baking dish. In a large bowl, whisk the eggs, milk, basil, oregano and pepper. Slowly pour over crouton mixture. Sprinkle with ham.

Bake, uncovered, at 325° for 60-65 minutes or until a knife inserted near the center comes out clean. Let stand for 10 minutes before cutting. **Yield:** 12-14 servings.

SPECIAL STUFFED FRENCH TOAST
(Pictured above)

Robin Perry, Seneca, Pennsylvania

For a sunrise sensation, just whip up this Texas toast with cream cheese and a sweet-tart cherry sauce.

      1 cup plus 2 tablespoons sugar, *divided*
      2 tablespoons cornstarch
    3/4 cup water
      4 cups pitted frozen tart cherries, thawed
      1 package (8 ounces) cream cheese,
         softened
      1 cup confectioners' sugar
     12 slices Texas toast
      1 egg
      1 cup milk

Combine 1 cup sugar and cornstarch in a small saucepan. Stir in water until smooth. Add cherries. Bring to a boil; cook and stir for 1-2 minutes or until thickened. Remove from heat; set aside.

In a small mixing bowl, beat cream cheese and confectioners' sugar. Spread over six slices of bread; top with remaining bread. In a shallow bowl, whisk the egg, milk and remaining sugar. Dip both sides of bread into egg mixture.

In large nonstick skillet coated with nonstick cooking spray, grill toast on both sides until golden brown. Serve with sauce. **Yield:** 6 servings.

◼◼◼◼◼◼◼◼◼◼◼◼◼◼

HEARTY PASTA CASSEROLE
(Pictured below)

*This Italian-inspired bake from our Test Kitchen is
loaded with roasted veggies. It's a great "to-go" dish
because it transports easily and retains heat well.*

✓ Uses less fat, sugar or salt. Includes
Nutrition Facts.

2 cups cubed peeled butternut squash
1/2 pound fresh brussels sprouts, halved
1 medium onion, cut into wedges
2 teaspoons olive oil
1 package (13-1/4 ounces) whole wheat
penne *or* medium tube pasta
1 pound Italian turkey sausage links,
casings removed
2 garlic cloves, minced
2 cans (14-1/2 ounces *each*) Italian
stewed tomatoes
2 tablespoons tomato paste
1-1/2 cups (6 ounces) shredded part-skim
mozzarella cheese, *divided*
1/3 cup shredded Asiago cheese, *divided*

In a large bowl, combine the squash, brussels
sprouts and onion; drizzle with oil and toss to coat.
Spread vegetables in a single layer in two 15-in.
x 10-in. x 1-in. baking pans coated with nonstick cooking spray. Bake, uncovered, at 425° for
30-40 minutes or until tender.

Meanwhile, cook pasta according to package
directions. In a large nonstick skillet, cook sausage
and garlic over medium heat until meat is no
longer pink; drain. Add tomatoes and tomato
paste; cook and stir over medium heat until slightly thickened, about 5 minutes.

Drain pasta and return to the pan. Add sausage

mixture, 1 cup mozzarella, 1/4 cup Asiago and
roasted vegetables; mix well. Transfer to a 13-in.
x 9-in. x 2-in. baking dish coated with nonstick
cooking spray.

Cover and bake at 350° for 30-40 minutes or
until heated through. Uncover; sprinkle with remaining cheeses. Bake 5 minutes longer or until
cheese is melted. **Yield:** 8 servings.

Nutrition Facts: 1-1/4 cups equals 416 calories,
13 g fat (5 g saturated fat), 47 mg cholesterol,
816 mg sodium, 53 g carbohydrate, 7 g fiber, 24 g
protein.

◼◼◼◼◼◼◼◼◼◼◼◼◼◼

SALMON WITH CUCUMBER SAUCE
Carole Holder, Norman, Oklahoma

*This grilled entree may sound fancy, but it's actually
a fuss-free way to prepare salmon. You can easily
make the sauce in advance and store it in the refrigerator until mealtime.*

✓ Uses less fat, sugar or salt. Includes Nutrition
Facts and Diabetic Exchanges.

1/4 cup lemon juice
2 tablespoons canola oil
1 teaspoon dill weed
1 teaspoon grated lemon peel
1 garlic clove, minced
4 salmon fillets (4 ounces *each*)
CUCUMBER SAUCE:
2/3 cup finely chopped seeded peeled
cucumber
1/3 cup reduced-fat sour cream
1 tablespoon chopped green onion
1-1/2 teaspoons reduced-fat mayonnaise
1/2 teaspoon lemon juice
1/8 teaspoon salt
1/8 teaspoon white pepper
1/8 teaspoon Worcestershire sauce

In a large resealable plastic bag, combine the
first five ingredients; add the salmon. Seal bag and
turn to coat; refrigerate for 30 minutes, turning
occasionally. Meanwhile, in a bowl, combine the
cucumber sauce ingredients. Cover and refrigerate until serving.

Coat grill rack with nonstick cooking spray before starting the grill. Drain and discard marinade.
Place salmon skin side down on grill rack.

Grill, covered, over medium heat for 12-15
minutes or until fish flakes easily with a fork.
Serve with cucumber sauce. **Yield:** 4 servings.

Nutrition Facts: 1 fillet with 2 tablespoons
sauce equals 261 calories, 16 g fat (4 g saturated
fat), 74 mg cholesterol, 172 mg sodium, 3 g carbohydrate, trace fiber, 24 g protein. **Diabetic Exchanges:** 3 meat, 2 fat.

Peach-Glazed Ribs
(Pictured above)

Sharon Taylor, Columbia, South Carolina

For a mouth-watering alternative to the usual barbecue sauce for ribs, try this slightly spicy recipe. The peaches add just the right touch of sweetness and a lovely color. After one taste, you'll never want to use store-bought sauce again!

  3 to 4 pounds pork baby back ribs, cut into serving-size pieces
  1 can (15-1/4 ounces) peach halves, drained
1/3 cup soy sauce
1/4 cup vegetable oil
1/4 cup honey
  2 tablespoons brown sugar
  1 teaspoon sesame seeds, toasted
  1 garlic clove, peeled
1/4 teaspoon ground ginger

Prepare grill for indirect heat, using a drip pan. Place ribs over drip pan. Grill, covered, over indirect medium heat for 60 minutes, turning occasionally.

Meanwhile, in a blender or food processor, combine the peaches, soy sauce, oil, honey, sugar, seeds, garlic and ginger. Cover and process until smooth. Baste ribs with some of the sauce. Grill 15-20 minutes longer or until meat is tender and juices run clear, basting occasionally with remaining sauce. **Yield:** 6 servings.

Sausage Spinach Manicotti

Donna Moyer, Grants Pass, Oregon

My young granddaughter likes to help stuff the manicotti shells for this rich and delicious casserole.

  2 cups (8 ounces) shredded part-skim mozzarella cheese, *divided*
1-1/2 cups (12 ounces) small-curd cottage cheese
  1 package (10 ounces) frozen chopped spinach, thawed and squeezed dry
1/2 cup grated Parmesan cheese
  1 egg, lightly beaten
1/4 teaspoon dried oregano
  1 garlic clove, minced
 10 uncooked manicotti shells
  1 pound bulk Italian sausage
  1 jar (26 ounces) spaghetti sauce
3/4 cup water

In a large bowl, combine 1 cup mozzarella, cottage cheese, spinach, Parmesan, egg, oregano and garlic; stuff into uncooked manicotti shells. Place in a greased 13-in. x 9-in. x 2-in. baking dish.

Crumble sausage into a large skillet; cook over medium heat until no longer pink. Drain. Stir in spaghetti sauce; pour over manicotti. Pour water along sides of pan. Cover and bake at 350° for 1 hour. Uncover; sprinkle with remaining mozzarella. Bake 5-8 minutes longer or until cheese is melted. Let stand for 10 minutes before serving. **Yield:** 5 servings.

utes. Divide mixture between two greased 8-in. square baking dishes. Cover and refrigerate until firm, about 1-1/2 hours.

In a large skillet, cook the beef, onion, green pepper and garlic over medium heat until meat is no longer pink; drain. Stir in the tomatoes, tomato sauce, mushrooms, herbs and hot pepper sauce; bring to a boil. Reduce heat; simmer, uncovered, for 20 minutes or until thickened.

Loosen one polenta from sides and bottom of dish; invert onto a waxed paper-lined baking sheet and set aside. Spoon half of the meat mixture over the remaining polenta that is still in a dish. Sprinkle with half the mozzarella and half the Parmesan cheese. Top with reserved polenta and remaining meat mixture.

Cover and bake at 350° for 40 minutes or until heated through. Uncover; sprinkle with remaining cheese. Bake 5 minutes longer or until cheese is melted. Let stand for 10 minutes before cutting. **Yield:** 6 servings.

Nutrition Facts: 1 serving equals 345 calories, 14 g fat (7 g saturated fat), 62 mg cholesterol, 874 mg sodium, 29 g carbohydrate, 4 g fiber, 25 g protein.

OLE POLENTA CASSEROLE
(Pictured above)

Angela Biggin, Lyons, Illinois

With plenty of ground beef and cheese, this layered bake goes over big on the dinner table. Adjust the amount of hot pepper sauce to suit your taste.

☑ Uses less fat, sugar or salt. Includes Nutrition Facts.

    1 cup yellow cornmeal
    1 teaspoon salt
    4 cups water, *divided*
    1 pound ground beef
    1 cup chopped onion
1/2 cup chopped green pepper
    2 garlic cloves, minced
    1 can (14-1/2 ounces) diced tomatoes,
        undrained
    1 can (8 ounces) tomato sauce
1/2 pound sliced fresh mushrooms
    1 teaspoon *each* dried basil, oregano and
        dill weed
Dash hot pepper sauce
1-1/2 cups (6 ounces) shredded part-skim
        mozzarella cheese
1/4 cup grated Parmesan cheese

For polenta, in a small bowl, whisk cornmeal, salt and 1 cup water until smooth. In a large saucepan, bring remaining water to a boil. Add cornmeal mixture, stirring constantly. Bring to a boil; cook and stir for 3 minutes or until thickened.

Reduce heat to low; cover and cook for 15 min-

BEEF CASSOULET

Virginia Whaley
Oswego, New York

Chock-full of both beef and Italian sausages, this stew will satisfy even the heartiest of appetites. While the meat simmers, pop some bread or rolls in the oven to round out your meal.

    6 Italian sausage links (about 1 pound)
1-1/2 to 2 pounds boneless beef chuck roast,
        cut into 1-inch cubes
    1 large onion, sliced
    2 garlic cloves, minced
    1 teaspoon dried basil
1/2 teaspoon salt
1/4 teaspoon pepper
    2 medium green peppers, seeded and cut
        into chunks
    4 medium potatoes, peeled and cut into
        quarters
    2 cans (16 ounces *each*) kidney beans,
        rinsed and drained
    1 cup beef broth

In a heavy skillet, brown sausages well; cut into bite-size pieces; set aside. In same skillet, brown beef in about 2 tablespoons of sausage fat. Add onion and garlic during last part of browning. Season with basil, salt and pepper. Cover and simmer about 1 hour or until meat is almost tender.

In a 3-qt. baking dish, combine all ingredients. Cover and bake at 350° for 75 minutes or until meat and potatoes are tender.

Editor's Note: This casserole could be made in a Dutch oven on the stovetop. Instead of baking, simmer gently on low heat for 1 hour or until potatoes are tender.

BUTTERMILK MEAT LOAF
(Pictured below)

Elizabeth Mason, Goleta, California

Barbecue sauce is a Southwestern staple, and I use it instead of ketchup in meat loaf. This main course always gets rave reviews.

     2 eggs
     1 cup soft bread crumbs
   1/2 cup finely chopped red onion
     6 tablespoons barbecue sauce, *divided*
   1/4 cup buttermilk
     2 tablespoons minced fresh parsley
     1 teaspoon garlic salt
   1/4 teaspoon pepper
 1-1/2 pounds ground beef

In a large bowl, lightly beat the eggs. Stir in the bread crumbs, onion, 4 tablespoons barbecue sauce, buttermilk, parsley, garlic salt and pepper. Crumble beef over mixture and mix well. Shape into a loaf. Place in a greased 11-in. x 7-in. x 2-in. baking dish.

Bake, uncovered, at 350° for 50 minutes. Spread with remaining barbecue sauce. Bake 10

minutes longer or until meat is no longer pink and a meat thermometer reads 160°. Drain; let stand for 10 minutes before slicing. **Yield:** 6 servings.

TACO SUPPER IN A BOWL
(Pictured above)

Linda Frisk, Roseburg, Oregon

This recipe is high on my family's list of favorites. They love the popular taco ingredients and great south-of-the-border flavor.

 1-1/2 pounds ground beef
     2 large onions, chopped
     2 garlic cloves, minced
     2 cans (28 ounces *each*) stewed tomatoes
     4 cups water
     1 can (28 ounces) kidney beans, drained
     2 tablespoons canned chopped green chilies
 1-1/2 teaspoons ground cumin
     1 teaspoon dried oregano
   1/2 teaspoon salt
     1 package (15-1/2 ounces) tortilla chips
     2 medium ripe avocado, peeled and chopped
     8 cups shredded lettuce
     4 cups shredded sharp cheddar cheese
Salsa

In a soup kettle or Dutch oven, cook the beef, onions and garlic over medium heat until meat is no longer pink; drain. Add the tomatoes, water, beans, chilies, cumin, oregano and salt. Bring to a boil. Reduce heat; simmer, uncovered, for 1 hour.

To serve, break tortilla chips into soup bowls; top with avocados and lettuce. Spoon soup over lettuce. Garnish with cheese and salsa. **Yield:** 12-14 servings.

SEAFOOD ENCHILADAS
(Pictured below)

Mary Halpin, King George, Virginia

When you want a change from the usual beef and chicken enchiladas, try these tortillas stuffed with crab, shrimp and scallops. They're cheesy, creamy and absolutely delicious!

- 1/2 pound fresh *or* frozen crabmeat, flaked and cartilage removed
- 1/2 pound uncooked medium shrimp, peeled and deveined
- 1/2 pound bay scallops
- 1 medium onion, chopped
- 2 tablespoons butter
SAUCE:
- 1/2 cup butter, cubed
- 1 teaspoon grated onion
- 1/4 cup chicken broth
- 3 egg yolks, lightly beaten
- 1 cup heavy whipping cream
- 1 tablespoon tomato paste
- 8 flour tortillas (6 inches)
- 2 cups (8 ounces) shredded Monterey Jack cheese *or* Colby cheese

In a large skillet, cook the seafood and onion in butter over medium heat for 4-5 minutes or until onion is tender and shrimp turn pink. Remove from the heat; set aside.

For sauce, melt butter in a small saucepan. Add onion and broth. Combine the egg yolks and cream; stir into broth mixture. Cook and stir until a thermometer reads 160°. Stir in tomato paste.

Remove from heat. Spoon 1/2 cup into a greased 13-in. x 9-in. x 2-in. baking dish.

Spoon 1/3 cup seafood mixture down the center of each tortilla; top with 1 tablespoon sauce and 2 tablespoons cheese. Roll up and place seam side down in dish. Top with remaining sauce and cheese. Bake uncovered, at 350° for 20-25 minutes or until heated through. **Yield:** 8 servings.

LINGUINE WITH HERBED CLAM SAUCE

Carolee Snyder, Hartford City, Indiana

This impressive pasta looks and tastes so much like fancy restaurant fare, you'll want to serve it to guests. But the recipe is so easy to prepare that you can enjoy it just about anytime.

- 1 can (10 ounces) whole baby clams
- 1 can (6-1/2 ounces) minced clams
- 1/2 cup finely chopped onion
- 1/4 cup olive oil
- 1/4 cup butter
- 1/3 cup minced fresh parsley
- 4 garlic cloves, minced
- 2 tablespoons cornstarch
- 1/2 cup white wine *or* chicken broth
- 1/4 cup minced fresh basil *or* 4 teaspoons dried basil
Dash pepper
Dash cayenne pepper
Hot cooked linguine
Shredded Parmesan cheese

Drain baby and minced clams, reserving juice; set clams and juice aside. In a large skillet, saute onion in oil and butter until tender. Add parsley and garlic; saute for 2 minutes. Add reserved clams; saute 2 minutes longer.

Combine cornstarch and reserved clam juice until smooth; stir into skillet with wine or broth. Bring to a boil; cook and stir for 1-2 minutes or until thickened. Stir in the basil, pepper and cayenne. Serve over linguine; sprinkle with Parmesan cheese. **Yield:** 4 servings.

ORANGE GARLIC SPARERIBS

Cindy Unger, Olds, Alberta

The meat on these zesty ribs is fall-off-the-bone tender, and the rich dark sauce has hints of orange and garlic. We like to spoon extra sauce over rice.

- 4 pounds pork spareribs
Salt and pepper

1 cup orange juice
1 cup red wine vinegar
2/3 cup ketchup
2/3 cup soy sauce
1/2 cup honey
1 teaspoon ground mustard
1 teaspoon paprika
1/2 teaspoon hot pepper sauce
1 garlic clove, minced

Place ribs in a 13-in. x 9-in. x 2-in. baking pan; season with salt and pepper. Cover tightly with foil; bake at 350° for 45 minutes. Drain off any fat. In a saucepan, combine the remaining ingredients; bring to a boil. Pour over ribs. Bake, uncovered, for 45-60 minutes or until ribs are tender, basting frequently. **Yield:** 6-8 servings.

▰▰▰▰▰▰▰▰▰▰▰

SALMON RICE PUFF
(Pictured above)

Frances Paige, York, Pennsylvania

This salmon recipe dates back to the 1930s and is just as good today as it was back then. My mother often served it with creamed vegetables.

2 eggs
1/2 cup milk
1 can (14-3/4 ounces) salmon, drained, bones and skin removed
1 cup cooked long grain rice
1/4 cup chopped green onion
1/4 cup chopped celery
4 tablespoons lemon juice
1/2 teaspoon Worcestershire sauce
1/2 cup shredded cheddar cheese

In a bowl, whisk the eggs and milk. Stir in the salmon, rice, onion, celery, lemon juice and Worcestershire sauce.

Transfer to a greased shallow 1-1/2-qt. baking dish. Bake, uncovered, at 375° for 20 minutes. Sprinkle with the shredded cheddar cheese; bake 10 minutes longer or until the cheese is melted. **Yield:** 3-4 servings.

▰▰▰▰▰▰▰▰▰▰▰

CARIBBEAN ROAST PORK LOIN
(Pictured below)

Denise Albers, Freeburg, Illinois

Here's a different but fuss-free treatment for a boneless pork loin roast. You simply combine the oil and seasonings, rub it over the roast and bake.

2 teaspoons olive oil
1 teaspoon pepper
3/4 teaspoon ground cinnamon
3/4 teaspoon ground nutmeg
1 boneless rolled pork loin roast (3-1/2 pounds)

Combine the oil, pepper, cinnamon and nutmeg; rub over roast. Place on a rack in a shallow roasting pan. Bake at 350° for 1-1/2 to 2 hours or until a meat thermometer reads 160°. Let stand for 10 minutes before slicing. **Yield:** 10-12 servings.

boil. Reduce heat; cover and simmer for 30 minutes or until pork is tender.

Add the sauerkraut; heat through. Combine the flour and water until smooth; stir into the pork mixture. Bring to a boil; cook and stir for 2 minutes or until thickened. Remove from the heat; stir in the sour cream and dill. Return to the heat; cook on low for 1-2 minutes or until heated through (do not boil). Serve over boiled potatoes. **Yield:** 6 servings.

***

GINGER SPICED PORK

Beth Walton, Columbus, Indiana

Flavor a few pork tenderloins with this easy rub before putting them on the grill, and you're in for a terrific treat. They make an extra-special summer meal.

✓ Uses less fat, sugar or salt. Includes Nutrition Facts and Diabetic Exchanges.

     1 small onion, finely chopped
     2 tablespoons brown sugar
 1-1/2 teaspoons ground ginger
   1/2 teaspoon salt
   1/2 teaspoon ground allspice
   1/2 teaspoon ground cinnamon
   1/2 teaspoon minced garlic
   1/4 teaspoon pepper
   1/8 teaspoon cayenne pepper
     2 pork tenderloins (1 pound *each*)

Combine the first nine ingredients; rub over the pork tenderloins. Cover pork and refrigerate for at least 2 hours.

Prepare grill for indirect heat. Coat grill rack with nonstick cooking spray before starting the grill. Grill pork, covered, over indirect medium heat for 30 minutes or until a meat thermometer reads 160°. Let stand for 5 minutes before slicing. **Yield:** 6 servings.

Nutrition Facts: 4 ounces cooked pork equals 210 calories, 6 g fat (2 g saturated fat), 90 mg cholesterol, 261 mg sodium, 6 g carbohydrate, trace fiber, 32 g protein. **Diabetic Exchanges:** 4 very lean meat, 1/2 starch, 1/2 fat.

***

HUNGARIAN PORK GOULASH
(Pictured above)

Barbara Lundgren, New Brighton, Minnesota

Because of the sauerkraut in this goulash, my husband was hesitant to try it, but he ended up eating every last bite. If you prefer, grind or crush the caraway seeds before adding them to the pot.

     2 pounds boneless pork, cut into 3/4-inch
       cubes
     1 tablespoon vegetable oil
     2 medium onions, chopped
     1 garlic clove, minced
     3 cups chicken broth
     1 to 2 tablespoons paprika
     1 teaspoon caraway seeds
     1 teaspoon salt
   1/4 teaspoon pepper
     2 cans (14 ounces *each*) sauerkraut,
       rinsed and well drained
     2 tablespoons all-purpose flour
   1/4 cup water
 1-1/2 cups (12 ounces) sour cream
     2 tablespoons minced fresh dill *or*
     2 teaspoons dill weed
Hot boiled potatoes

In a Dutch oven or soup kettle, brown pork in oil over medium heat. Add onions and garlic; cook until onions are tender. Add the broth, paprika, caraway seeds, salt and pepper; bring to a

***

TENDERLOIN TIPS

Because pork tenderloin defrosts and cooks quickly, it is a good cut to keep in the freezer for last-minute meals. Thaw pork tenderloin using the "defrost" cycle of your microwave according to the manufacturer's instructions.

WILD RICE BRUNCH CASSEROLE
(Pictured below)

Meredith Berg, Hudson, Wisconsin

This saucy breakfast bake is a deliciously different way to start your day. People love the combination of rice, ham, eggs, cheese and asparagus.

      1 package (4 ounces) wild rice
1-1/2 pounds fresh asparagus, trimmed and
         cut into 1-inch pieces
      2 cups cubed fully cooked ham
      5 tablespoons butter, *divided*
     12 eggs
    1/2 cup milk
      1 teaspoon salt
    1/4 teaspoon pepper
CHEESE SAUCE:
      2 tablespoons vegetable oil
      3 tablespoons all-purpose flour
      1 cup milk
      2 cups (8 ounces) shredded Colby *or*
         Gouda cheese
    1/2 teaspoon ground ginger
Dash white pepper

Cook the wild rice according to the package directions. Spread in a greased 13-in. x 9-in. x 2-in. baking dish; set aside.

Place asparagus and 1/2 in. of water in a large saucepan; bring to a boil. Reduce heat; cover and simmer for 3-5 minutes or until crisp-tender. Drain and set aside.

In a large skillet, saute ham in 2 tablespoons butter until lightly browned. Spoon over wild rice. In a large bowl, beat the eggs, milk, salt and pep-

per. In the same skillet, cook egg mixture in remaining butter until set, stirring occasionally. Spoon over ham; top with asparagus.

For sauce, heat oil in a saucepan. Stir in flour until smooth. Gradually stir in milk. Bring to a boil; cook and stir for 2 minutes or until thickened. Reduce heat; add the cheese, ginger and pepper. Cook and stir 2 minutes longer or until cheese is melted.

Pour over casserole. Cover and bake at 325° for 30 minutes. Uncover; bake 10-15 minutes longer or until heated through. **Yield:** 10-12 servings.

CAJUN CATFISH WITH FRUIT SALSA
(Pictured above)

Katherine Nelson, Palmdale, California

I got the idea for this entree from my brother-in-law, Brett, who's a fabulous cook. Even the pickiest of eaters will want a second helping of this fish, so you might want to double the recipe!

      6 catfish fillets (6 ounces *each*)
      3 tablespoons butter, melted
      2 tablespoons Cajun seasoning
SALSA:
      2 medium navel oranges, peeled,
         sectioned and diced
      1 cup diced cantaloupe
    1/2 cup diced honeydew
      2 tablespoons lime juice

Brush both sides of fillets with butter; sprinkle with Cajun seasoning. Place on a broiler pan; broil 6 in. from the heat for 8-10 minutes or until fish flakes easily with a fork.

For salsa, in a small bowl, combine the remaining ingredients. Serve with fish. **Yield:** 6 servings.

ENHANCE *any main course you like with the appetizing accompaniments that take center stage in this chapter.*

STANDOUT SIDE. California-Style Spanish Rice (p. 73).

Side Dishes & Condiments

CALIFORNIA-STYLE SPANISH RICE
(Pictured at left)

Renee Randall, Port Richey, Florida

Back in the 1920s, this was one of the family-size dishes my great-aunt relied on to help feed her four children. The flavorful rice still proves popular today.

      4 bacon strips, diced
  3/4 cup chopped onion
      2 tablespoons olive oil
      1 cup uncooked long grain rice
      1 can (14-1/2 ounces) beef broth
      1 cup diced green pepper
      1 cup diced sweet red pepper
      1 can (14-1/2 ounces) stewed tomatoes

In a large skillet, cook bacon until crisp; remove to paper towels. Drain, reserving 2 tablespoons drippings. In the drippings, saute onion until tender. Remove and set aside.

In the small skillet, heat oil over medium heat. Add rice; cook and stir until golden brown. Reduce heat; stir in broth. Cover and simmer for 20 minutes. Stir in the bacon, onion, peppers and tomatoes. Cover and simmer 25-30 minutes longer or until rice is tender and most of the liquid is absorbed. **Yield:** 8-10 servings.

GRILLED GARDEN VEGGIES

Holly Wilhelm, Madison, South Dakota

This nicely seasoned veggie medley offers a wonderful taste of summer. The dish is also on the lighter side, so you can enjoy it guilt-free.

☑ Uses less fat, sugar or salt. Includes Nutrition Facts and Diabetic Exchanges.

      2 tablespoons olive oil, *divided*
      1 small onion, chopped
      2 garlic cloves, minced
      1 teaspoon dried rosemary, crushed, *divided*
      2 small zucchini, sliced
      2 small yellow summer squash, sliced
  1/2 pound medium fresh mushrooms, quartered
      1 large tomato, diced

  3/4 teaspoon salt
  1/4 teaspoon pepper

Drizzle 1 tablespoon of oil over a double thickness of heavy-duty foil (about 24 in. x 12 in.). Combine the onion, garlic and 1/2 teaspoon rosemary; spoon over foil. Top with the zucchini, yellow squash, mushrooms and tomato; drizzle with the remaining oil. Sprinkle with salt, pepper and remaining rosemary.

Fold foil around vegetables; seal tightly. Grill, covered, over medium heat for 15-20 minutes or until vegetables are tender. **Yield:** 8 servings.

Nutrition Facts: 3/4 cup equals 61 calories, 4 g fat (1 g saturated fat), 0 cholesterol, 227 mg sodium, 6 g carbohydrate, 2 g fiber, 2 g protein. **Diabetic Exchanges:** 2 vegetable, 1/2 fat.

PARMESAN PASTA AND CORN

Frank Hilliard, East Liverpool, Ohio

This simple crowd-pleaser can easily be doubled for potlucks, picnics or other occasions when you're serving a large group. I like this best with fresh corn.

      8 ounces uncooked small shells pasta
      1 medium onion
      1 medium green pepper, diced
  1/4 cup butter
  3-1/3 cups fresh *or* frozen corn, thawed
      1 teaspoon salt
  1/8 teaspoon pepper
      3 tablespoons grated Parmesan cheese

Cook pasta according to package directions; drain. In a large skillet, saute the onion and green pepper in butter until tender. Add the pasta, corn, salt and pepper; heat through. Sprinkle with Parmesan cheese. **Yield:** 10 servings.

COOKOUT CLEANUP
Cleaning the grill rack is easier if I scrub it after each use while it's still warm. I've found that a wire-bristled brass brush works great.
—*Pattie Ann Forssberg, Logan, Kansas*

Getting Creative with Cranberries

CRAVING something other than the usual cranberry sauce for your Thanksgiving or Christmas dinner? Try any of the creative dishes here to give cranberries a tongue-tingling twist.

ACORN SQUASH WITH CRANBERRY STUFFING
(Pictured below)

Dorothy Pritchett, Wills Point, Texas

If you have squash or cranberry lovers at your table, you can't go wrong with this impressive dish. The blend of flavors is delicious and goes wonderfully with a turkey or chicken entree.

2 medium acorn squash
1/4 cup chopped celery
2 tablespoons chopped onion
2 tablespoons butter
1 medium tart apple, peeled and diced
1/2 teaspoon salt
1/2 teaspoon lemon juice
1/8 teaspoon pepper
1 cup fresh *or* frozen cranberries
1/2 cup sugar
2 tablespoons water

Cut squash in half; discard seeds. Cut a thin slice from the bottom of squash halves so they sit flat. Place squash hollow side down in an ungreased 13-in. x 9-in. x 2-in. baking dish. Add 1/2 in. of water. Cover and bake at 375° for 45 minutes.

Meanwhile, in a small skillet, saute celery and onion in butter until tender. Add the apple, salt, lemon juice and pepper. Cook, uncovered, over medium-low heat until apple is tender, stirring occasionally. Stir in the cranberries, sugar and water. Cook and stir until berries pop and liquid is syrupy.

Turn squash halves over; fill with cranberry mixture. Cover and bake 10-15 minutes longer or until squash is tender. **Yield:** 4 servings.

CRANBERRY CHERRY RELISH

B. J. Reimer, Fowler, Kansas

With gorgeous color and three kinds of tangy fruit, this ruby-red relish is always a highlight of holiday menus. Enjoy it straight from the stove or chilled, whichever your family prefers.

2 cups fresh *or* frozen cranberries
1 can (14-1/2 ounces) pitted tart cherries
1 medium navel orange, peeled and chopped
3/4 cup sugar
1/2 cup packed brown sugar
1 teaspoon grated orange peel
1/2 teaspoon ground cinnamon
1/4 teaspoon salt

1/4 teaspoon crushed red pepper flakes
1/2 teaspoon vanilla extract

In a large saucepan, combine the first nine ingredients. Cook over medium heat until berries pop, about 15 minutes. Remove from the heat; stir in vanilla. Serve warm or chilled. Refrigerate leftovers. **Yield:** 3 cups.

PRETZEL-TOPPED SWEET POTATOES
(Pictured above)

Sue Mallory, Lancaster, Pennsylvania

I've shared this recipe with a number of friends, and they all say it's become their favorite way to prepare sweet potatoes. The mingled sweet, tart and salty tastes are an unusual and delectable treat.

2 cups chopped pretzel rods (about 13)
1 cup chopped pecans
1 cup fresh *or* frozen cranberries
1 cup packed brown sugar
1 cup butter, melted, *divided*
1 can (2-1/2 pounds) sweet potatoes, drained
1 can (5 ounces) evaporated milk
1/2 cup sugar
1 teaspoon vanilla extract

In a large bowl, combine the pretzel pieces, pecans, cranberries, brown sugar and 1/2 cup butter; set aside.

In a large mixing bowl, beat the sweet potatoes. Add the milk, sugar, vanilla and remaining butter; mix well. Spoon into a greased shallow 2-qt. baking dish; sprinkle with pretzel mixture. Bake, uncovered, at 350° for 25-30 minutes or until the edges are bubbly. **Yield:** 10-12 servings.

CHILI SEASONED POTATO WEDGES

Irene Marshall, Nampa, Idaho

When I tried out these roasted potato wedges on my family, it was love at first taste! Since I usually have the onion soup mix and seasonings on hand, the recipe couldn't be easier to fix. Feel free to adjust the spice amounts to your liking.

    1 tablespoon onion soup mix
    1 tablespoon chili powder
  1/4 teaspoon salt
  1/4 teaspoon garlic powder
  1/4 teaspoon pepper
    4 large baking potatoes
    2 tablespoons vegetable oil

In a large resealable plastic bag, combine the soup mix, chili powder, salt, garlic powder and pepper. Cut each potato into eight wedges; place in the bag and shake to coat.

Arrange the potato wedges in a single layer in a greased 15-in. x 10-in. x 1-in. baking pan. Drizzle with the oil. Bake, uncovered, at 425° for 20 minutes. Turn; bake 15-20 minutes longer or until crisp. **Yield:** 8 servings.

HERBED BAKED SPINACH
(Pictured above)

Verna Hart, Seattle, Washington

Parmesan cheese and garlic really liven up this spinach, which goes well with meat entrees and main-dish casseroles. Sometimes I use broccoli as a spinach substitute, and the results are just as good.

  1/2 cup chopped onion
    1 garlic clove, minced
    2 tablespoons butter
    2 packages (10 ounces *each*) frozen chopped spinach, thawed and squeezed dry
  1/2 cup heavy whipping cream
  1/3 cup milk
    5 tablespoons shredded Parmesan cheese, *divided*
  1/4 cup dry bread crumbs
  1/2 teaspoon salt
  1/4 teaspoon dried marjoram
  1/8 teaspoon pepper

In a large skillet, saute onion and garlic in butter until onion is tender. Stir in the spinach, cream and milk. Remove from the heat; stir in 4 tablespoons Parmesan cheese, bread crumbs, salt, marjoram and pepper.

Spoon into a greased 1-qt. baking dish. Sprinkle with remaining cheese. Bake, uncovered, at 350° for 40-45 minutes or until cheese is lightly browned. **Yield:** 6 servings.

GRILLED CHEESY POTATOES

Julie McQuiston, Bradenton, Florida

When you're grilling a main course, toss this side dish on as well...you'll be glad you did! The rich red potatoes are wonderful with many different meats.

      3 cups cubed red potatoes
      5 tablespoons water, *divided*
1-1/2 cups cubed process cheese (Velveeta)
      1 large onion, finely chopped
      1 tablespoon Worcestershire sauce
    1/2 teaspoon salt
    1/4 teaspoon garlic powder
    1/4 teaspoon pepper
      2 tablespoons butter

Place potatoes and 3 tablespoons water in a microwave-safe bowl. Cover and microwave on high for 3-4 minutes or until almost tender; drain.

In a large bowl, combine the cheese and onion. Stir in the potatoes. Transfer to a double thickness of greased heavy-duty foil (about 18 in. square).

Combine the Worcestershire sauce, salt, garlic powder, pepper and remaining water; sprinkle over potatoes. Dot with butter.

Fold foil around potato mixture and seal tightly. Grill, covered, over medium heat for 8-10 minutes or until potatoes are tender and cheese is melted. **Yield:** 4 servings.

GARDEN VEGETABLE MEDLEY
(Pictured at right)

Betty Shepherd, Bear, Delaware

If you're looking for a way to use up your bumper crop of zucchini, consider this quick-and-easy side dish. The tomatoes and corn add eye-catching color while the oregano provides great flavor.

    1/2 cup sliced onion
      1 teaspoon salt
    1/4 teaspoon pepper
    1/2 teaspoon dried oregano
    1/4 cup butter
      2 pounds zucchini, julienned
      3 medium tomatoes, cut into thin wedges
      1 cup whole kernel corn

In a large skillet, saute the onion, salt, pepper and oregano in butter until onion is crisp-tender. Add the zucchini, tomatoes and corn. Cook until the vegetables are tender, about 8 minutes. **Yield:** 6 servings.

POMADORO SAUCE
(Pictured below)

JoAnn Renze, Omaha, Nebraska

A friend shared the recipe for this fresh, garlicky tomato mixture. It can be enjoyed like bruschetta—on top of Italian or French bread. You could also toss it with pasta or serve it with poultry, fish or pork.

      4 large tomatoes, seeded and chopped
    1/4 cup olive oil
      4 garlic cloves, minced
      3 tablespoons minced fresh basil
    1/2 teaspoon salt
Freshly ground pepper to taste
Thinly sliced French bread, toasted, optional

In a small bowl, combine the tomatoes, oil, garlic, basil, salt and pepper. Cover and let stand at room temperature for 20 minutes. Serve as topping on bread if desired or as a sauce. **Yield:** 3 cups.

BARBECUE SEASONING

Rose Rainier, Sheridan, Wyoming

This rub is terrific on country-style ribs, pork chops and chicken. If you don't use the whole batch right away, it will keep for the next time.

    1/4 cup beef bouillon granules
    1/4 cup chili powder
    1/4 cup paprika
      1 tablespoon sugar
      1 tablespoon garlic salt
      1 tablespoon onion salt
      1 teaspoon celery salt
      1 teaspoon cayenne pepper
      1 teaspoon pepper
    1/2 teaspoon curry powder
    1/2 teaspoon dried oregano

In a small bowl, combine all of the ingredients. Store in an airtight container in a cool dry place for up to 6 months. Use as a rub for ribs, chicken or pork. **Yield:** 1 cup.

WILD RICE CHESTNUT STUFFING
(Pictured at top right)

Mildred Sherrer, Roanoke, Texas

If you're a fan of rice stuffing and nuts, you'll love this flavorful version featuring chestnuts. The recipe yields enough to stuff a 10- to 12-pound turkey.

12 cups water, *divided*
 2 cups uncooked wild rice
 2 teaspoons chicken bouillon granules
 2 pounds sweet chestnuts
 3 celery ribs, chopped
 1 medium onion, chopped
 6 tablespoons butter
 1 teaspoon rubbed sage
1/2 teaspoon salt
1/2 teaspoon dried thyme

In a large saucepan, bring 4 cups water, rice and bouillon to a boil. Reduce heat; cover and simmer for 50-60 minutes or until rice is tender.

Meanwhile, with a small sharp knife, score an "X" on the flat side of each chestnut, being careful not to cut through the nutmeat. In a Dutch oven, bring the remaining water to a boil. Add chestnuts. Return to a boil; cook, uncovered, for 15 minutes.

Drain and return the chestnuts to the pan; cover and keep warm. With a kitchen towel or pot holder, remove one or two chestnuts at a time. Peel and discard the outer shell and inner skin. Coarsely chop the nutmeats.

Drain the rice. In a large skillet, saute the celery and onion in butter until tender. Gently stir in the sage, salt, thyme, rice and chestnuts. Spoon into a greased 3-qt. baking dish. Cover and bake at 325° for 40-50 minutes or until heated through. **Yield:** 10 cups (enough to stuff one 10- to 12-pound turkey).

HARVEST STUFFING
(Pictured at bottom right)

Ruth Hastings, Louisville, Illinois

Chock-full of colorful veggies and dried fruits, this unique stuffing boasts the best of autumn's harvest. It's delicious served with poultry or pork.

1-1/2 cups water, *divided*
 1 cup *each* chopped carrots, celery and
   onion
10 dried plums, halved
10 dried apricots, halved
 1 teaspoon salt-free herb seasoning blend
1/2 teaspoon salt

 8 slices cinnamon-raisin bread, cubed
1/4 cup unsweetened apple juice

In a large saucepan, combine 1 cup water, carrots, celery, onion, plums, apricots, seasoning blend and salt. Bring to a boil. Reduce heat; cover and simmer for 15-20 minutes or until fruit and vegetables are tender.

Meanwhile, place bread cubes in a single layer on baking sheets. Bake at 350° for 8-10 minutes or until lightly toasted. Transfer vegetable mixture to a large bowl. Stir in bread, apple juice and remaining water; toss gently to combine.

Transfer to a greased 1-1/2-qt. baking dish. Cover and bake at 350° for 30 minutes. Uncover; bake 10-15 minutes longer or until heated through. **Yield:** 6 servings.

OYSTER SAUSAGE STUFFING
(Pictured at center right)

Page Alexander, Baldwin City, Kansas

I've had this wonderful recipe for more than 30 years and always prepare it for special occasions. But it's so rich and buttery, I often make it on other days, too. Try it with pork roast...or use it to stuff pork chops.

 1 envelope onion soup mix
 2 cups boiling water
1/2 cup butter, cubed
10 cups cubed day-old bread, toasted
 1 can (8 ounces) whole oysters, drained
1/2 pound bulk pork sausage, cooked and
   drained
1/2 cup minced fresh parsley
3/4 teaspoon poultry seasoning

Place soup mix in a bowl; add boiling water and let stand for 5 minutes. In a Dutch oven, melt butter. Stir in bread cubes and soup mixture. Cover and cook over low heat for 5 minutes, stirring occasionally. Gently stir in remaining ingredients.

Transfer to a greased 2-1/2-qt. baking dish. Cover and bake at 375° for 40-50 minutes or until heated through. **Yield:** 9 cups (enough to stuff an 8- to 10-pound turkey).

THE RIGHT STUFF
You can prepare stuffing ahead of time and keep it in the refrigerator, but do not stuff poultry until you're ready to bake it. Loosely spoon the stuffing into the neck and body cavities to allow for expansion as the poultry roasts.

Side Dishes & Condiments

milk, half of the cream cheese and 1 tablespoon butter. Add the onions, 3/4 teaspoon salt and pepper; mix well. Spoon into a greased 13-in. x 9-in. x 2-in. baking dish.

Drain sweet potatoes; mash with the thyme and remaining milk, cream cheese, butter and salt. Spread over Yukon Gold potato mixture. Cut through layers with a knife to swirl. Bake, uncovered, at 350° for 25-30 minutes or until heated through. **Yield:** 7 servings.

STRAWBERRY PEACH JAM
(Pictured below)

Gwen Frankhouser, El Cajon, California

This chunky, luscious toast-topper really captures the flavors of summer. The jam can be stored in the freezer for up to a year and makes a nice housewarming or hostess gift.

      2 cups sliced fresh strawberries
1-1/4 cups finely chopped peeled peaches
      1 package (1-3/4 ounces) powdered fruit
        pectin
      5 cups sugar

In a large saucepan, combine the strawberries, peaches and pectin. Cook and stir until mixture

 ## SWIRLED POTATO BAKE
(Pictured above)

Mary Ann Dell, Phoenixville, Pennsylvania

Potato lovers will go crazy for this scrumptious bake from my mother-in-law. I think the creamy combination of Yukon Golds and sweet potatoes goes especially well with poultry or roasts.

2-1/2 pounds sweet potatoes, peeled and
        cubed
2-1/2 pounds Yukon Gold potatoes, peeled
        and cubed
1-1/2 cups milk, *divided*
      1 package (8 ounces) cream cheese,
        softened, *divided*
      2 tablespoons butter, *divided*
      2 green onions, finely chopped
1-1/2 teaspoons salt, *divided*
    1/4 teaspoon pepper
    1/2 teaspoon dried thyme

Place sweet potatoes in a large saucepan; cover with water. Bring to a boil. Reduce heat; cover and cook for 20-25 minutes or just until tender.

Meanwhile, place the Yukon Gold potatoes in another large saucepan; cover with water. Bring to a boil. Reduce heat; cover and cook for 15-20 minutes or until tender. Drain; mash with 3/4 cup

comes to a full rolling boil. Stir in sugar; return to a full rolling boil. Boil and stir for 1 minute. Remove from the heat; skim off foam if necessary.

Pour into jars or freezer containers. Cool to room temperature, about 1 hour. Cover and let stand overnight or until set, but not longer than 24 hours. Refrigerate for up to 3 weeks or freeze for up to 1 year. **Yield:** about 3-1/2 pints.

STIR-FRIED ASPARAGUS
(Pictured above)

Marie Hattrup, The Dalles, Oregon

Here's one of my favorite recipes for that first early-spring asparagus. Stir-frying keeps the texture crisp but tender, and the almonds add a pleasant crunch.

  1 tablespoon olive oil
  3 cups cut fresh asparagus (1-inch pieces)
  1 small onion, sliced
  1 garlic clove, minced
  2 tablespoons sliced almonds, toasted
  2 teaspoons lemon juice
  1 teaspoon soy sauce
1/2 teaspoon grated lemon peel
  1 tablespoon shredded Parmesan cheese

In a skillet or wok, heat oil; stir-fry the asparagus, onion and garlic over medium-high heat until tender. Add the almonds, lemon juice, soy sauce and lemon peel; toss gently to coat. Sprinkle with Parmesan cheese. **Yield:** 4 servings.

QUICK 'N' EASY BEAN POT

Marion Foster, Kirkton, Ontario

With this recipe that conveniently uses canned beans, I don't have to cook beans from scratch. This crowd-pleasing dish turns out great every time.

  4 bacon strips, diced
  1 medium onion, chopped
  2 cans (15-3/4 ounces *each*) pork and
     beans
  2 tablespoons packed brown sugar
  2 teaspoons ground mustard
  1 teaspoon instant coffee

In a large skillet, cook the bacon and onion over medium heat until bacon is crisp; drain. Stir in the beans, brown sugar, mustard and coffee. Pour into an ungreased 1-1/2-qt. baking dish. Cover and bake at 350° for 30 minutes. Uncover and bake 30 minutes longer. **Yield:** 6-8 servings.

FOUR-CHEESE SPINACH BAKE

Trish Nelson, Lynn Center, Illinois

It's tradition for me to prepare this rich, crustless quiche on Christmas Eve. But because it's so yummy, my family asks for it year-round.

    8 eggs, beaten
    4 cups small-curd cottage cheese
    1 carton (15 ounces) ricotta cheese
  1/3 cup all-purpose flour
  1/2 teaspoon salt, optional
    1 package (10 ounces) frozen chopped spinach, thawed and squeezed dry
    2 cups (8 ounces) shredded cheddar cheese
    2 cups (8 ounces) shredded part-skim mozzarella cheese
  1/2 cup finely chopped green onions

In a large bowl, combine the eggs, cottage cheese, ricotta cheese, flour and salt if desired. Add the remaining ingredients; mix well. Pour into a greased 13-in. x 9-in. x 2-in. baking dish.

Bake, uncovered, at 350° for 40-45 minutes or until a knife inserted near the center comes out clean. Let stand for 10 minutes before cutting. **Yield:** 10-12 servings.

BAKED SWEET POTATOES AND APPLES

(Pictured above)

Etta Johnson, South Hadley, Massachusetts

For a pretty and pleasing side dish, try this combination of sweet potatoes and apples sprinkled with gingersnap crumbs. It's one of my favorites to serve with our holiday turkey.

    6 medium sweet potatoes
    2 medium tart apples, peeled, cored and cut into rings
  1/2 cup packed brown sugar
  1/4 cup butter
    2 tablespoons unsweetened apple juice
  2/3 cup finely crushed gingersnap cookies (about 10 cookies)

Place the sweet potatoes in a Dutch oven; cover with water. Cover and bring to a boil; cook for 30 minutes or just until tender. Drain; cool slightly. Peel the potatoes and cut into 1/2-in. slices. Arrange half of the slices in a greased 13-in. x 9-in. x 2-in. baking dish. Top with the apples and remaining sweet potato slices.

In a small saucepan, bring the brown sugar, butter and apple juice to a boil, stirring constantly. Pour over potatoes and apples. Bake, uncovered, at 325° for 30 minutes or until apples are tender. Sprinkle with gingersnap crumbs. Bake 15 minutes longer. **Yield:** 8-10 servings.

 ## DILLY STUFFED POTATOES

Koreen Ogg
Ste. Rose du Lac, Manitoba

Dill and cream cheese make these twice-baked spuds extra special. You can stuff the potato shells ahead of time, chill them and finish baking later.

    4 large baking potatoes
  1/4 cup finely chopped onion
  1/4 cup butter, cubed
    1 cup (4 ounces) shredded cheddar cheese
    4 ounces cream cheese, cubed
    1 teaspoon dill weed
    4 bacon strips, cooked and crumbled

Scrub and pierce potatoes. Bake at 400° for 1 hour or until tender. Meanwhile, in a small skillet, saute onion in butter until tender; set aside.

When potatoes are cool enough to handle, cut a thin slice off the top of each and discard. Scoop out pulp, leaving a thin shell. In a bowl, mash the pulp with cheddar cheese, cream cheese and dill. Stir in the bacon and reserved onion mixture. Spoon into potato shells. Place on a baking sheet. Bake at 400° for 30-35 minutes or until heated through. **Yield:** 4 servings.

SCALLOPED PARSNIPS
(Pictured below)

Elaine Sabacky, Litchfield, Minnesota

With Colby-Monterey Jack and crumbled bacon, this side dish always goes over well. It comes out of the oven golden brown and delicious.

- 1 pound parsnips, peeled and thinly sliced
- 3 tablespoons dry bread crumbs
- 1/4 cup shredded Colby-Monterey Jack cheese
- 1/2 teaspoon salt
- 1/8 teaspoon white pepper
- 1 cup half-and-half cream
- 4 bacon strips, cooked and crumbled

Place parsnips in a saucepan; cover with water. Bring to a boil. Reduce heat; cover and simmer for 8 minutes. Drain.

Place half of the parsnips in a greased 1-qt. baking dish. Combine the bread crumbs, cheese, salt and pepper; sprinkle half over parsnips. Repeat layers. Pour cream over the top; sprinkle with bacon. Bake, uncovered, at 350° for 30-35 minutes or until golden brown and bubbly. **Yield: 4-6 servings.**

SPINACH SUPREME
(Pictured above)

Cyndi Gavin, Blackfoot, Idaho

This is the best spinach recipe I've ever tasted! It's cheesy, creamy and flavorful. If there are any leftovers, I use them to make small appetizer turnovers using phyllo dough.

- 2 packages (10 ounces *each*) frozen chopped spinach, thawed and squeezed dry
- 2 cups (8 ounces) shredded Monterey Jack cheese
- 1 can (10-3/4 ounces) condensed cream of potato soup, undiluted
- 1 cup (8 ounces) sour cream
- 1/2 cup grated Parmesan cheese

In a large bowl, combine all of the ingredients. Transfer to a greased 11-in. x 7-in. x 2-in. baking dish. Bake, uncovered, at 325° for 25-30 minutes or until edges are lightly browned and bubbly. **Yield: 4-6 servings.**

PARSNIP TIPS

Buy smooth, firm parsnips that feel heavy for their size and have unblemished skins. Keep unwashed parsnips in a plastic bag in the refrigerator crisper drawer for up to 1 week.

GOLDEN MASHED POTATO BAKE
(Pictured above)

Cathy Hanehan, Saratoga Springs, New York

My husband and his brother are partners in a dairy farm, so I use a lot of dairy products in my cooking. These comforting, home-style potatoes complement many main dishes.

    8 medium potatoes, peeled and cubed
    1 package (8 ounces) cream cheese, cubed
    2 eggs
    2 tablespoons all-purpose flour
    2 tablespoons minced fresh parsley *or* 2 teaspoons dried parsley flakes
    2 tablespoons minced chives
    2 teaspoons salt
  1/4 teaspoon pepper
    1 can (2.8 ounces) french-fried onions

Place potatoes in a saucepan and cover with water; cover and bring to a boil over medium-high heat. Cook for 20-25 minutes or until very tender; drain well. In a mixing bowl, beat the potatoes and cream cheese until smooth. Add the eggs, flour, parsley, chives, salt and pepper; mix well.

Transfer to a greased 3-qt. baking dish. Bake, uncovered, at 325° for 45 minutes or until a thermometer reads 160°. Sprinkle with onions; bake 5-10 minutes longer or until golden brown. **Yield:** 12 servings.

FRIED CABBAGE
(Pictured below)

Bernice Morris, Marshfield, Missouri

A favorite menu in my family is fried cabbage with potatoes, deviled eggs, corn bread and blackberry cobbler for dessert. I always liked this meal best when we used garden-grown cabbage and potatoes, plus wild blackberries we picked from the woods.

✓ Uses less fat, sugar or salt. Includes Nutrition Facts.

    2 tablespoons butter
    1 teaspoon sugar
  1/2 teaspoon salt
  1/4 teaspoon crushed red pepper flakes
  1/8 teaspoon pepper
    6 cups coarsely chopped cabbage
    1 tablespoon water

In a large skillet, melt the butter over medium heat. Stir in the sugar, salt, crushed red pepper flakes and pepper. Add the cabbage and water. Cook for 5-6 minutes or until tender, stirring occasionally. **Yield:** 6 servings.

Nutrition Facts: 1 cup equals 59 calories, 4 g fat (2 g saturated fat), 10 mg cholesterol, 251 mg sodium, 6 g carbohydrate, 2 g fiber, 1 g protein.

CANDIED GINGER SWEET POTATOES
(Pictured above)

Ingrid Hamm, Chatham, Ontario

I normally don't care for sweet potatoes, so when my cousin served these on Thanksgiving, I tried some just to be polite. The blend of maple, apricot and ginger flavors was so good, I went back for seconds!

> 4 pounds sweet potatoes, peeled and cubed
> 2 tablespoons olive oil
> 1/2 cup maple syrup
> 1/3 cup chopped crystallized ginger
> 1/3 cup apricot jam
> 2 tablespoons butter
> 1/2 teaspoon salt

Place sweet potatoes in a 15-in. x 10-in. x 1-in. baking pan. Drizzle with oil; toss to coat. Bake, uncovered, at 450° for 30 minutes, stirring twice.

In a microwave-safe bowl, combine the maple syrup, crystallized ginger, jam, butter and salt. Cover and microwave on high for 1-2 minutes or until heated through. Pour the mixture over the sweet potatoes; toss to coat. Bake 10-15 minutes longer or until tender. **Yield:** 10 servings.

ONIONS ON THE GRILL

Pattie Ann Forssberg, Logan, Kansas

It's almost hard to believe that such a satisfying side dish can be so easy to make. This recipe calls for just four basic ingredients.

> 3 large onions, sliced
> 2 tablespoons honey
> 1/2 teaspoon salt
> 1/2 teaspoon ground mustard

In a large bowl, combine all of the ingredients; toss to coat. Place on a double thickness of heavy-duty foil (about 18 in. square). Fold foil around onion mixture and seal tightly. Grill, covered, over medium heat for 20-25 minutes or until onions are tender, turning once. **Yield:** 6 servings.

HONEY OF AN IDEA

Combine extra honey, salt and ground mustard left from Onions on the Grill to make a honey-mustard dipping sauce for chicken.

YOUR FAMILY and friends won't be able to resist these fresh-from-the-oven loaves, scones, muffins and more.

GOLDEN-BROWN GOODNESS. Cherry Crescent Coffee Cake (p. 89).

Breads & Rolls

▰▰▰▰▰▰▰▰▰▰▰

CHERRY CRESCENT COFFEE CAKE
(Pictured at left)

Valerie Belley, St. Louis, Missouri

A can of pie filling and a few tubes of crescent rolls help me assemble this sweet treat. It's the perfect addition to hot cups of coffee and good conversation.

1 package (8 ounces) cream cheese, softened
3/4 cup confectioners' sugar, *divided*
1 egg
1/2 teaspoon vanilla extract
2 tubes (8 ounces *each*) refrigerated crescent rolls
1 can (21 ounces) cherry pie filling
2 to 3 teaspoons milk

In a small mixing bowl, beat cream cheese and 1/4 cup confectioners' sugar until smooth. Add egg; beat just until combined. Stir in vanilla; set aside.

Unroll crescent dough and separate into triangles. Set four triangles aside. Place remaining triangles on a greased 14-in. pizza pan, forming a ring with wide ends facing outer edge of pan and pointed ends toward the center; leave a 3-in. hole in the center. Lightly press seams together.

Spread cream cheese mixture over dough to within 1/2 in. of edges. Top with pie filling to within 1/2 in. of cream cheese edges. Cut reserved triangles into thirds, starting at the wide end and ending at the point. Arrange over pie filling with points facing outer edge of pan, forming spokes. Press ends at center and outer edge to seal.

Bake at 375° for 15-20 minutes or until golden brown. Cool on a wire rack. Combine remaining confectioners' sugar and enough milk to achieve drizzling consistency; drizzle over coffee cake. **Yield:** 12 servings.

▰▰▰▰▰▰▰▰▰▰▰

NEW YORK STATE APPLE MUFFINS

Lillian Davis, Berkshire, New York

I used to work at an apple orchard before retiring. We gave this recipe to customers, and so many of them came back telling us how good the muffins were.

2 cups all-purpose flour
3/4 cup packed brown sugar
1/2 cup sugar
2 teaspoons baking soda
1-1/2 teaspoons ground cinnamon
1/2 teaspoon salt
1/4 to 1/2 teaspoon ground cloves
1/8 teaspoon ground nutmeg
3 eggs
1/2 cup butter, melted
1 package (3 ounces) cream cheese, cut into 1/4-inch cubes and softened
1/2 teaspoon vanilla extract
2 cups chopped peeled apples
1/2 cup raisins
1/2 cup chopped walnuts
TOPPING:
1/2 cup packed brown sugar
1/2 cup finely chopped walnuts
1/4 cup all-purpose flour
2 tablespoons butter, melted
1 teaspoon ground cinnamon
1 teaspoon grated lemon peel

In a large bowl, combine the first eight ingredients. Combine the eggs, butter, cream cheese and vanilla extract; stir into the dry ingredients just until moistened (the batter will be stiff). Fold in the apples, raisins and walnuts. Fill greased or paper-lined muffin cups two-thirds full. Combine the ingredients for the topping; sprinkle over the batter.

Bake at 375° for 20-25 minutes or until a toothpick comes out clean. Cool for 5 minutes before removing from pans to wire racks. **Yield:** 2 dozen.

MEMORABLE MUFFINS

A lumpy batter will yield more tender muffins, so avoid overmixing the batter. Unless the recipe states otherwise, muffins should go into the oven as soon as the batter is mixed.

Check muffins for doneness 5-7 minutes before the end of the baking time to avoid overbaking. Muffins are done if a toothpick inserted near the center comes out clean.

Turn dough onto a lightly floured surface; divide in half. Roll each portion into a 3-in. x 9-in. rectangle. Dot with butter; sprinkle with cinnamon. Spread about 1/3 cup prune filling down the center of each. Fold a third of the dough lengthwise over filling. Fold remaining dough over top; pinch seams to seal and tuck ends under. Place seam side down in two greased 15-in. x 10-in. x 1-in. baking pans. Cover and let rise in a warm place for 2 hours or until doubled.

Bake at 350° for 25-30 minutes or until golden brown. Remove from pans to wire racks to cool. Combine the glaze ingredients; drizzle over loaves. **Yield:** 2 loaves.

▄▜▆▜▆▜▆▜▆▜▆▜▄

TWO-GRAIN YEAST ROLLS

Susan Plumb, Acworth, Georgia

Our weekly menu always features these homemade oatmeal-potato rolls. Depending on the meal, I may sprinkle them with cinnamon and brown sugar or brush on garlic butter.

 1/2 cup cubed peeled potatoes
 1/2 cup quick-cooking oats
 1/2 cup butter, softened, *divided*
  2 packages (1/4 ounce *each*) active dry yeast
  1 cup warm water (110° to 115°)
  2 eggs
 2/3 cup sugar
  1 teaspoon salt
  4 cups bread flour
  1 to 1-1/4 cups whole wheat flour
Poppy seeds *or* sesame seeds, optional

Place potatoes in a small saucepan and cover with water. Bring to a boil; cook until tender. Drain, reserving 3 tablespoons water. Combine oats and reserved water (mixture will be crumbly). In a bowl, mash the potatoes. Stir in 6 tablespoons butter until blended (potatoes will be very soft). Stir in oat mixture.

In a large mixing bowl, dissolve yeast in warm water. Add the eggs, sugar, salt, 2 cups bread flour and potato mixture. Beat until smooth. Stir in remaining bread flour and enough whole wheat flour to form a stiff dough. Turn onto a floured surface; knead until smooth and elastic, about 6-8 minutes. Place in a greased bowl, turning once to grease top. Cover and refrigerate overnight.

Punch dough down. Turn onto a lightly floured surface; divide into 32 pieces. Shape each piece into a ball. Place in two greased 9-in. round baking pans. Cover and let rise in a warm place until doubled, about 1 hour.

▄▜▆▜▆▜▆▜▆▜▆▜▄

 ## GREAT-GRANDMA'S PRUNE ROLL

(Pictured above)

Marci Kulla, Brush Prairie, Washington

Here's an old-fashioned favorite that's sure to bring back memories of home cooking. The vanilla glaze adds a perfect hint of sweetness.

  1 package (1/4 ounce) active dry yeast
  1 cup warm milk (110° to 115°)
 1/2 cup butter, softened
 1/2 cup shortening
  3 tablespoons sugar
  1 teaspoon salt
  3 egg yolks
  4 cups all-purpose flour
FILLING:
  2 cups dried pitted prunes
 1/2 cup water
 1/2 cup sugar
  2 tablespoons lemon juice
 1/4 cup butter
 1/2 teaspoon ground cinnamon
GLAZE:
  1 cup confectioners' sugar
 1/4 teaspoon vanilla extract
  2 to 3 tablespoons water

In a large mixing bowl, dissolve yeast in warm milk. Add the butter, shortening, sugar and salt; mix well. Add egg yolks and flour to form a soft dough. Cover and refrigerate overnight.

In a saucepan, cook prunes in water 12-15 minutes or until liquid is absorbed. Mash; add sugar and lemon juice. Cook for 8-10 minutes over low heat until thickened. Cool and refrigerate.

Bake at 350° for 24-30 minutes or until golden brown. Remove from pans to wire racks. Melt remaining butter; brush over rolls. Sprinkle with poppy seeds or sesame seeds if desired. **Yield:** 32 rolls.

ORANGE CRANBERRY GEMS
(Pictured below)

Diane Jordan, Albemarle, North Carolina

I often bake these muffins ahead of time so I can reheat them later for a quick breakfast treat. They have wonderful fruit flavor.

> 2 cups all-purpose flour
> 1/2 cup sugar
> 3/4 teaspoon baking soda
> 1/2 teaspoon salt
> 1 egg
> 2/3 cup buttermilk
> 1/3 cup orange juice
> 1/3 cup butter, melted
> 2 teaspoons grated orange peel
> 3/4 cup dried cranberries *or* raisins
> 1/2 cup chopped pecans

In a bowl, combine the flour, sugar, baking soda and salt. In another bowl, beat the egg, buttermilk, orange juice, butter and orange peel; stir into dry ingredients just until moistened. Fold in cranberries and pecans.

Fill greased muffin cups three-fourths full. Bake at 375° for 18-20 minutes or until a toothpick comes out clean. Cool for 5 minutes before removing from pan to wire rack. **Yield:** 1 dozen.

CINNAMON DATE SCONES
(Pictured above)

Roni Goodell, Spanish Fork, Utah

My kids love to help make these scones for Sunday morning breakfast. They also love to eat them! The dates are chewy and sweet.

> 2 cups all-purpose flour
> 4 tablespoons sugar, *divided*
> 2-1/2 teaspoons baking powder
> 1/2 teaspoon salt
> 5 tablespoons cold butter
> 2/3 cup chopped dates
> 2 eggs, lightly beaten
> 1/3 cup milk
> 1/4 teaspoon ground cinnamon

In a bowl, combine the flour, 2 tablespoons sugar, baking powder and salt. Cut in butter until the mixture resembles fine crumbs. Stir in dates. Combine eggs and milk; stir into crumb mixture just until blended (dough will be soft).

Turn onto a lightly floured surface. With lightly floured hands, gently knead dough 10 times. Pat into a 9-in. x 6-in. rectangle. Using a floured knife, cut into six 3-in. squares; cut each square diagonally in half.

Place on a greased baking sheet. Combine the cinnamon and remaining sugar; sprinkle over scones. Bake at 400° for 12-14 minutes or until lightly browned. Remove to a wire rack. **Yield:** 1 dozen.

Peanut Butter Banana Bread
(Pictured below)

Juanita Sisco, New Port Richey, Florida

Bananas and chunky peanut butter complement each other in this quick bread, which bakes to a beautiful golden brown. It's a fun change of pace from typical banana breads.

- 1/2 cup butter, softened
- 1 cup sugar
- 2 eggs
- 1 cup mashed ripe banana (about 2 medium)
- 3/4 cup chunky peanut butter
- 2 cups all-purpose flour
- 1 teaspoon salt
- 1 teaspoon baking soda

In a mixing bowl, cream butter and sugar. Add eggs, one at a time, beating well after each addition. Add bananas and peanut butter; mix well. Combine the flour, salt and baking soda; add to creamed mixture.

Transfer to a greased 9-in. x 5-in. x 3-in. loaf pan. Bake at 350° for 70-75 minutes or until a toothpick inserted near the center of bread comes out clean. Cool for 10 minutes before removing from the pan to a wire rack to cool completely. **Yield:** 1 loaf.

Cheesy Rye Bread

Arline Hofland, Deer Lodge, Montana

Cubed cheddar cheese is a flavorful addition to these country-style loaves. When you feel like a jazzed-up version of rye bread, this recipe is perfect.

- 1-3/4 cups water
- 1/2 cup cornmeal
- 2 teaspoons salt
- 1/4 cup butter, cubed
- 1/2 cup molasses
- 2 tablespoons active dry yeast
- 1/2 cup warm water (110° to 115°)
- 2 cups rye flour
- 3 cups all-purpose flour
- 1/2 pound cheddar cheese, cut into 1/4-inch cubes

Additional cornmeal

In a saucepan over medium heat, bring water, cornmeal and salt to a boil; stir until thickened. Remove from the heat; stir in butter and molasses. Cool to room temperature. In a large mixing bowl, dissolve yeast in warm water. Add the cornmeal mixture, rye flour and 1 cup all-purpose flour; beat until smooth. Stir in enough remaining all-purpose flour to form a stiff dough.

Turn onto a floured surface; knead until smooth and elastic, about 6-8 minutes. Place in a greased bowl, turning once to grease top. Cover; let rise in a warm place until doubled, about 1-1/2 hours.

Punch the dough down. Turn onto a floured surface; knead cheese cubes into the dough. Divide into three portions; shape each portion into a 5-in. round loaf. Sprinkle greased baking sheets with cornmeal. Place loaves on prepared pans. Cover and let rise until doubled, about 1 hour. Bake at 350° for 40-45 minutes or until golden brown. Remove from pans to wire racks to cool. Store in the refrigerator. **Yield:** 3 loaves.

Lemon Easter Bread
(Pictured above right)

Elizabeth Imblum, Warren, Ohio

This yeast bread is an Easter tradition at my house, but I also bake it at other times of the year. The aroma of the loaves in the oven is fantastic!

- 1 package (1/4 ounce) active dry yeast
- 1/2 cup warm water (110° to 115°)
- 1 cup warm milk (110° to 115°)
- 1/4 cup butter, softened
- 1 package (3.4 ounces) instant lemon pudding mix

3 eggs, lightly beaten
5 to 5-1/2 cups all-purpose flour

In a large mixing bowl, dissolve yeast in warm water. Add the milk, butter, pudding mix, eggs and 3 cups flour; beat until smooth. Stir in enough remaining flour to form a soft dough. Turn onto a floured surface; knead until smooth and elastic, about 6-8 minutes. Place in a greased bowl, turning once to grease top. Cover and let rise in a warm place until doubled, about 1 hour.

Punch the dough down. Turn onto a lightly floured surface; divide in half. Shape into two loaves. Place in two greased 8-in. x 4-in. x 2-in. loaf pans. Cover and let rise until doubled, about 30 minutes. Bake at 350° for 25-30 minutes or until golden brown. Remove from the pans to wire racks to cool. **Yield:** 2 loaves.

◼◼◼◼◼◼◼◼◼◼◼

BUTTER CORNSTICKS

Carolyn Baer, Conrath, Wisconsin

Crusty on the outside and tender on the inside, these breadsticks go well with soups, stews and casseroles. The recipe has been a family favorite for generations.

1/3 cup butter
2-1/4 cups all-purpose flour
2 tablespoons sugar
4 teaspoons baking powder
1 teaspoon salt
1 cup canned cream-style corn
1/4 cup milk

Place butter in a 13-in. x 9-in. x 2-in. baking pan; heat in a 425° oven until melted. Tilt to coat bottom of pan; set aside.

In a large bowl, combine the flour, sugar, baking powder and salt. Stir in corn and milk. Turn onto a lightly floured surface; knead 10-12 times.

Roll into a 10-in. x 8-in. rectangle, about 1/2 in. thick. Cut into 4-in. x 1-in. strips. Place in melted butter and turn to coat. Bake for 18-20 minutes or until cornsticks are crispy and golden brown. **Yield:** 20 cornsticks.

◼◼◼◼◼◼◼◼◼◼◼

WHOLE WHEAT PUMPKIN BREAD
(Pictured below)

Arvilla McKenzie, Bellingham, Washington

I created this recipe after tasting a similar loaf. The pumpkin and pudding mix add moistness while the whole wheat flour makes the bread hearty.

4 eggs
1 cup sugar
1-1/4 cups vegetable oil
1 can (15 ounces) solid-pack pumpkin
2 cups whole wheat flour
2 packages (3 ounces *each*) cook-and-serve vanilla pudding mix
1 teaspoon baking soda
1 teaspoon ground cinnamon
1/2 teaspoon salt

In a large mixing bowl, beat eggs and sugar. Add oil and pumpkin; mix well. Combine the flour, pudding mixes, baking soda, cinnamon and salt; stir into pumpkin mixture just until moistened. Pour into two greased 8-in. x 4-in. x 2-in. loaf pans.

Bake at 325° for 70-75 minutes or until a toothpick inserted near the center comes out clean. Cool for 10 minutes before removing from pans to wire racks. **Yield:** 2 loaves.

PLUM QUICK BREAD
(Pictured above)

Gloria Peters, Portland, Oregon

Plums are an interesting alternative to the fruit fillings usually found in breads. I top off these pretty loaves with cinnamon-sugar and pecans.

   1 cup sugar
  1/2 cup packed brown sugar
  3/4 cup vegetable oil
   1 egg
   1 teaspoon grated lemon peel
   2 cups all-purpose flour
   1 teaspoon baking soda
  1/4 teaspoon salt
   1 cup buttermilk
1-1/2 cups chopped pitted fresh plums (about
     9 small)
TOPPING:
   2 tablespoons sugar
   2 tablespoons chopped pecans
  1/4 teaspoon ground cinnamon

In a mixing bowl, combine the sugars, oil, egg and lemon peel; mix well. Combine the flour, baking soda and salt; add to sugar mixture alternately with buttermilk. Stir in plums. Pour into two greased 8-in. x 4-in. x 2-in. loaf pans.

For the topping, combine the sugar, pecans and cinnamon; sprinkle over batter. Bake at 350° for 60-70 minutes or until a toothpick inserted near the center comes out clean. Cool for 10 minutes before removing from the pans to wire racks to cool completely. **Yield:** 2 loaves.

DILLY BRAN REFRIGERATOR ROLLS

Dorothea Kampfe, Gothenburg, Nebraska

These crowd-pleasing, overnight rolls are perfect to make when you're having company for dinner or serving a holiday meal. I've also found that any leftover baked rolls freeze well.

1-1/2 cups boiling water
   1 cup All-Bran
   2 packages (1/4 ounce *each*) active dry
     yeast
  1/4 cup warm water (110° to 115°)
  1/2 cup butter, melted
  1/2 cup sugar
1-1/2 teaspoons salt
   1 teaspoon dill seed
   2 eggs
5-1/2 to 6 cups all-purpose flour

In a small bowl, combine boiling water and bran; set aside. In a large bowl, dissolve yeast in warm water. Stir in the butter, sugar, salt, dill, eggs, 2 cups flour and bran mixture; beat until smooth. Stir in enough of the remaining flour to form a firm dough.

Turn onto a floured surface; knead until smooth and elastic, about 5-7 minutes. Place in a greased bowl, turning once to grease top. Cover and refrigerate for 8 hours or overnight.

Punch dough down. Turn onto a lightly floured surface; divide into thirds. Shape each portion into 12 balls; place in three greased 9-in. round baking pans. Cover and let rise until doubled, about 1 to 1-1/2 hours.

Bake at 375° for 18-20 minutes or until lightly browned. Remove from pans to wire racks. **Yield:** 3 dozen.

CHERRY CREAM CHEESE COFFEE CAKE
(Pictured at right)

Linda Guiles, Belvidere, New Jersey

You'll love the texture of this tender coffee cake. The sour cream pairs well with the sweet cherries, and the crunchy almonds in the streusel topping make a nice accent. Everyone who tries this treat discovers the same thing—it's hard to eat only one slice!

2-1/4 cups all-purpose flour
  3/4 cup sugar
  3/4 cup cold butter, cubed
  1/2 teaspoon baking powder
  1/2 teaspoon baking soda
  1/2 teaspoon salt

1 egg, lightly beaten
3/4 cup sour cream
1 teaspoon almond extract
FILLING:
1 package (8 ounces) cream cheese, softened
1/4 cup sugar
1 egg, lightly beaten
1 can (21 ounces) cherry pie filling
1/2 cup slivered almonds

In a large bowl, combine the flour and sugar. Cut in the butter until crumbly. Reserve 3/4 cup crumb mixture.

For the crust, add the baking powder, baking soda and salt to the remaining crumb mixture. Stir in the egg, sour cream and almond extract until blended. Press the mixture onto the bottom and 1 in. up the sides of an ungreased 9-in. springform pan with removable bottom.

For the filling, in a large mixing bowl, beat the cream cheese and sugar for 1 minute. Add the egg; mix well. Spread over the prepared crust. Carefully top with pie filling. Sprinkle with almonds and reserved crumb mixture.

Bake at 350° for 50-60 minutes or until the center is set. Cool on a wire rack. Carefully run a knife around the edge of the pan to loosen; remove the sides of the pan. Store coffee cake in the refrigerator. **Yield:** 8-10 servings.

■■■■■■■■■■■■■■

RUM SWEET ROLLS
(Pictured above)

Karen Hughes, Chester, Virginia

These plump, tender goodies are a yummy choice for breakfast or a coffee break...and they're easy to make, too. I also bake batches for holidays and other special occasions. Replace the packaged mix with your favorite recipe for yeast rolls if you'd like.

1 package (16 ounces) hot roll mix
3 tablespoons butter, softened
2 cups confectioners' sugar
4-1/2 teaspoons water
3-1/2 teaspoons rum extract
1/2 teaspoon ground cinnamon

Prepare hot roll mix according to package directions. Turn dough onto a lightly floured surface; gently knead for 5 minutes. Cover with a bowl and let rest for 5 minutes. Roll into a 12-in. x 10-in. rectangle. Spread with butter to within 1/2 in. of edges.

In a bowl, combine the confectioners' sugar, water and extract until smooth. Spread half of the mixture over butter. Sprinkle with cinnamon. Roll up jelly-roll style, starting with a long side; pinch seam to seal. Cut into 12 rolls. Place cut side up in a greased 11-in. x 7-in. x 2-in. baking dish. Cover and let rest until nearly doubled, about 25 minutes.

Bake at 375° for 20-25 minutes or until golden brown. Cool for 5 minutes before removing from pan to a wire rack. Cool for 15 minutes. Drizzle with remaining confectioners' sugar mixture. Serve warm. **Yield:** 1 dozen.

MARASCHINO CHERRY ALMOND BREAD

(Pictured below)

Mrs. Gertrudis Miller, Evansville, Indiana

Pretty cherry bits peek out of every piece of this bread, turning its moist interior bright pink. Spread on some almond butter and enjoy!

> 1 jar (10 ounces) maraschino cherries
> 1/2 cup butter, softened
> 3/4 cup sugar
> 2 eggs
> 1 teaspoon vanilla extract
> 2 cups all-purpose flour
> 1 teaspoon baking powder
> 1/2 teaspoon salt
> 1/2 cup slivered almonds

ALMOND BUTTER:

> 1/2 cup butter, softened
> 1 tablespoon slivered almonds, finely chopped
> 1/2 teaspoon almond extract

Drain cherries, reserving juice; add enough water to juice to measure 1/2 cup. Cut cherries into quarters; blot dry and set aside. In a large mixing bowl, cream butter and sugar. Add eggs, one at a time, beating well after each addition. Beat in vanilla. Combine flour, baking powder and salt; gradually add to creamed mixture alternately with reserved juice. Stir in cherries and almonds.

Pour into a greased 9-in. x 5-in. x 3-in. loaf pan. Bake at 350° for 50-60 minutes or until a toothpick inserted near center comes out clean. Cool for 10 minutes before removing from pan to a wire rack to cool completely. In a small bowl, combine butter ingredients. Serve with bread. **Yield:** 1 loaf (1/2 cup almond butter).

CHOCOLATE CHIP BUTTERMILK SCONES

Reba Starling-Silvey, Versailles, Missouri

Chocolate chips make these scones a hit with everyone who tries them. The confectioners' sugar glaze is a simple way to dress them up a bit.

> 3 cups self-rising flour
> 2/3 cup sugar
> 3 teaspoons baking powder
> 1/2 cup cold butter
> 1 cup (6 ounces) semisweet chocolate chips
> 1 cup buttermilk

GLAZE:

> 1 cup confectioners' sugar
> 3 tablespoons water
> 1 teaspoon vanilla extract

In a large bowl, combine the flour, sugar and baking powder. Cut in butter until mixture is crumbly. Add the chocolate chips; stir in buttermilk just until blended.

Turn dough onto a floured surface; knead gently 8-10 times. Pat into a 9-in. circle. Cut with a floured 2-in. biscuit cutter. Place 1 in. apart on greased baking sheets. Bake at 450° for 8-10 minutes or until golden brown. Remove to wire racks.

In a small bowl, combine glaze ingredients until smooth. Drizzle over scones. Serve warm. **Yield:** about 1-1/2 dozen.

Editor's Note: As a substitute for each cup of self-rising flour, place 1-1/2 teaspoons baking powder and 1/2 teaspoon salt in a measuring cup. Add all-purpose flour to measure 1 cup.

ORANGE ROLLS

(Pictured above right)

Mary Kibbe, Randall, Kansas

Perfect for breakfast, lunch or an evening snack, these delightful bites will be requested time and again in your home.

> 1 package (1/4 ounce) active dry yeast
> 1/4 cup warm water (110° to 115°)
> 1 cup sugar, *divided*
> 1 teaspoon salt

2 eggs
1/2 cup sour cream
1/2 cup butter, melted, *divided*
3-1/2 cups flour
2 tablespoons grated orange peel
GLAZE:
3/4 cup sugar
1/2 cup sour cream
2 tablespoons frozen orange juice
concentrate, thawed
1/4 cup butter

In large mixing bowl, dissolve yeast in warm water. Beat in 1/4 cup sugar, salt, eggs, sour cream and 6 tablespoons melted butter. Gradually add 2 cups flour; beat until smooth. Knead remaining flour into dough. Cover and let rise in warm place until doubled, about 2 hours.

Punch dough down; knead on floured surface about 15 times. Divide in half; roll one half into 12-in. circle. Combine remaining sugar and peel. Brush dough with 1 tablespoon melted butter and sprinkle with half of the sugar mixture. Cut into 12 wedges; roll each into crescent shape. Repeat with second half of dough. Place rolls, point side down, on a greased baking sheet. Cover and let rise until doubled, about 1 hour. Bake at 350° for 20 minutes or until golden brown.

In a small saucepan, combine the glaze ingredients; bring to boil, stirring constantly for 3 minutes. Pour warm glaze over rolls immediately after removing from oven. **Yield:** 12 rolls.

 ## MASHED POTATO KOLACHKES
(Pictured at right)

Jan Wagner-Cuda, Deer Park, Washington

My husband's Bohemian mother brought a kolachke recipe with her when she came to America, so these rolls are a part of our family heritage.

1 medium potato, peeled and cubed
1-1/4 teaspoons active dry yeast
2 tablespoons warm water (110° to 115°)
3/4 cup sugar
1/2 cup warm milk (110° to 115°)
1/4 cup shortening
6 tablespoons butter, softened, *divided*
1 egg, beaten
3/4 teaspoon salt
3 to 4 cups all-purpose flour
1/3 cup apricot filling
1/3 cup raspberry filling
2/3 cup confectioners' sugar
4 teaspoons milk

Place potato in a saucepan and cover with water. Bring to a boil. Reduce heat; cover and cook for 15-20 minutes or until tender. Drain, reserving 1/2 cup cooking liquid. Mash potato; set aside 1/2 cup (discard or save remaining potato for another use).

In a large mixing bowl, dissolve yeast in warm water. Add sugar, milk, shortening, 4 tablespoons butter, egg, reserved cooking liquid and mashed potato. Beat in 2 cups flour until smooth. Stir in enough of remaining flour to form a soft dough. Turn onto a floured surface; knead until smooth and elastic, about 6-8 minutes. Place in a greased bowl, turning once to grease top. Cover; let rise in a warm place until doubled, about 45 minutes.

Turn onto a well-floured surface. Shape into 1-1/2-in. balls; place 2 in. apart on greased baking sheets. Flatten to 1/2-in. thickness. Cover and let rise for 15 minutes or until almost doubled. Melt the remaining butter.

Using the end of a wooden spoon handle, make an indentation in the center of each ball; brush with butter and fill with a rounded teaspoon of filling. Bake at 400° for 10-15 minutes or until lightly browned. Remove from pans to wire racks. Combine confectioners' sugar and milk; drizzle over rolls. **Yield:** about 2 dozen.

DREAMY DESSERTS *of all kinds are just waiting for you here. Enjoy cakes, pies, cookies and much more!*

TEMPTING RECIPE. Triple-Layer Lemon Cake (p. 99).

Sweet Treats

TRIPLE-LAYER LEMON CAKE
(Pictured at left)

Connie Jurjevich, Atmore, Alabama

A smooth and silky citrus filling separates the three layers of my lemon cake. It's a homemade favorite that friends and family never tire of. Serve it after a special spring or summer meal.

  2 cups sugar
3/4 cup vegetable oil
  4 eggs, *separated*
  1 teaspoon vanilla extract
  3 cups all-purpose flour
  3 teaspoons baking powder
1/4 teaspoon salt
  1 cup milk
FILLING:
3/4 cup sugar
  2 tablespoons cornstarch
1/8 teaspoon salt
1/2 cup water
  1 egg, lightly beaten
1/3 cup lemon juice
1-1/2 teaspoons grated lemon peel
  1 tablespoon butter, softened
FROSTING:
  1 cup butter, softened
  6 cups confectioners' sugar
  2 tablespoons lemon juice
  1 teaspoon grated lemon peel
  4 to 6 tablespoons heavy whipping cream

In a mixing bowl, beat the sugar and oil. Add the egg yolks and vanilla extract; beat well. Combine the dry ingredients; add to the sugar mixture alternately with the milk.

In a mixing bowl, beat egg whites until stiff peaks form; fold into batter. Pour into three greased and waxed paper-lined 9-in. round baking pans. Bake at 350° for 20-25 minutes or until a toothpick comes out clean. Cool for 10 minutes; remove to wire racks to cool.

For filling, in a saucepan, combine sugar, cornstarch and salt. Stir in water until smooth. Cook and stir over medium-high heat until thickened and bubbly. Reduce heat; cook and stir 2 minutes longer. Remove from the heat. Stir a small amount of hot filling into egg; return to all the

pan, stirring constantly. Bring to a gentle boil; cook and stir 2 minutes longer. Remove from the heat. Gently stir in lemon juice, peel and butter. Cool to room temperature without stirring. Cover and refrigerate.

In a mixing bowl, combine the frosting ingredients. Spread filling between cake layers. Frost top and sides of cake. Store in the refrigerator. **Yield:** 12-14 servings.

CAKE-TOPPED STRAWBERRY-RHUBARB DESSERT

Ruth Johnson, Elkton, Maryland

Here's a delightful way to use up your harvest of rhubarb. Fresh from the oven, the bubbling dessert is wonderful with a dollop of whipped cream or a scoop of vanilla ice cream.

  3 cups sliced fresh *or* frozen rhubarb
  2 cups sliced fresh strawberries
1-1/2 cups sugar, *divided*
  3 tablespoons quick-cooking tapioca
  2 teaspoons lemon juice
  2 tablespoons plus 1/4 cup butter, softened, *divided*
  1 egg
1-1/2 cups all-purpose flour
1-1/2 teaspoons baking powder
1/2 teaspoon salt
1/2 cup milk
Heavy whipping cream, optional

In a large bowl, combine the rhubarb, strawberries, 1 cup sugar, tapioca and lemon juice. Pour into a greased 8-in. square baking dish. Dot with 2 tablespoons butter.

In a large mixing bowl, cream the remaining butter and sugar. Beat in egg. Combine the flour, baking powder and salt; add to creamed mixture alternately with milk. Spoon over fruit mixture. Bake at 350° for 40-45 minutes or until a toothpick inserted near the center comes out clean. Serve warm with whipped cream if desired. **Yield:** 9 servings.

Editor's Note: If using frozen rhubarb, measure rhubarb while still frozen, then thaw completely. Drain in a colander, but do not press liquid out.

PUMPKIN CHEESECAKE PIE
(Pictured below)

Sharon Crockett, La Palma, California

If you're looking for a classic autumn dessert, try this pumpkin treat in a gingersnap crust. To create the lacy design on top, lay a clean paper doily over the pie before sprinkling on the cinnamon.

1-1/2 cups crushed gingersnap cookies
　　1 tablespoon sugar
　1/4 cup butter, melted
FILLING:
　　2 packages (8 ounces *each*) cream cheese, softened
　3/4 cup sugar
　　1 can (15 ounces) solid-pack pumpkin
　　1 teaspoon ground cinnamon
　1/4 teaspoon ground ginger
　1/4 teaspoon ground nutmeg
　1/8 teaspoon salt
　　2 eggs, lightly beaten
TOPPING:
　　1 cup (8 ounces) sour cream
　1/4 cup sugar
　　1 teaspoon vanilla extract
Ground cinnamon, optional

In a small bowl, combine the gingersnap crumbs and sugar. Stir in butter. Press onto the bottom and up the sides of a greased 9-in. deep-dish pie plate. Bake at 350° for 8-10 minutes or until lightly browned.

In a large mixing bowl, beat cream cheese until smooth. Gradually beat in sugar. Add pumpkin, cinnamon, ginger, nutmeg and salt. Beat in eggs just until combined. Pour into crust. Bake for

35-40 minutes or until center is almost set.

In a small bowl, combine the sour cream, sugar and vanilla. Spread over pie. Bake 8-12 minutes longer or until set. Cool on a wire rack. Cover and refrigerate for at least 4 hours. Sprinkle with cinnamon if desired. **Yield:** 8-10 servings.

CARROT PECAN CAKE

Margie Blank, Cuero, Texas

My from-scratch carrot cake is dressed up with a hint of citrus flavor, plenty of nuts and a delectable cream cheese frosting. I like to bake the cake ahead of time, wrap it tightly in foil before frosting it, then let it sit like that for a day or two to let the flavors blend.

　　1 cup butter, softened
　　1 cup packed light brown sugar
　　1 cup sugar
　　4 eggs
　　3 cups all-purpose flour
　　2 teaspoons baking powder
　　1 teaspoon baking soda
　　1 teaspoon ground cinnamon
　1/2 teaspoon salt
　　2 tablespoons grated lemon peel
　　2 tablespoons grated orange peel
　　2 tablespoons lemon juice
　　2 tablespoons orange juice
　　1 pound grated carrots
　　1 cup chopped pecans
　　1 cup raisins
FROSTING:
　　1 package (8 ounces) cream cheese, softened
1-1/2 cups confectioners' sugar
　　1 teaspoon vanilla extract
Milk as needed
　1/2 cup chopped pecans

In a large mixing bowl, cream butter and sugars until light and fluffy, about 3 minutes. Add eggs, one at a time, beating well after each addition.

Combine flour, baking powder, baking soda, cinnamon and salt; add to creamed mixture alternately with lemon peel, orange peel, lemon juice and orange juice. Beat just until smooth, about 1 minute. Stir in carrots, pecans and raisins. Pour into a lightly greased and floured 10-in. tube pan.

Bake at 350° for 60-70 minutes or until a toothpick inserted near center comes out clean. Cool for 10 minutes before removing from pan to a wire rack. Cool completely before frosting.

Combine cream cheese, sugar and vanilla. Add milk to achieve desired spreading consistency. Frost cake; sprinkle with chopped pecans. **Yield:** 12-16 servings.

CHOCOLATE POTATO CAKE
(Pictured above)

Catherine Hahn, Winamac, Indiana

I won grand champion honors in a potato festival baking contest with this moist chocolate cake. Feel free to double the amount of caramel icing if you have an extra-strong sweet tooth!

  1 cup butter, softened
  2 cups sugar
  2 eggs
  1 cup cold mashed potatoes (without added milk and butter)
  1 teaspoon vanilla extract
  2 cups all-purpose flour
1/2 cup baking cocoa
  1 teaspoon baking soda
  1 cup milk
  1 cup chopped walnuts *or* pecans
CARAMEL ICING:
1/2 cup butter, cubed
  1 cup packed brown sugar
1/4 cup evaporated milk
  2 cups confectioners' sugar
1/2 teaspoon vanilla extract

In a large mixing bowl, cream butter and sugar. Add eggs, one at a time, beating well after each addition. Add potatoes and vanilla. Combine the flour, cocoa and baking soda; add to creamed mixture alternately with milk. Stir in nuts.

Pour into two greased and floured 9-in. round baking pans. Bake at 350° for 25-30 minutes or until a toothpick inserted near the center comes out clean. Cool for 10 minutes before removing from pans to wire racks to cool completely.

For the icing, in a saucepan over low heat, cook the butter and brown sugar until the butter is melted and the mixture is smooth. Stir in the evaporated milk; bring to a boil, stirring constantly. Remove from the heat; cool to room temperature. Stir in the confectioners' sugar and vanilla until smooth. Spread between the layers and over top of cake. **Yield:** 10-12 servings.

PECAN ANGEL FOOD CAKE
(Pictured below)

Margaret Wampler, Butler, Pennsylvania

Chopped pecans add a delightfully nutty taste and texture to my angel food cake, making it a unique variation from the traditional variety.

1-1/2 cups egg whites (about 12)
    1 cup all-purpose flour
    1 teaspoon cream of tartar
    2 teaspoons vanilla extract
1-1/2 cups sugar
1-1/2 cups finely chopped pecans
Whipped cream, optional

Place egg whites in a large mixing bowl; let stand at room temperature for 30 minutes. Sift flour twice; set aside. Add cream of tartar and vanilla to egg whites; beat on medium speed until soft peaks form. Gradually beat in sugar, about 2 tablespoons at a time, on high until stiff glossy peaks form. Gradually fold in flour, about 1/4 cup at a time. Fold in pecans. Gently spoon into an ungreased 10-in. tube pan. Cut through batter with a knife to remove air pockets.

Bake on lowest oven rack at 350° for 35-40 minutes or until lightly browned and entire top appears dry. Immediately invert pan; cool completely, about 1 hour. Run a knife around side and center tube of pan; remove cake. Serve with whipped cream if desired. **Yield:** 12-16 servings.

CANDY BAR CHEESECAKE

(Pictured above)

Melissa Pirtle, Fresno, California

I am a cheesecake fanatic! When I found this version featuring Butterfinger candy bars, I knew it was for me. Our pastor's wife asked me to share the recipe so she could make it to impress her family and friends back home…she couldn't believe something so elegant was such a snap to prepare.

> 2 cups chocolate wafer crumbs (about 35 wafers)
> 1/3 cup butter, melted
> 4 packages (8 ounces *each*) cream cheese, softened
> 1 cup sugar
> 3 tablespoons heavy whipping cream
> 1-1/2 teaspoons vanilla extract
> 5 eggs, lightly beaten
> 3 Butterfinger candy bars (2.1 ounces *each*), frozen and chopped

TOPPING:

> 1 Butterfinger candy bar (2.1 ounces), frozen and chopped
> 2 tablespoons butterscotch ice cream topping

In a small bowl, combine the wafer crumbs and butter. Press onto the bottom and 1-1/2 in. up the sides of greased 9-in. springform pan; set aside.

In a large mixing bowl, beat cream cheese and sugar until smooth. Beat in the cream and vanilla. Add eggs; beat on low speed just until combined. Stir in chopped candy bars. Pour into the crust. Place pan on a baking sheet. Bake at 325° for 60-70 minutes or until the center is almost set.

Cool on a wire rack for 10 minutes. Carefully run a knife around edge of pan to loosen; cool 1 hour longer. Refrigerate overnight.

Remove sides of pan. Sprinkle chopped candy bar over cheesecake; drizzle with butterscotch topping. Refrigerate leftovers. **Yield:** 12 servings.

GRILLED APPLE CRISP

Margaret Hanson-Maddox
Montpelier, Indiana

The first time I tasted this old-fashioned crisp, I was amazed it was made on the grill. Topped with vanilla ice cream, the warm dessert earns rave reviews.

> 10 cups thinly sliced peeled tart apples (about 8 medium)
> 1 cup old-fashioned oats
> 1 cup packed brown sugar
> 1/4 cup all-purpose flour
> 3 teaspoons ground cinnamon
> 1 teaspoon ground nutmeg
> 1/4 teaspoon ground cloves
> 1/4 cup cold butter

Vanilla ice cream, optional

Place the apple slices on a double thickness of heavy-duty foil (about 24 in. x 12 in.). In a small bowl, combine the oats, brown sugar, flour, cinnamon, nutmeg and cloves; cut in butter until mixture is crumbly. Sprinkle over apples.

Fold foil around apple mixture and seal tightly. Grill, covered, over medium heat for 20-25 minutes or until apples are tender. Serve warm with ice cream if desired. **Yield:** 6 servings.

SWISS APPLE PIE

Ruth Johnson, Williamson, Iowa

Looking for a pie that's quick and easy to fix? Don't fuss with a pastry crust! Simply combine these ingredients and pour it all into a pie plate.

    1 egg
3/4 cup sugar
1/2 teaspoon vanilla extract
1/2 cup all-purpose flour
    1 teaspoon baking powder
1/8 teaspoon salt
    1 cup chopped peeled tart apple
1/2 cup chopped walnuts

In a bowl, combine the egg, sugar and vanilla. Combine the flour, baking powder and salt; stir into egg mixture just until moistened. Fold in apples and walnuts. Transfer to a greased 9-in. pie plate. Bake at 350° for 30 minutes or until golden brown and a toothpick inserted near the center comes out clean. Cool on a wire rack. **Yield:** 6-8 servings.

HOLSTEIN CRINKLES

Kim Hebert, Gueydan, Louisiana

Ever since I was a teenager, I've been surprising my family with my baking experiments. These fudgy cookies are among my favorite successes.

    2 cups sugar
1/2 cup vegetable oil
    4 squares (1 ounce *each*) unsweetened
       chocolate, melted and cooled
    2 teaspoons vanilla extract
    4 eggs
    2 cups all-purpose flour
    2 teaspoons baking powder
1/2 teaspoon salt
    1 cup miniature semisweet chocolate
       chips
3/4 to 1 cup confectioners' sugar

In a large mixing bowl, combine the sugar, oil, chocolate and vanilla. Add eggs, one at a time, beating well after each addition. Combine the flour, baking powder and salt; gradually add to chocolate mixture and beat until smooth. Stir in chocolate chips. Cover and refrigerate for 4 hours or until easy to handle.

Working with 1 cup of dough at a time, shape into 1-in. balls. Roll in confectioners' sugar. Place 2 in. apart on greased baking sheets. Bake at 350° for 10-12 minutes or until set. Remove to wire racks to cool. **Yield:** 6 dozen.

SUGAR-TOPPED MOCHA CUPCAKES
(Pictured below)

Jennifer Kraft, Hastings, Nebraska

I prepared this recipe for a school carnival, and now it's the only dessert my daughter requests. Moist and tender, the cupcakes don't need frosting thanks to the sparkly cinnamon-sugar topping.

2-1/2 cups all-purpose flour
1-1/2 cups plus 1/3 cup sugar, *divided*
    1/2 cup baking cocoa
       2 teaspoons baking soda
    1/2 teaspoon salt
    2/3 cup olive oil
       2 tablespoons cider vinegar
       1 teaspoon vanilla extract
       2 cups cold brewed coffee
    1/2 teaspoon ground cinnamon

In a large mixing bowl, combine the flour, 1-1/2 cups sugar, cocoa, baking soda and salt. Add the oil, cider vinegar and vanilla; beat on low speed until blended. Add the coffee; beat on medium for 2 minutes.

Fill paper-lined muffin cups two-thirds full. Combine cinnamon and remaining sugar; sprinkle half of the mixture over batter. Bake at 350° for 20-25 minutes or until a toothpick comes out clean. Immediately sprinkle remaining cinnamon-sugar over cupcakes. Cool for 10 minutes before removing from pans to wire racks to cool completely. **Yield:** about 2-1/2 dozen.

Editor's Note: This recipe does not use eggs.

Prize-Winning Pies

BLUE RIBBONS abound in this scrumptious salute to one of the country's best-loved desserts. With one bite, you'll know why these tantalizing pies were judged prize winners!

CRANBERRY PEAR PIE
(Pictured below)

Helen Toulantis, Wantagh, New York

When my family is invited to a gathering, this pie usually comes along. The recipe is very versatile—you can prepare it with a double crust or replace the pears with baking apples.

Pastry for single-crust pie (9 inches)
- 2 tablespoons all-purpose flour
- 1/2 cup maple syrup

- 2 tablespoons butter, melted
- 5 cups sliced peeled fresh pears
- 1 cup fresh *or* frozen cranberries

TOPPING:
- 1/2 cup all-purpose flour
- 1/4 cup packed brown sugar
- 1 teaspoon ground cinnamon
- 1/3 cup cold butter
- 1/2 cup chopped walnuts

Line a 9-in. pie plate with the pastry; trim and flute the edges. Set aside. In a large bowl, combine the flour, maple syrup and butter until smooth. Add the pears and cranberries; toss to coat. Spoon into the pastry crust.

For topping, combine the flour, brown sugar and cinnamon; cut in butter until crumbly. Stir in walnuts. Sprinkle over filling.

Cover the edges of crust loosely with foil to prevent overbrowning. Bake at 400° for 15 minutes. Reduce the heat to 350°. Remove the foil; bake 35-40 minutes longer or until the crust is golden brown and the filling is bubbly. Cool on a wire rack. **Yield:** 6-8 servings.

WHITE CHOCOLATE MOUSSE CHERRY PIE

Bernice Janowski, Stevens Point, Wisconsin

A cookie crust is topped with a cherry-almond filling and light-as-air mousse in this delectable dessert. It makes any dinner extra special.

- 14 cream-filled chocolate sandwich cookies
- 3/4 cup chopped macadamia nuts
- 2 tablespoons butter, melted

FILLING:
- 1 tablespoon cornstarch
- 2 tablespoons water
- 1 can (21 ounces) cherry pie filling
- 1/2 teaspoon almond extract

WHITE CHOCOLATE MOUSSE:
- 1 cup cold milk
- 1 package (3.3 ounces) instant white chocolate pudding mix

1 envelope unflavored gelatin
3 cups heavy whipping cream, *divided*
1/4 cup sugar
1/4 teaspoon almond extract
Chocolate curls, optional

For the crust, in a food processor, combine the chocolate sandwich cookies and macadamia nuts; cover and process until the cookies are finely chopped. Add the butter; cover and pulse until mixture begins to hold together. Press onto the bottom and up the sides of an ungreased 9-in. deep-dish pie plate. Bake at 350° for 8-10 minutes or until set. Cool on a wire rack.

For filling, combine cornstarch and water in a saucepan until smooth. Stir in pie filling. Bring to a boil; cook and stir for 1 minute or until slightly thickened. Remove from the heat; stir in extract. Cool completely.

For mousse, in a large bowl, whisk milk and pudding mix for 2 minutes; set aside. In a small saucepan, sprinkle gelatin over 1/2 cup cream; let stand for 1 minute. Heat over low heat, stirring until gelatin is completely dissolved. Remove from the heat.

In a large mixing bowl, beat remaining cream until it begins to thicken. Add sugar and extract; beat until soft peaks form. Gradually beat in gelatin mixture. Fold into pudding. Refrigerate until slightly firm, about 30 minutes.

Spread the cooled filling into the crust; top with the mousse. Refrigerate for 2 hours or until firm. Garnish pie with chocolate curls if desired. **Yield:** 8-10 servings.

LEMON PIE IN MERINGUE SHELL
(Pictured above right)

Carol Mumford, Casstown, Ohio

Cool and refreshing, this out-of-the-ordinary lemon pie is a part of all our family's celebrations. Its sunny yellow filling and whipped cream topping make everyone want to dig right in.

3 egg whites
1/4 teaspoon cream of tartar
1-1/2 cups sugar, *divided*
4 egg yolks
3 tablespoons lemon juice
1 tablespoon grated lemon peel
1/8 teaspoon salt
2 cups heavy whipping cream, **whipped**

Place egg whites in a small mixing bowl; let stand at room temperature for 30 minutes. Add cream of tartar; beat until soft peaks form. Gradually add 1 cup sugar, beating until stiff peaks form. Spread onto the bottom and up the sides of a greased 9-in. pie plate. Bake at 350° for 25-30 minutes. Cool on a wire rack.

In a large saucepan, combine the egg yolks, lemon juice and peel, salt and remaining sugar. Cook and stir over medium heat until thickened and bubbly. Reduce heat; cook and stir 2 minutes longer. Remove from the heat. Cool to room temperature without stirring.

Fold half of the whipped cream into lemon filling; spread into meringue shell. Top with remaining whipped cream. Refrigerate leftovers. **Yield:** 6-8 servings.

BAKED CHERRY PUDDING
(Pictured below)

Loretta Broderick, Plattsburg, Missouri

My mother's recipes always went over big with the whole family. One of my brothers was especially fond of her cherry pudding. Every time he came home, Mom would bake this cake-like treat. Now, I surprise him with it whenever he visits me.

1-2/3 cups sugar, *divided*
   1 cup all-purpose flour
   2 teaspoons baking powder
1/8 teaspoon salt
2/3 cup milk
   1 can (14-1/2 ounces) pitted tart
     cherries, undrained
   1 tablespoon butter

In a small bowl, combine 2/3 cup sugar, flour, baking powder and salt. Stir in milk. Spread into a greased 11-in. x 7-in. x 2-in. baking dish; set aside.

In a small saucepan, combine the cherries, butter and remaining sugar. Bring to a boil; cook and stir for 1-2 minutes or until sugar is dissolved. Spoon over crust. Bake at 350° for 30-35 minutes or until golden brown. Serve warm. **Yield:** 6 servings.

APPLE CHEDDAR CHEESECAKE

Kay Coffey, Exeter, Nebraska

With a lemon-flavored crust, heavenly filling and tangy glaze, this delightful dessert gets a warm welcome wherever I serve it. The combination of apples and cheddar cheese is a real crowd-pleaser, especially during the fall and winter.

1/2 cup all-purpose flour
   2 tablespoons sugar
1/2 teaspoon grated lemon peel
1/4 cup butter
   1 egg yolk, lightly beaten
1/4 teaspoon vanilla extract
FILLING:
   2 packages (8 ounces *each*) cream
     cheese, softened
   1 cup (4 ounces) shredded cheddar
     cheese
1/4 cup milk
3/4 cup sugar
   2 tablespoons all-purpose flour
   2 eggs, lightly beaten
APPLE GLAZE:
1-1/2 cups water
  3/4 cup sugar, *divided*
Dash salt
   3 cups sliced peeled tart apples
   2 teaspoons cornstarch
1/2 teaspoon ground cinnamon

For the crust, combine the flour, sugar and lemon peel; cut in the butter until the mixture is crumbly. Stir in the beaten egg yolk and vanilla until the mixture forms a dough. Lightly coat fingertips with butter or flour; press the dough over the bottom only of a 9-in. springform pan. Bake the crust at 400° for 5-6 minutes.

In a mixing bowl, beat cream cheese and cheddar cheese with milk until fluffy. Combine sugar and flour; gradually beat into cheese mixture. Add eggs, beating to blend. Pour into crust. Bake at 375° for 30-35 minutes. Cool on a wire rack for 10 minutes. Carefully run a knife around the edge of pan to loosen; cool 1 hour longer.

For the glaze, in a large saucepan, combine the water, 1/2 cup sugar and salt. Bring to a boil. Reduce heat; add apples and cook for 5-6 minutes or until apples are crisp-tender. Drain apples, reserving 1/3 cup liquid.

In a small saucepan, combine cornstarch, cinnamon and remaining sugar; stir in reserved apple liquid. Cook, stirring until mixture comes to a boil and thickens slightly; cool. Arrange apple slices over top of cheesecake; spoon the glaze between apple slices. Refrigerate several hours before serving. **Yield:** 12-14 servings.

CRAN-APPLE RAISIN PIE
(Pictured below)

Kathe Gardner, Bruce, Wisconsin

Raisins added to the cranberry-apple filling make this pie unique. Northwestern Wisconsin is known for its bountiful cranberry harvest, so this recipe represents my region well.

Pastry for double-crust pie (9 inches)
1-1/2 cups sugar
   1 cup packed brown sugar
  1/2 cup all-purpose flour
   3 tablespoons cornstarch
1-1/2 teaspoons ground cinnamon
   1 teaspoon ground nutmeg
  1/2 teaspoon ground allspice
  1/4 teaspoon salt
   3 cups thinly sliced peeled tart apples
    (about 3 medium)
   2 cups fresh *or* frozen cranberries, thawed
   2 cups raisins
  1/4 cup butter, melted

Line a 9-in. pie plate with bottom pastry; trim even with edge of plate. Set aside. In a large bowl, combine the sugars, flour, cornstarch, cinnamon, nutmeg, allspice and salt. Add the apples, cranberries and raisins; toss to coat. Pour into crust. Drizzle with butter.

Roll out remaining pastry to fit top of pie; place over filling. Trim, seal and flute edges. Cut slits in pastry. Cover edges loosely with foil. Bake at 400° for 20 minutes. Remove foil; bake 30-35 minutes longer or until crust is golden brown and filling is bubbly. Cool on a wire rack. **Yield:** 6-8 servings.

APRICOT CHIP COOKIES
(Pictured above)

Shirley Steele, San Jose, California

Our state has an abundance of apricots and walnuts, both of which dress up the irresistible goodies here. They're great when you want something other than the usual chocolate chip cookie.

1/4 cup butter, softened
1/4 cup shortening
1/3 cup sugar
1/3 cup packed brown sugar
  1 egg
1/2 teaspoon vanilla extract
  1 cup all-purpose flour
1/2 teaspoon salt
1/2 teaspoon baking soda
2/3 cup chopped dried apricots
1/2 cup semisweet chocolate chips
1/2 cup chopped walnuts

In a mixing bowl, cream the butter, shortening and sugars. Add egg and vanilla; mix well. Combine the flour, salt and baking soda; add to the creamed mixture. Stir in the apricots, chocolate chips and walnuts.

Drop by tablespoonfuls 2 in. apart onto ungreased baking sheets. Bake at 375° for 8-10 minutes or until golden brown. Remove to wire racks to cool. **Yield:** about 3 dozen.

MIXING COOKIE DOUGH

If your mixer starts to strain because your drop cookie dough has become thick, use a wooden spoon to stir in the last of the flour or ingredients such as chocolate chips and nuts.

pan comes out clean. Cool on a wire rack.

For frosting, combine the butter, cream cheese, milk and vanilla in a mixing bowl; beat until smooth. Gradually beat in confectioners' sugar. Spread over bars. Store in the refrigerator. **Yield:** about 2 dozen.

░░░░░░░░░░░░

SWEET CHERRY CHEESE DESSERT

Diane Lombardo, New Castle, Pennsylvania

I love the combination of this dessert's soft, creamy filling, crunchy cookie crust and wonderful pecan flavor. The layer of ruby-red cherries on top makes for a beautiful presentation.

> 1/2 cup cold butter, cubed
> 2-1/2 cups crushed pecan shortbread cookies
> 2 cans (21 ounces *each*) cherry pie filling
> 1 teaspoon almond extract
> 1 teaspoon vanilla extract
> 1 package (8 ounces) cream cheese, softened
> 2 cups confectioners' sugar
> 1 carton (12 ounces) frozen whipped topping, thawed

In a large bowl, cut butter into crushed cookies until mixture resembles coarse crumbs. Press into an ungreased 13-in. x 9-in. x 2-in. baking pan. Bake at 350° for 15-18 minutes or until crust is lightly browned. Cool on a wire rack.

In a large bowl, combine the pie filling and extracts; set aside. In a large mixing bowl, beat cream cheese and confectioners' sugar until fluffy. Fold in whipped topping. Spread over crust. Top with filling. Cover and refrigerate for 1-2 hours or until set. **Yield:** 15 servings.

░░░░░░░░░░░░

CRANBERRY CASHEW JUMBLES

Mary Wilhelm, Sparta, Wisconsin

I've baked these from-scratch cookies for the Cranberry Festival Cooking Contest in nearby Warrens, where cranberry is "king." Folks really go for them.

> 1/2 cup butter, softened
> 1 cup packed brown sugar
> 1/2 cup sour cream
> 1 egg
> 1 teaspoon vanilla extract
> 2 cups all-purpose flour
> 3/4 teaspoon baking powder
> 1/4 teaspoon baking soda
> 1/4 teaspoon salt
> 1 package (6 ounces) dried cranberries
> 1 cup chopped cashews

░░░░░░░░░░░░

 ## RAISIN PUMPKIN BARS
(Pictured above)

Mrs. J.B. Hendrix, Ganado, Texas

These moist, nutty treats keep well…that is, if your family doesn't eat them all right away! They're nice to take to a potluck supper, serve for dessert or enjoy anytime as a snack.

> 2 cups sugar
> 1 can (15 ounces) solid-pack pumpkin
> 1 cup vegetable oil
> 4 eggs
> 2 cups all-purpose flour
> 2 teaspoons baking powder
> 1 teaspoon baking soda
> 1 teaspoon ground cinnamon
> 1 teaspoon ground nutmeg
> 1/2 teaspoon salt
> 1/8 teaspoon ground cloves
> 1/2 cup raisins
> 1/3 cup chopped pecans *or* walnuts

FROSTING:

> 1/3 cup butter, softened
> 1 package (3 ounces) cream cheese, softened
> 1 tablespoon milk
> 1 teaspoon vanilla extract
> 2 cups confectioners' sugar

In a large mixing bowl, beat the sugar, pumpkin, oil and eggs. Combine the flour, baking powder, baking soda, cinnamon, nutmeg, salt and cloves; gradually add to pumpkin mixture and mix well. Stir in raisins and nuts.

Pour the batter into a greased 15-in. x 10-in. x 1-in. baking pan. Bake at 350° for 25-30 minutes or until a toothpick inserted near the center of

GLAZE:
    1 cup confectioners' sugar
    2 tablespoons orange juice

In a large mixing bowl, cream butter and brown sugar. Add the sour cream, egg and vanilla; mix well. Combine the flour, baking powder, baking soda and salt; gradually add to creamed mixture. Stir in cranberries and cashews.

Drop by tablespoonfuls 2 in. apart onto ungreased baking sheets. Bake at 375° for 10-12 minutes or until lightly browned. Remove to wire racks to cool. Combine the glaze ingredients; drizzle over cookies. **Yield:** 5 dozen.

CITRUS TARTLETS
(Pictured below)

Sandra Kea, Nashville, North Carolina

These little desserts are always popular at church bake sales and get-togethers. The men in my family can be hard to please, but they enjoy these tiny bites. Even when I make extra tarts, they all disappear.

    1 package (3 ounces) cream cheese, softened
    1 can (14 ounces) sweetened condensed milk
1/4 cup orange juice concentrate
    3 tablespoons lemon juice
    3 drops yellow food coloring, optional
    1 cup heavy whipping cream, whipped
    2 packages (6 count *each*) individual graham cracker tart shells
Additional whipped cream
    2 teaspoons grated orange peel
    2 teaspoons grated lemon peel

In a large mixing bowl, beat cream cheese until smooth. Gradually add milk, beating until smooth. Stir in juice concentrate, lemon juice and food coloring if desired. Fold in whipped cream.

Spoon into tart shells; chill for several hours or overnight. Garnish with whipped cream; sprinkle with orange peel and lemon peel. **Yield:** 12 tarts.

BLUEBERRY SYRUP
(Pictured above)

Pam Duncan, Summer, Arkansas

With its great blueberry flavor, this simple syrup is as delicious over vanilla ice cream and pound cake as it is on pancakes and waffles.

✓ Uses less fat, sugar or salt. Includes Nutrition Facts.

1-3/4 cups fresh blueberries, *divided*
    1 cup corn syrup
    1 tablespoon cornstarch

In a blender, combine 1 cup blueberries and corn syrup; cover and process for 30 seconds or until blueberries are almost smooth.

Place cornstarch in a small saucepan; gradually whisk in the blueberry mixture. Bring to a boil over medium heat; cook and stir for 1 minute or until thickened. Remove from the heat; stir in the remaining blueberries and cool. Store in the refrigerator. **Yield:** 2 cups.

Nutrition Facts: 2 tablespoons equals 69 calories, trace fat (trace saturated fat), 0 cholesterol, 25 mg sodium, 18 g carbohydrate, trace fiber, trace protein.

CREAMY CARAMEL FLAN

(Pictured above)

Pat Forte, Miami, Florida

If you're unfamiliar with flan, think of it as a tasty variation on custard. One warning, though…it's very rich. A small slice goes a long way!

- 3/4 cup sugar
- 1 package (8 ounces) cream cheese, softened
- 5 eggs
- 1 can (14 ounces) sweetened condensed milk
- 1 can (12 ounces) evaporated milk
- 1 teaspoon vanilla extract

In a heavy saucepan, cook and stir sugar over medium-low heat until melted and golden, about 15 minutes. Quickly pour into an ungreased 2-qt. round baking or souffle dish, tilting to coat the bottom; let stand for 10 minutes.

In a mixing bowl, beat the cream cheese until smooth. Beat in eggs, one at a time, until thoroughly combined. Add remaining ingredients; mix well. Pour over caramelized sugar.

Place dish in a larger baking pan. Pour boiling water into larger pan to a depth of 1 in. Bake at 350° for 50-60 minutes or until center is just set (mixture will jiggle). Remove dish from pan to a wire rack; cool for 1 hour. Refrigerate overnight.

To unmold, run a knife around edges and invert onto a large rimmed serving platter. Cut into wedges or spoon onto dessert plates; spoon sauce over each serving. **Yield:** 8-10 servings.

ROASTED ROSEMARY FRUIT TOPPING

Mildred Sherrer, Roanoke, Texas

Chunks of peach and plum are mixed with tart cherries and a little rosemary for this bubbling sensation.

✓ Uses less fat, sugar or salt. Includes Nutrition Facts.

- 1 medium fresh peach
- 1 medium fresh plum
- 2 cups pitted fresh *or* frozen tart cherries, thawed
- 2 tablespoons butter, melted
- 2 tablespoons sugar
- 1 tablespoon lime juice
- 1 to 2 teaspoons minced fresh rosemary
- 2 cups reduced-fat vanilla ice cream *or* frozen yogurt

Prick the skin of peach and plum with a fork. Cut in half; remove pits. Cut each half into eight slices. Place in a greased 15-in. x 10-in. x 1-in. baking pan. Add the cherries.

In a small bowl, combine the butter, sugar, lime juice and rosemary. Spoon over fruit. Bake at 400° for 13-15 minutes or until fruit is tender, stirring occasionally. Serve over ice cream or frozen yogurt. Drizzle with pan juices. **Yield:** 4 servings.

Nutrition Facts: 1/2 cup equals 227 calories, 9 g fat (5 g saturated fat), 25 mg cholesterol, 117 mg sodium, 36 g carbohydrate, 2 g fiber, 4 g protein.

CHERRY ANGEL FOOD CAKE

Estelle Hardin, Washington, Utah

With only 1 gram of fat but delectable flavor, this divine dessert is sure to tempt the taste buds of everyone sitting at your dinner table—whether they're watching their weight or not.

✓ Uses less fat, sugar or salt. Includes Nutrition Facts.

- 1-3/4 cups egg whites (about 13)
- 1 cup all-purpose flour
- 1-1/2 teaspoons cream of tartar
- 1-1/2 teaspoons vanilla extract
- 1/2 teaspoon almond extract
- 1/4 teaspoon salt
- 1-1/2 cups plus 2 tablespoons sugar, *divided*
- 1/2 cup maraschino cherries (about 30), coarsely chopped and drained
- 3/4 cup reduced-fat whipped topping

Place egg whites in a large mixing bowl; let stand at room temperature for 30 minutes. Sift flour twice; set aside. Add cream of tartar, extracts and salt to egg whites; beat on medium speed until soft peaks form. Gradually beat in 3/4 cup sugar, about 2 tablespoons at a time, on high until stiff glossy peaks form and sugar is dissolved.

Combine the flour and remaining sugar; gradually fold into the batter, 1/4 cup at a time. Fold

in cherries. Gently spoon into an ungreased 10-in. tube pan. Cut through the batter with a knife to remove air pockets.

Bake on lowest oven rack at 350° for 30-35 min. or until cake springs back when lightly touched. Immediately invert pan; cool completely, about 1 hour. Run a knife around sides and center tube of pan. Remove cake to a plate. Serve with whipped topping. **Yield:** 12 servings.

Nutrition Facts: 1 piece equals 186 calories, 1 g fat (1 g saturated fat), 0 cholesterol, 108 mg sodium, 40 g carbohydrate, trace fiber, 5 g protein.

CHERRY CREAM CHEESE ICE CREAM
(Pictured below)

Ruby Nelson, Mountain Home, Arkansas

This delightfully rich and velvety ice cream was an instant hit in our home. It's great on hot summer days, but we can't resist making it year-round.

        2 eggs, lightly beaten
1-1/4 cups sugar
2-1/2 cups half-and-half cream, *divided*
      12 ounces cream cheese, softened
        1 tablespoon lemon juice
        1 teaspoon vanilla extract
      1/2 teaspoon grated lemon peel
        2 cups pitted sweet cherries, quartered

In a heavy saucepan, combine the eggs and sugar. Gradually add 1-3/4 cups cream. Cook and stir over low heat until mixture reaches at least 160° and coats the back of a metal spoon. Remove from the heat. Cool quickly by placing pan in a bowl of ice water; stir for 2 minutes.

In a mixing bowl, beat cream cheese until

smooth. Gradually beat in the egg mixture. Add the lemon juice, vanilla, lemon peel and remaining cream. Press plastic wrap onto surface of custard. Refrigerate for several hours or overnight.

Stir in cherries. Fill cylinder of ice cream freezer two-thirds full; freeze according to manufacturer's directions. Refrigerate remaining mixture until ready to freeze. Allow to ripen in ice cream freezer or firm up in refrigerator freezer for 2-4 hours before serving. **Yield:** about 1-1/2 quarts.

FLUTED LEMON CAKE
(Pictured above and on front cover)

Gail Mast, Clarkson, Kentucky

Apricot nectar gives a surprising taste twist to this lovely lemon cake. Topped with a simple citrus glaze, slices are scrumptious with coffee or tea.

        1 package (18-1/4 ounces) yellow cake
          mix
        1 package (3.4 ounces) instant lemon
          pudding mix
        1 cup apricot nectar
      1/2 cup vegetable oil
        4 eggs
        1 teaspoon lemon extract
LEMON GLAZE:
        1 cup confectioners' sugar
        2 tablespoons lemon juice

In a large mixing bowl, combine the cake and pudding mix, apricot nectar, oil, eggs and extract. Beat on medium speed for 2 minutes. Pour into a greased and floured 10-in. fluted tube pan.

Bake at 350° for 45-55 minutes or until a toothpick inserted near the center comes out clean. Cool for 10 minutes before removing from pan to a wire rack to cool completely. In a small bowl, combine glaze ingredients until smooth; drizzle over cake. **Yield:** 12 servings.

move from the heat. Stir a small amount of hot liquid into egg; return all to the pan, stirring constantly. Bring to a gentle boil; cook and stir 2 minutes longer.

Remove from the heat. Stir in coconut and pecans. Pour over filling. Cool on a wire rack. Cover and chill for at least 3 hours. Refrigerate leftovers. **Yield:** 8 servings.

SPICED POUND CAKE

Tracy Dranttel, Fuquay-Varina, North Carolina

From the first time my mother baked this cake years ago, it's been a family favorite. The fruit and spices add a twist to a traditional pound cake, and the glaze has a delicious hint of lemon.

- 1/2 cup shortening
- 2 cups sugar
- 4 eggs
- 2 cups self-rising flour
- 1 teaspoon ground cinnamon
- 1/4 teaspoon ground nutmeg
- 1/4 teaspoon ground cloves
- 5 jars (2-1/2 ounces *each*) peach baby food
- 1 cup chopped walnuts

GLAZE:
- 3/4 cup confectioners' sugar
- 1 to 2 tablespoons lemon juice

In a large mixing bowl, cream shortening and sugar. Add eggs, one at time, beating well after each addition. Combine the flour, cinnamon, nutmeg and cloves; add to creamed mixture alternately with baby food. Fold in walnuts. Transfer to a greased and floured 10-in. fluted tube pan.

Bake at 325° for 60-65 minutes or until a toothpick inserted near the center comes out clean. Cool for 10 minutes before removing from pan to a wire rack. Combine the glaze ingredients; drizzle over warm cake. Cool completely. **Yield:** 10-12 servings.

Editor's Note: As a substitute for each cup of self-rising flour, place 1-1/2 teaspoons baking powder and 1/2 teaspoon salt in a measuring cup. Add all-purpose flour to measure 1 cup.

GERMAN CHOCOLATE PIE
(Pictured above)

Debbie Clay, Farmington, New Mexico

Thanksgiving dinner at our house includes an average of 25 guests and a dozen different pies. This one has all the luscious flavor of German chocolate cake.

- 1 package (4 ounces) German sweet chocolate
- 1 tablespoon butter
- 1 teaspoon vanilla extract
- 1/3 cup sugar
- 3 tablespoons cornstarch
- 1-1/2 cups milk
- 2 egg yolks, lightly beaten
- 1 pastry shell (9 inches), baked

TOPPING:
- 2/3 cup evaporated milk
- 1/2 cup sugar
- 1/4 cup butter, cubed
- 1 egg, lightly beaten
- 1-1/3 cups flaked coconut, toasted
- 1/2 cup chopped pecans, toasted

In a microwave-safe bowl, melt chocolate and butter; stir until smooth. Stir in vanilla; set aside.

In a small saucepan, combine sugar, cornstarch and milk until smooth. Cook and stir over medium-high heat until thickened and bubbly. Reduce heat; cook and stir 2 minutes longer. Remove from the heat. Stir a small amount of hot filling into egg yolks; return all to the pan, stirring constantly. Bring to a gentle boil; cook and stir 2 minutes longer. Remove from the heat. Gently stir in chocolate mixture. Spoon into pastry shell.

In a small saucepan, combine the evaporated milk, sugar and butter. Cook and stir until butter is melted and mixture just comes to a boil. Re-

---

SELF-RISING FLOUR

Some cake recipes call for self-rising flour instead of all-purpose flour. Self-rising flour contains the leavening agent and salt, so you only need to measure one ingredient.

STRAWBERRY CHEESECAKE TRIFLE
(Pictured below)

Diane Evens, George, Washington

I like to serve desserts that look as great as they taste, and trifles are so attractive. Even after a big meal, I always have room for a few bites of this treat.

>   2 packages (8 ounces *each*) cream cheese, softened
>   2 cups confectioners' sugar
>   1 cup (8 ounces) sour cream
> 1-1/2 teaspoons vanilla extract, *divided*
> 1/4 teaspoon almond extract
>   1 cup heavy whipping cream
>   1 tablespoon sugar
>   1 prepared angel food cake, torn into bite-size pieces
>   2 quarts fresh strawberries, thinly sliced
>   3 tablespoons sugar
>   3 tablespoons amaretto *or* 1 teaspoon almond extract

In a large bowl, beat the cream cheese and sugar until fluffy; add sour cream, 1/2 teaspoon vanilla and almond extract. Set aside. In a small, deep bowl, whip the cream, remaining vanilla and sugar. Fold whipped cream into cream cheese mixture. Add cake pieces; set aside.

Combine berries, sugar and amaretto or almond extract. Layer berries and cake mixture in a large glass bowl, starting and ending with berries. Cover with plastic wrap; chill well. **Yield:** 24 servings.

DRIED CHERRY BISCOTTI
(Pictured above)

Sharon Martin, Manistee, Michigan

Want holiday goodies that aren't too sweet? Try my cherry biscotti. The cherries and almonds add color and texture while a sprinkling of confectioners' sugar dresses up each piece.

☑ Uses less fat, sugar or salt. Includes Nutrition Facts and Diabetic Exchanges.

>   2 tablespoons butter, softened
> 1/2 cup sugar
>   4 egg whites
>   2 teaspoons almond extract
>   2 cups all-purpose flour
>   2 teaspoons baking powder
> 1/4 teaspoon salt
> 1/2 cup dried cherries
> 1/4 cup chopped almonds, toasted
>   2 teaspoons confectioners' sugar

In a small mixing bowl, beat butter and sugar for 2 minutes or until crumbly. Beat in egg whites and extract. Combine the flour, baking powder and salt; gradually add to sugar mixture. Stir in cherries and almonds (dough will be stiff).

Press into an 8-in. square baking dish coated with nonstick cooking spray. Bake at 375° for 15-20 minutes or until lightly browned. Cool for 5 minutes. Remove from pan to a cutting board; cut biscotti in half with a serrated knife. Cut each half into 1/2-in. slices.

Place slices cut side down on baking sheets coated with nonstick cooking spray. Bake for 8-10 minutes or until light golden brown, turning once. Remove to wire racks to cool. Sprinkle with confectioners' sugar. **Yield:** 2-1/2 dozen.

Nutrition Facts: 2 cookies equals 135 calories, 3 g fat (1 g saturated fat), 4 mg cholesterol, 123 mg sodium, 24 g carbohydrate, 1 g fiber, 3 g protein.
Diabetic Exchanges: 1-1/2 starch, 1/2 fat.

CHOCOLATE-CHERRY CREAM CREPES
(Pictured below)

Kimberly Witt, Minot, North Dakota

My teenage son calls me a gourmet whenever I make these golden crepes. Sometimes I substitute apple pie filling and drizzle them with warm caramel sauce.

1-1/4 cups milk
3 eggs
2 tablespoons butter, melted
3/4 cup all-purpose flour
1 tablespoon sugar
1/4 teaspoon salt
1 package (8 ounces) cream cheese, softened
1/2 cup confectioners' sugar
1 teaspoon vanilla extract
1 can (21 ounces) cherry pie filling
Chocolate fudge ice cream topping and whipped topping

In a large mixing bowl, combine the milk, eggs and butter. Combine the flour, sugar and salt; add to egg mixture. Cover and refrigerate for 1 hour. For filling, in a small mixing bowl, beat cream cheese until smooth. Beat in the confectioners' sugar and vanilla until smooth; set aside.

Heat a lightly greased 8-in. nonstick skillet; pour 2 tablespoons batter into the center of skillet. Lift and tilt pan to evenly coat bottom. Cook until top appears dry; turn and cook 15-20 seconds longer. Remove to a wire rack. Repeat with remaining batter, greasing skillet as needed. Stack crepes with waxed paper between. Cover and freeze 10 crepes for another use. Crepes may be frozen for up to 3 months.

Pipe filling onto the center of each remaining crepe. Top with 2 tablespoons pie filling. Fold side edges of crepe to the center. Drizzle with fudge topping and garnish with whipped topping. Serve immediately. **Yield:** 8 servings.

BABY SHOWER SUGAR COOKIES

Joyce Leach, Armstrong, Iowa

These crisp treats shaped with hand and foot cookie cutters are a sure hit at baby showers. What a yummy way to celebrate the pitter-patter of tiny feet!

1 cup butter, softened
1-1/2 cups sugar
1 egg
1 teaspoon vanilla extract
1/2 teaspoon almond extract
2-1/2 cups all-purpose flour
1 teaspoon baking soda
1 teaspoon cream of tartar
Pink and blue colored sugar

In a large mixing bowl, cream butter and sugar. Add egg; beat well. Beat in extracts. Combine the flour, baking soda and cream of tartar; gradually add to the creamed mixture. Cover and refrigerate for 2 hours or until easy to handle.

On a lightly floured surface, roll out to 1/8-in. thickness. Cut into small hands and feet or desired shapes. Place on greased baking sheets. Sprinkle with colored sugar. Bake at 375° for 6-8 minutes or until edges are lightly browned. Remove to wire racks to cool. **Yield:** about 5 dozen.

CHERRY CHOCOLATE CAKE

LaJune Holton, Sterling, Michigan

A cake mix and canned frosting make it easy to serve this dessert, even on busy weeknights. It has a hint of almond that complements the cherries and nuts.

1 package (18-1/4 ounces) chocolate cake mix
1/2 cup sour cream
2 eggs
1 teaspoon almond extract
1 can (21 ounces) cherry pie filling
1 can (16 ounces) chocolate frosting
1/2 cup chopped walnuts, optional

In a large mixing bowl, beat the cake mix, sour cream, eggs and extract. Stir in pie filling. Pour into a greased 13-in. x 9-in. x 2-in. baking pan.

Bake at 350° for 40-45 minutes or until a toothpick inserted near the center comes out clean.

Cool on a wire rack. Frost cake; sprinkle with nuts if desired. **Yield:** 12-15 servings.

GRAPEFRUIT PIE
(Pictured above)

Debbie Phillips, Pittsburg, Texas

Grapefruit may be surprising in a pie, but this one has been popular in our house for years. Marshmallows and whipped cream offset the fruit's tartness.

- 32 large marshmallows
- 1/2 cup grapefruit juice, *divided*
- 3 large red grapefruit
- 1 cup heavy whipping cream, whipped
- 1 pastry shell (9 inches), baked
- 1/4 cup flaked coconut, toasted

In a heavy saucepan, combine the marshmallows and 1/4 cup grapefruit juice. Cook and stir over low heat until marshmallows are melted. Cool to room temperature.

Peel the grapefruit and cut into sections (about 2-1/2 cups). Stir the grapefruit, whipped cream and remaining grapefruit juice into marshmallow mixture. Pour into crust. Sprinkle with coconut. Refrigerate for 3 hours or until set. **Yield:** 6-8 servings.

PEANUT BUTTER 'N' JELLY CAKE
(Pictured at right)

Linda Graybill, Sebring, Florida

Kids of any age have a hard time resisting peanut butter and jelly...especially when it comes in cake! I made this fun treat for my son's first birthday.

- 1/2 cup butter, softened
- 1/4 cup peanut butter
- 1-1/2 cups sugar
- 2 eggs
- 1 teaspoon vanilla extract
- 2 cups all-purpose flour
- 3 teaspoons baking powder
- 1 teaspoon salt
- 1 cup milk

FROSTING:
- 1/4 cup butter, softened
- 1/2 cup plus 1 tablespoon peanut butter
- 1-3/4 tablespoons vanilla extract
- 3 cups confectioners' sugar
- 4 to 6 tablespoons milk
- 3/4 cup grape jelly

In a large mixing bowl, cream the butter and peanut butter until smooth. Add sugar; mix well. Add the eggs, one at a time, beating well after each addition. Beat in vanilla. Combine the flour, baking powder and salt; add to peanut butter mixture alternately with milk.

Pour into two greased and floured 9-in. round baking pans. Bake at 350° for 35-40 minutes or until a toothpick inserted near the center comes out clean. Cool for 5 minutes before removing from pans to wire racks to cool completely.

For frosting, in a mixing bowl, beat the butter and peanut butter. Add the vanilla, confectioners' sugar and enough milk to achieve spreading consistency. Place one cake layer on a serving plate; spread with jelly. Top with the remaining cake layer; frost top and sides of cake with frosting. **Yield:** 12 servings.

PECAN PLUM CAKE

Betty Doane, Clackamas, Oregon

This moist, flavorful plum cake is topped with nuts and has a home-style look that's irresistible. The recipe is quite old and was given to me by one of the best cooks I know. It's a real treat served warm with a dollop of whipped topping.

    1 egg
3/4 cup vegetable oil
    1 cup sugar
1/2 cup packed brown sugar
    1 teaspoon grated orange peel
    2 cups all-purpose flour
    1 teaspoon baking powder
1/4 teaspoon baking soda
1/4 teaspoon salt
1-1/2 cups chopped canned plums, drained
       and patted dry
TOPPING:
1/4 cup chopped pecans
    2 tablespoons sugar
    1 teaspoon ground cinnamon

In a large mixing bowl, beat the egg, oil, sugars and peel. In another bowl, combine the flour, baking powder, baking soda and salt; add to sugar mixture (batter will be thick). Fold in plums.

Spread the batter into a greased 11-in. x 7-in. x 2-in. baking dish. Combine the topping ingredients; sprinkle over the batter. Bake at 350° for 35-40 minutes or until a toothpick inserted near the center of cake comes out clean. Cool on a wire rack. **Yield:** 12 servings.

BLACK FOREST BROWNIES

Heidi Stouffer, Bradford, Ontario

A brownie mix and canned pie filling help me fix these layered bars fast. Everyone loves the combination of chocolate and cherries.

    1 package fudge brownie mix (13-inch x
       9-inch pan size)
    1 package (8 ounces) cream cheese,
       softened
1/3 cup sugar
1/2 teaspoon vanilla extract
1/3 cup heavy whipping cream
    1 can (21 ounces) cherry pie filling
    2 squares (1 ounce *each*) semisweet
       chocolate

Prepare and bake brownies according to package directions. Cool on a wire rack.

In a large mixing bowl, beat the cream cheese,

GRASSHOPPER PIE
(Pictured above)

Sally Vandermus, Rochester, Minnesota

After a hearty meal, this chocolate-mint pie is wonderfully refreshing. I make it at Christmas and whenever my son comes to visit.

2/3 cup semisweet chocolate chips
    2 tablespoons heavy whipping cream
    2 teaspoons shortening
    1 cup finely chopped walnuts
FILLING:
  35 large marshmallows
1/4 cup milk
1/4 teaspoon salt
    3 tablespoons green creme de menthe
    3 tablespoons clear creme de cacao
1-1/2 cups heavy whipping cream, whipped
Chocolate curls, optional

Line a 9-in. pie plate with foil; set aside. In a large heavy saucepan, combine the chocolate chips, cream and shortening; cook over low heat until chips are melted. Stir in walnuts. Pour into prepared pie plate; spread evenly over bottom and sides of plate. Refrigerate for 1 hour or until set.

In a large heavy saucepan, combine the marshmallows, milk and salt; cook over low heat until marshmallows are melted, stirring occasionally. Remove from the heat; stir in creme de menthe and creme de cacao. Refrigerate for 1 hour or until slightly thickened.

Carefully remove foil from crust and return crust to plate. Fold whipped cream into filling; pour into crust. Refrigerate overnight. Garnish with chocolate if desired. **Yield:** 6-8 servings.

sugar and vanilla until smooth. In a small mixing bowl, beat cream until stiff peaks form; fold into cream cheese mixture. Spread over brownies. Top with pie filling. In a microwave or small heavy saucepan, melt chocolate; stir until smooth. Drizzle over brownies. Refrigerate for 10 minutes or until chocolate is set. **Yield:** 2 dozen.

SWEET POTATO MINI CAKES
(Pictured below)

Joyce Larson, New Market, Iowa

Whenever I make these cute desserts, I think of my grandmother. She used sweet potatoes from her garden in pies, breads and cakes...and added black walnuts from her trees for good measure!

- 2 cups all-purpose flour
- 1 cup sugar
- 1 cup packed brown sugar
- 1 teaspoon salt
- 1 teaspoon baking soda
- 1 teaspoon baking powder
- 1 teaspoon ground cinnamon
- 1 teaspoon pumpkin pie spice
- 4 eggs
- 1-1/4 cups vegetable oil
- 3 cups shredded peeled sweet potatoes
- 1 teaspoon rum extract
- 1 can (8 ounces) crushed pineapple, drained
- 1 cup golden raisins
- 1 cup chopped walnuts

FROSTING:
- 1 package (8 ounces) cream cheese, softened
- 1 cup butter, softened
- 5 cups confectioners' sugar

- 4 teaspoons brown sugar
- 1 teaspoon vanilla extract
- 1/2 teaspoon rum extract
- 1-1/2 cups ground walnuts

In a large mixing bowl, combine the first eight ingredients. Add eggs, oil, potatoes and extract; beat until combined. Stir in the pineapple, raisins and walnuts. Fill 12 greased or paper-lined jumbo muffin cups three-fourths full. Bake at 350° for 25-30 minutes or until a toothpick comes out clean. Cool for 10 minutes before removing from pans to wire racks to cool completely.

For frosting, in a large mixing bowl, beat cream cheese and butter until fluffy. Beat in the sugars and extracts until smooth. Frost sides of cakes; roll in walnuts. Place cakes upside down and frost tops with remaining frosting. **Yield:** 1 dozen.

BLENDER EGG CUSTARD
(Pictured above)

Ivy Praytor, Mobile, Alabama

Egg custard is a traditional Southern recipe. I think this yummy version is foolproof—you just blend the ingredients, pour and bake.

- 2 cups milk
- 1/4 cup butter, melted
- 4 eggs
- 1 cup sugar
- 1/2 cup all-purpose flour
- 1/2 teaspoon vanilla extract
- 1/4 to 1/2 teaspoon ground nutmeg

In a blender, combine all of the ingredients. Cover and process until well blended. Pour into a greased 9-in. pie plate. Bake at 325° for 55-65 minutes or until a knife inserted near the center comes out clean. Serve warm or chilled. Refrigerate leftovers. **Yield:** 6-8 servings.

Fun with Food

PLAYING with your food is perfectly fine when you assemble these fun-filled and festive treats. They'll delight kids of all ages.

■▬■▬■▬■▬■▬■▬■

BUMBLEBEE BANANA CUPCAKES
(Pictured below)

Beatrice Richard, Posen, Michigan

These adorable, easy cupcakes are simply irresistible. They're wonderful for school treats or even for outdoor summer events.

> 1 package (14 ounces) banana quick
>   bread and muffin mix
> 1 cup milk

1/2 cup vegetable oil
  2 eggs
  1 can (16 ounces) vanilla frosting
  5 drops yellow food coloring
12 large yellow gumdrops
1/2 cup chocolate frosting
12 semisweet chocolate chips
24 miniature semisweet chocolate chips
12 large white gumdrops
Black shoestring licorice, cut into 1-inch pieces

In a large bowl, combine the muffin mix, milk, oil and eggs. Fill 12 greased or paper-lined muffin cups two-thirds full. Bake at 375° for 15-18 minutes or until a toothpick comes out clean. Cool for 5 minutes before removing from pan to a wire rack to cool completely.

In a mixing bowl, combine vanilla frosting and food coloring. Frost cupcakes. Cut yellow gumdrops in half widthwise. Use the rounded tops for heads. Flatten remaining portions into ovals for bodies. Place one head and one body on each cupcake.

Place chocolate frosting in a resealable plastic bag; cut a small hole in a corner of the bag. Pipe stripes on gumdrop bodies to resemble a bumblebee. For the stinger, place one chocolate chip at the end of body with pointed end facing out. Position two mini chocolate chips in front of head for eyes. Cut white gumdrops in half lengthwise; position next to bodies for wings. Insert two licorice pieces for antennae. **Yield:** 1 dozen.

■▬■▬■▬■▬■▬■▬■

HAMBURGER COOKIES
(Pictured above right)

Julie Wellington, Youngstown, Ohio

My husband loves peppermint patties, and our son is crazy for vanilla wafers. So I put the two together to make a cookie that looks just like a burger. Children and adults alike get a kick out of them.

1/2 cup vanilla frosting
Red and yellow paste *or* gel food coloring
40 vanilla wafers

20 peppermint patties
1 teaspoon corn syrup
1 teaspoon sesame seeds

Place 1/4 cup frosting in each of two bowls. Tint one red and the other yellow. Frost the bottoms of 20 vanilla wafers yellow; top with a peppermint patty. Spread with red frosting. Brush tops of the remaining vanilla wafers with corn syrup; sprinkle with sesame seeds. Place over red frosting. **Yield:** 20 cookies.

★★★★★★★★★★★★

SWEET JACK-O'-LANTERNS
(Pictured at right)

Hannah Bjerkseth, Three Hills, Alberta

There's no trick to making these Halloween-themed cupcakes. Using a convenient cake mix, you can turn them out in a jiffy. Simplify them even more by starting with canned white frosting.

  1 package (18-1/4 ounces) yellow cake
     mix *or* cake mix of your choice
3-3/4 cups confectioners' sugar

3 tablespoons butter, softened
2/3 to 3/4 cup milk
1 to 1-1/2 teaspoons orange paste food
   coloring
4 green gumdrops
12 black jujubes

Prepare and bake cake according to package directions for cupcakes. Fill 24 greased muffin cups two-thirds full. Bake at 350° for 15-18 minutes or until a toothpick comes out clean. Cool for 5 minutes before removing from pans to wire racks to cool completely.

For frosting, in a small bowl, combine confectioners' sugar, butter and enough milk to achieve spreading consistency. Stir in food coloring. Cut a thin slice off the top of each cupcake. Spread frosting on 12 cupcakes. Invert remaining cupcakes and place on top; frost top and sides.

For stems, cut each gumdrop into three lengthwise wedges; place one piece on top of each cupcake. Cut jujubes into thin slices; use a bottom slice for each mouth.

From remaining jujube slices, cut one large triangle and two smaller ones. Position two small triangles and a large triangle on each cupcake for eyes and nose. **Yield:** 1 dozen.

UPSIDE-DOWN APPLE PIE
(Pictured below)

Susan Frisch, Germansville, Pennsylvania

This pie has won eight ribbons at area fairs. People say it looks and tastes like a giant apple-cinnamon bun! I bake pies during the holidays for family and friends, and this is a favorite.

2 cups all-purpose flour
1/2 teaspoon salt
6 tablespoons shortening
2 tablespoons cold butter
5 to 7 tablespoons orange juice
FILLING:
6 tablespoons butter, melted, *divided*
1/2 cup packed brown sugar
1/2 cup chopped pecans
1 cup sugar
1/3 cup all-purpose flour
3/4 teaspoon ground cinnamon
1/4 teaspoon ground nutmeg
8 cups thinly sliced peeled Golden Delicious apples (about 1/8 inch thick)
GLAZE:
1/2 cup confectioners' sugar
2 to 3 teaspoons orange juice

In a bowl, combine flour and salt; cut in shortening and butter until crumbly. Gradually add orange juice, tossing with a fork until dough forms a ball. Divide dough into two balls. Wrap in plastic wrap; refrigerate for at least 30 minutes.

Line a 9-in. deep-dish pie plate with heavy-duty foil, leaving 1-1/2 in. beyond edge; coat the foil with nonstick cooking spray. Combine 4 tablespoons butter, brown sugar and pecans; spoon in-to prepared pie plate. In a large bowl, combine the sugar, flour, cinnamon, nutmeg, apples and remaining butter; toss gently.

On waxed paper, roll out one ball of pastry to fit pie plate. Place pastry over nut mixture, pressing firmly against mixture and sides of plate; trim to 1 in. beyond plate edge. Fill with apple mixture. Roll out remaining pastry to fit top of pie; place over filling. Trim to 1/4 in. beyond plate edge. Fold bottom pastry over top pastry; seal and flute edges. Cut four 1-in. slits in top pastry.

Bake at 375° for 20 minutes. Cover edges loosely with foil. Bake 30 minutes longer or until apples are tender and crust is golden brown. Cool for 15 minutes on a wire rack. Invert onto a serving platter; carefully remove foil. Combine glaze ingredients; drizzle over pie. **Yield:** 6-8 servings.

PECAN CARAMEL BARS

Cheryl Guzman, Monroe, Georgia

My co-workers request these goodies all the time, so I bring them for our potlucks. Butterscotch chips make these pecan bars different from most.

1 package (12 ounces) vanilla wafers, crushed
2 tablespoons sugar
3/4 cup butter, melted
1 can (14 ounces) sweetened condensed milk
1 egg
1/2 teaspoon maple flavoring
1 cup butterscotch chips
1-1/2 cups coarsely chopped pecans

In a small bowl, combine the wafer crumbs, sugar and butter. Press into a greased 13-in. x 9-in. x 2-in. baking pan. Bake at 350° for 8-10 minutes or until lightly browned and set. Cool for 10 minutes on a wire rack.

In a small mixing bowl, beat the milk, egg and maple flavoring. Stir in the butterscotch chips. Spread over crust. Sprinkle with pecans. Bake for 18-22 minutes or until golden brown. Cool on a wire rack. Cut into bars. **Yield:** 3 dozen.

FLUTED PIE CRUST

To flute the edge of a pie crust, position your thumb on the inside of the crust. With your other hand on the outside edge, pinch the pastry around your thumb to form a "V" shape. Continue around the edge of the pie.

SAUCY CHERRY ENCHILADAS
(Pictured below)

Helen Craft, Robstown, Texas

Enchiladas for dessert? When they're filled with fruit and covered with a sweet syrup and pecans, why not? These yummy tortillas are also good with apple or blueberry pie filling instead of cherry.

> 2 cups sugar
> 1-1/2 cups water
> 1 cup butter, cubed
> 2 tablespoons lemon juice
> 1 can (21 ounces) cherry, apple *or* blueberry pie filling
> 16 flour tortillas (6 inches)
> 1 cup chopped pecans
> 1 teaspoon ground cinnamon
> Vanilla ice cream

In a large saucepan, bring the sugar, water, butter and lemon juice to a boil over medium heat. Reduce heat; simmer, uncovered, for 30 minutes or until mixture has the consistency of syrup. Remove from the heat; set aside.

Spoon about 3 tablespoons of pie filling off-center on each tortilla; fold sides and ends over filling and roll up. Place in a greased 13-in. x 9-in. x 2-in. baking dish. Pour sugar syrup over tortillas; let stand at room temperature for 30 minutes.

Bake, uncovered, at 350° for 30 minutes. Sprinkle with pecans and cinnamon. Bake 15 minutes longer or until golden brown and sauce bubbles around the edges. Serve warm with ice cream. **Yield:** 16 servings.

PEANUT BUTTER PIE
(Pictured above)

Lillibell Welter, Rainier, Oregon

Although I prepare this fudgy peanut butter pie regularly for luncheons at our church, I have yet to eat a whole piece. Usually, there's nothing left to take home with me but crumbs!

> 1 package (8 ounces) cream cheese, softened
> 1 cup plus 2 tablespoons creamy peanut butter, *divided*
> 1/2 cup sugar
> 1 carton (12 ounces) frozen whipped topping, thawed, *divided*
> 1 chocolate crumb crust (8 inches)
> 2/3 cup plus 2 tablespoons hot fudge ice cream topping, *divided*

In a large mixing bowl, beat the cream cheese until smooth. Add 1 cup peanut butter and sugar; mix well. Fold in 3 cups whipped topping; spoon into chocolate crumb crust.

In a microwave-safe bowl, heat 2/3 cup hot fudge topping for 30 seconds. Pour over the peanut butter layer and spread to the edges of the crust. Refrigerate for 2 hours.

Spread remaining whipped topping over pie. Cut into slices. Place the remaining hot fudge topping and peanut butter in two separate plastic bags. Cut a small hole in the corner of each bag; pipe topping and peanut butter over each slice of pie. **Yield:** 8 servings.

WHEN LESS *is more, you can rely on the pared-down yet delicious recipes here. They're sure to go over big!*

SIZED JUST RIGHT. From top: Spiced Iced Tea, Roasted Corn Muffins, Broccoli Salad and Old-Country Sauerkraut 'n' Ribs (all recipes on p. 123).

Cooking for Two

OLD-COUNTRY SAUERKRAUT 'N' RIBS

Helen Wentz, North Fort Myers, Florida

This simple, one-pan dish is a complete meal and takes little time to prepare. Whenever I serve it, I know I'm setting a hearty meal on the table.

    1 medium baking potato, cut into
        1-1/2-inch chunks
    1 can (8 ounces) sauerkraut, rinsed and
        well drained
    1 pound pork baby-back ribs
    1/4 cup ketchup
    1/4 cup molasses
    3 tablespoons Worcestershire sauce

Layer the potato, sauerkraut and ribs in a greased 11-in. x 7-in. x 2-in. baking dish. Combine the ketchup, molasses and Worcestershire sauce; pour over the ribs. Cover and bake at 350° for 1-1/4 hours. Uncover; bake 15 minutes longer or until meat is tender. Remove ribs and cut into two-rib portions before serving. **Yield:** 2 servings.

ROASTED CORN MUFFINS

Dorinda Bruce, Bixby, Oklahoma

I have never gone back to my old corn bread recipe after finding this one. Adding corn to the batter gives this small batch of muffins extra color and flavor.

    1/4 cup butter, softened
    1/3 cup sugar
    1 egg
    2 tablespoons honey
    1/4 teaspoon salt
    3/4 cup all-purpose flour
    1/2 cup yellow cornmeal
    1/4 teaspoon baking powder
    1/4 cup milk
    1/2 cup frozen corn

In a small mixing bowl, cream butter and sugar. Beat in egg, honey and salt. Combine flour, cornmeal and baking powder; add to creamed mixture alternately with milk. Fold in corn.

Fill greased or paper-lined muffin cups two-thirds full. Bake at 400° for 20-25 minutes or until a toothpick comes out clean. Cool for 5 minutes before removing from pan to a wire rack. Serve warm. **Yield:** 6 muffins.

BROCCOLI SALAD

Sara Sherlock, Pork Alice, British Columbia

After I sampled this salad at a barbecue, the recipe was given to me without any measurements. I can toss it together in a jiffy, and it always turns out great.

    1-1/2 cups fresh broccoli florets
    3/4 cup shredded cheddar cheese
    4 bacon strips, cooked and crumbled
    1/4 cup finely chopped onion
    3 tablespoons mayonnaise
    2 tablespoons white vinegar
    1 tablespoon sugar

In a bowl, combine the broccoli, cheese, bacon and onion. In another bowl, whisk the mayonnaise, vinegar and sugar. Pour over broccoli mixture and toss to coat. Cover and refrigerate for at least 1 hour before serving. **Yield:** 2 servings.

SPICED ICED TEA

Ellen Carlton, Mont Vernon, New Hampshire

I love to share my mother's iced tea recipe. Ice-cold pitchers of that refreshing drink had a special spot in our refrigerator every summer.

    4 cups boiling water
    4 individual tea bags
    1 cinnamon stick (3 inches)
    4 whole cloves
Sugar substitute equivalent to 4 teaspoons
    sugar
Ice cubes, fresh mint and lemon slices

Pour boiling water into a heat-proof pitcher. Add the tea bags, cinnamon, cloves and sugar substitute; steep tea for 15 minutes.

Discard the tea bags, cinnamon and cloves. Pour tea over ice in glasses; garnish with mint and lemon. **Yield:** 2-4 servings.

Editor's Note: This recipe was tested with Splenda No Calorie Sweetener.

LEMONY SHRIMP SANDWICHES
(Pictured below)

Catherine Fontana, Fox Lake, Illinois

After one bite of these wonderful sandwiches, you'll have found a new favorite that you'll turn to time and again. The no-fuss citrus spread really complements the shrimp.

☑ Uses less fat, sugar or salt. Includes Nutrition Facts.

　1/3　cup fat-free mayonnaise
　　1　teaspoon lemon juice
　3/4　teaspoon grated lemon peel
　1/4　teaspoon ground coriander
　1/8　teaspoon salt
　1/8　teaspoon pepper
　　2　slices sourdough bread (1/2 inch thick)
　　2　Boston lettuce leaves
　　1　medium tomato, cut into 1/4-inch slices
　　6　cooked large shrimp, peeled and deveined, butterflied
　1/2　medium ripe avocado, peeled and sliced
　　2　thin slices red onion

In a small bowl, combine the mayonnaise, lemon juice and peel, coriander, salt and pepper. Spread over both slices of bread. Layer each with lettuce, tomato, shrimp, avocado and onion. **Yield:** 2 servings.

Nutrition Facts: 1 sandwich equals 321 calories, 11 g fat (2 g saturated fat), 36 mg cholesterol, 907 mg sodium, 46 g carbohydrate, 6 g fiber, 11 g protein.

FRESH FLORET SALAD

Mary Tallman, Arbor Vitae, Wisconsin

This crisp veggie salad features a homemade dressing that blends refreshing lemon flavor with hearty Italian seasonings. It's perfect for a pair.

　　1　cup fresh broccoli florets
　　1　cup fresh cauliflowerets
　　3　tablespoons sliced celery
　　2　tablespoons finely chopped onion
　　1　hard-cooked egg, chopped
　1/3　cup prepared Italian salad dressing
　　2　tablespoons plain yogurt
2-1/2　teaspoons Italian salad dressing mix
　　2　teaspoons lemon juice

In a small bowl, combine the first five ingredients. In another bowl, whisk the salad dressing, yogurt, dressing mix and lemon juice. Pour over broccoli mixture and toss to coat. Cover and refrigerate for 4 hours or overnight. **Yield:** 2 servings.

FRUIT COMPOTE

Maxine Otis, Hobson, Montana

My kids always ate more fruit when I dressed it up this way. My mother used to make this yummy compote when I was a child.

　　1　cup apricot nectar, **divided**
Dash to 1/8 teaspoon ground cloves
Dash to 1/8 teaspoon ground cinnamon
　　1　tablespoon cornstarch
　　2　tablespoons lemon juice
　　1　firm banana, cut into 1/2-inch slices
　　4　fresh strawberries, sliced
　　1　kiwifruit, halved and thinly sliced

In a saucepan, bring 3/4 cup apricot nectar, cloves and cinnamon to a boil. Combine the cornstarch and remaining apricot nectar until smooth; gradually whisk into the nectar mixture. Return to a boil; cool and stir for 1-2 minutes or until thickened and bubbly. Remove from the heat; stir in the lemon juice. Cool.

　Stir in the banana, strawberries and kiwi. Cover and refrigerate for at least 1 hour before serving. **Yield:** 2 servings.

NEPTUNE PASTA SALAD
(Pictured above)

Deborah Baumgarten, Jacksonville, Florida

Here's a unique salad that's very easy to make. It's good for a light supper, and co-workers love it when I increase the recipe and bring it to potluck lunches.

3/4 cup uncooked tricolor spiral pasta
4 ounces imitation crabmeat, chopped
2 tablespoons chopped green onion
1/4 cup mandarin oranges
2 tablespoons sour cream
2 tablespoons mayonnaise
2 tablespoons orange juice
1/4 teaspoon salt
1/4 teaspoon dill weed

Cook pasta according to package directions; drain and rinse in cold water. In a bowl, combine the pasta, crab, onions and oranges. In another bowl, combine the sour cream, mayonnaise, orange juice, salt and dill. Add to the pasta mixture; toss to coat. Cover and refrigerate until serving. **Yield:** 2 servings.

BUYING BAKING APPLES

When you need tart baking apples, you have many varieties to choose from. They include Baldwin, Cortland, Golden Russet, Granny Smith, Ida Red, Jonathan, Lady Apple, McIntosh, Macoun, Newtown Pippin, Northern Spy, Rhode Island Greening, Rome Beauty, Winesap, Wolf River and York Imperial.

APPLE BUTTERSCOTCH CAKE
(Pictured below)

Nancy Zimmerman,
Cape May Court House, New Jersey

This delectable, old-fashioned cake baked in a small square pan won't leave you with leftovers for days on end. The combination of cinnamon, butterscotch, apples and pecans is just right.

1-1/4 cups all-purpose flour
1 teaspoon baking powder
1/2 teaspoon baking soda
1/2 teaspoon salt
1/2 teaspoon ground cinnamon
1 cup sugar
1/2 cup vegetable oil
2 eggs, beaten
2 cups chopped peeled tart apples
1/2 cup chopped pecans
1/2 cup butterscotch chips, *divided*

In a large bowl, combine the flour, baking powder, baking soda, salt and cinnamon. Combine the sugar, oil and eggs; stir into dry ingredients just until combined. Stir in the apples, pecans and 1/4 cup butterscotch chips.

Pour into a greased 8-in. square baking dish. Sprinkle with the remaining butterscotch chips. Bake at 350° for 40-45 minutes or until a toothpick inserted near the center comes out clean. Cool on a wire rack. **Yield:** 4-6 servings.

PAPRIKA POTATOES
(Pictured above)

Sandra Novotny, Windsor, Pennsylvania

Mildly seasoned with fresh parsley and the flavors of garlic and onion, this stovetop side dish goes well with just about any main course.

> 1 tablespoon olive oil
> 1 can (14-1/2 ounces) sliced potatoes, drained
> 1 small onion, cut into thin wedges
> 2 teaspoons minced fresh parsley
> 1/2 teaspoon paprika
> 1/4 teaspoon garlic powder
> 1/4 teaspoon onion powder

Pinch salt

In a small skillet, heat oil over medium heat. Add potatoes and onion; cook and stir for 10 minutes or until lightly browned. Combine the parsley, paprika, garlic powder, onion powder and salt; sprinkle over potato mixture and toss to coat.

Cook 5-10 minutes longer or until onion is tender. **Yield:** 2 servings.

PARMESAN ASPARAGUS
(Pictured above)

Julie Sumner, Plant City, Florida

A handful of kitchen staples are all you'll need for this tasty take on asparagus. It bakes in the oven in a mere 10 minutes.

> 10 fresh asparagus spears, trimmed
> 2 teaspoons olive oil
> 1/8 teaspoon garlic salt

Dash cayenne pepper

> 2 to 3 teaspoons grated Parmesan cheese

Place the asparagus in a shallow baking dish. Drizzle with oil; sprinkle with garlic salt, cayenne and Parmesan cheese. Bake, uncovered, at 425° for 8-10 minutes or until asparagus is crisp-tender. **Yield:** 2 servings.

Salmon with Tomato-Dill Sauce
(Pictured at left)

Janet Ryan, Thornton, Colorado

Dinner doesn't get much easier than it does with this lovely main course. The sauce comes together in a snap and complements the salmon nicely.

  2 salmon fillets (6 ounces *each*)
1/3 cup mayonnaise
1-1/2 teaspoons milk
1/2 teaspoon lemon-pepper seasoning
1/4 teaspoon dill weed
  1 plum tomato, diced

Place the salmon in a small greased baking dish. Bake, uncovered, at 350° for 20-25 minutes or until fish flakes easily with a fork. In a small bowl, combine the mayonnaise, milk, lemon-pepper and dill; stir in tomato. Spoon over salmon. Bake 5 minutes longer or until heated through. **Yield:** 2 servings.

Breaded Chicken with Ham 'n' Cheese

Laurie Mitchell, Indianapolis, Indiana

This recipe was adapted from one in an old cookbook and has become one of my all-time favorite chicken dishes. I like to serve it with rice pilaf along with some lightly steamed, fresh green beans.

  2 boneless skinless chicken breast halves
    (6 ounces *each*)
  4 thin slices prosciutto *or* deli ham
  2 slices Muenster cheese
1/4 cup all-purpose flour
  1 egg, lightly beaten
1/2 cup dry bread crumbs
  1 tablespoon grated Parmesan cheese
1/8 teaspoon garlic powder
1/8 teaspoon dried tarragon
  2 tablespoons butter
1/2 cup chicken broth
  2 tablespoons sherry *or* additional
    chicken broth
  1 teaspoon cornstarch
  2 teaspoons cold water

Flatten chicken to 1/4-in. thickness. Place two slices of prosciutto and one slice of cheese down the center of each chicken breast half; fold chicken over cheese and secure with toothpicks.

Place the flour and egg in separate shallow bowls. In another shallow bowl, combine the bread crumbs, Parmesan cheese, garlic powder and tarragon. Coat the chicken with flour, then dip in-

to the egg and coat with the crumb mixture. Let stand for 5 minutes.

In a large skillet, brown chicken in butter on all sides. Transfer to a 1-qt. baking dish. Bake, uncovered, at 350° for 25-30 minutes or until juices run clear.

Meanwhile, add broth and sherry or additional broth to the skillet; stir to loosen browned bits. Combine cornstarch and water until smooth; gradually stir into broth mixture. Bring to a boil; cook and stir for 2 minutes or until thickened. Serve over chicken. **Yield:** 2 servings.

Honey Banana Sundaes
(Pictured below)

Pauline Sledge, Hamilton, Ohio

This simple, comforting and nutritious dessert is a hit every time I make it. It tops the list of requested treats when my grandchildren come to visit.

  2 medium firm bananas, sliced
  1 teaspoon lemon juice
  1 tablespoon honey
  1 teaspoon toasted wheat germ
Vanilla ice cream

In a bowl, toss bananas with lemon juice. In a nonstick skillet, cook bananas over low heat for 3-5 minutes or until heated through. Add honey and wheat germ. Cover and cook for 2 minutes or until honey is melted. Serve over ice cream. **Yield:** 2 servings.

★★★★★★★★★★★★★★★★★

PEANUT BUTTER CHIP PANCAKES
(Pictured above)

Margaret Pache, Mesa, Arizona

One day, I added peanut butter chips and pecans to my pancake recipe. This enhanced the taste and gave the pancakes an unexpected crunch.

    3/4 cup pancake mix
      1 tablespoon sugar
      1 egg, lightly beaten
    1/2 cup milk
    1/3 cup peanut butter chips
    1/4 cup chopped pecans
Pancake syrup and fresh strawberries

In a bowl, combine pancake mix and sugar. Combine egg and milk; add to the dry ingredients just until moistened. Stir in the chips and nuts.

Pour batter by 1/4 cupfuls onto a greased hot griddle. Turn each pancake when bubbles form on top; cook until second side is golden brown. Serve with syrup and strawberries. **Yield:** 2 servings.

★★★★★★★★★★★★★★★★★

RAISIN-APPLE BREAD PUDDING

Cora Uden, Juniata, Nebraska

I got the idea for this old-fashioned dessert from a recipe in a farming magazine. The pudding is so homey and satisfying, especially served warm with cream.

      1 medium tart apple, peeled, cored and cut into thin rings
      1 tablespoon lemon juice
      1 tablespoon butter
1-1/2 teaspoons plus 1/2 cup sugar, *divided*
    1/8 teaspoon ground cinnamon
    1/8 teaspoon ground nutmeg
      3 slices day-old raisin bread, cubed
      2 tablespoons raisins
      2 eggs
      1 cup milk
Dash salt
    1/4 teaspoon vanilla extract
    1/4 teaspoon lemon extract *or* additional vanilla extract
Half-and-half cream, optional

In a small bowl, toss apple rings with lemon juice. In a small skillet, saute apple in butter for 3 minutes or just until tender. Remove from the heat. Combine 1-1/2 teaspoons sugar, cinnamon and nutmeg; sprinkle over apple. Toss to coat evenly; set aside.

Place bread cubes in a greased 8-in. x 4-in. x 2-in. loaf pan. Top with raisins and apple mixture. In a bowl, whisk the eggs and remaining sugar. In a small saucepan. combine milk and salt; cook just until the mixture begins to bubble around sides of pan. Gradually whisk into egg mixture. Stir in extracts. Pour over apple and raisins.

Place dish in an ungreased 11-in. x 7-in. x 2-in. baking dish. Bake, uncovered, at 350° for 40-50 minutes or until a knife inserted near the center comes out clean. Serve warm with cream if desired. **Yield:** 2-3 servings.

★★★★★★★★★★★★★★★★★

MASHED POTATO 'N' PARSNIP

Doreen Saunders, Kingston, Ontario

This root vegetable recipe came from my mother, who loved parsnips. I've continued the tradition of serving it for special occasions and Sunday dinners. Here's a down-sized version of the dish.

      1 large potato, peeled and cut into 1-inch pieces
      1 medium parsnip, peeled and cut into 1/2-inch pieces
      1 medium carrot, cut into 1/2-inch slices
      2 tablespoons milk
      1 tablespoon butter
      1 teaspoon brown sugar
    1/4 teaspoon salt

Place the potato, parsnip and carrot in a saucepan; cover with water. Bring to a boil. Reduce heat; cover and cook for 20-25 minutes or until tender. Drain. In a small bowl, mash the vegetables with the milk, butter, brown sugar and salt. **Yield:** 2 servings.

★★★★★★★★★★★★

PASTA BEAN SOUP
(Pictured below)

Barb Swatz, Davisburg, Michigan

My older relatives brought this recipe from Italy and prepared it often as I was growing up. It makes a comforting and balanced meal all by itself.

    1/4 cup chopped onion
      1 garlic clove, minced
      1 tablespoon butter
      1 teaspoon olive oil
      3 cups chicken broth
    1/4 cup uncooked ditalini *or* other small
        pasta
    1/2 cup canned white kidney *or* cannellini
        beans
    1/2 cup canned diced tomatoes
    1/2 cup torn fresh spinach
    1/4 teaspoon salt
Shredded Parmesan cheese

In a saucepan, saute the onion and garlic in butter and oil. Add the broth; bring to a boil. Add the pasta; reduce heat. Simmer, uncovered, for 10 minutes or until pasta is tender. Add the beans, tomatoes, spinach and salt. Cook 5 minutes

longer or until heated through. Serve with Parmesan cheese. **Yield:** 2 servings.

★★★★★★★★★★★★

APRICOT CHIP TRIANGLES
(Pictured above)

Kay Brune, Guymon, Oklahoma

After a trip to England, I was determined to learn how to make scones. This recipe is a combination of several from my search. I often get together with a couple of friends to enjoy a traditional English tea, and these triangles are always a hit.

    1-1/2 cups plus 2 tablespoons all-purpose
        flour
      1/4 cup sugar
    1-1/2 teaspoons baking powder
      1/2 teaspoon salt
        3 tablespoons cold butter
        1 egg, lightly beaten
      1/3 cup heavy whipping cream
    1-1/2 teaspoons vanilla extract
      3/4 cup chopped dried apricots
      3/4 cup chopped walnuts, toasted
      1/2 cup vanilla *or* white chips

In a bowl, combine the flour, sugar, baking powder and salt. Cut in butter until mixture resembles coarse crumbs. Combine the egg, cream and vanilla; stir into the crumb mixture until a soft dough forms. Add the apricots, nuts and chips.

Turn onto a lightly floured surface; knead gently 6-8 times. Shape into a 6-in. circle; cut into six wedges. Place on a greased baking sheet. Bake at 375° for 18-20 minutes or until golden brown. Remove to a wire rack. **Yield:** 6 scones.

STRAWBERRY CREAM PIE

Judith Kapcsos, Colorado City, Arizona

My mother treated us to strawberry desserts every spring, and this was the one we looked forward to most. I tried using a chocolaty cookie crust, and now I make it that way all the time.

  1/2 cup crushed cream-filled chocolate
      sandwich cookies (7 cookies)
    2 tablespoons sugar
    2 tablespoons butter, melted
FILLING:
    4 ounces cream cheese, softened
    2 tablespoons sugar
  1/2 teaspoon vanilla extract
  1/2 cup mashed fresh strawberries
  1/2 cup heavy whipping cream
    2 tablespoons confectioners' sugar

Combine the cookie crumbs, sugar and butter; press into a 7-in. pie plate. Bake at 375° for 8 minutes. Cool completely on a wire rack.

In a small mixing bowl, beat the cream cheese, sugar and vanilla until smooth. Stir in the strawberries. In another small mixing bowl, beat cream until it begins to thicken.

Gradually add confectioners' sugar, beating until stiff peaks form. Fold into the cream cheese mixture. Spoon into the crust. Refrigerate for 4 hours or overnight. **Yield:** 3-4 servings.

SWEET PEPPER RICE

Betty Nickeles, Tampa, Florida

This tasty, colorful side dish is a lovely complement to many entrees. The peppers and rice are a hit with everyone, and extra parsley adds a special touch.

  1/2 cup uncooked long grain rice
    1 garlic clove, minced
    1 tablespoon butter
    1 cup chicken broth
  1/4 cup chopped sweet red pepper
  1/4 cup chopped green pepper
  1/2 teaspoon dried oregano
  1/8 teaspoon salt
Pinch pepper
Minced fresh parsley

In a small skillet or saucepan, saute the rice and garlic in butter until rice is browned. Add broth; bring to a boil.

Reduce heat; add the peppers, oregano, salt and pepper. Cover and simmer for 15 minutes or until rice is tender. Fluff with a fork. Sprinkle with parsley. **Yield:** 2 servings.

TANGY GREEN BEANS

Beth Allard, Belmont, New Hampshire

Years ago, my mother helped put together a church cookbook, and this dish was submitted by a family friend. Mom tried it, and we all loved it. I've since discovered that the recipe works just as well with fresh, frozen or canned beans.

1-1/4 cups fresh green beans, trimmed
    2 tablespoons butter
    1 tablespoon cider vinegar
    1 teaspoon sugar
    1 teaspoon lemon juice
  1/2 teaspoon prepared mustard
  1/4 teaspoon salt

Place the green beans in a saucepan; cover with water. Bring to a boil over medium heat. Reduce the heat; simmer, uncovered, for 10 minutes or until tender.

In a small saucepan, melt the butter. Add the remaining ingredients. Cook and stir for 3 minutes or until heated through. Drain the beans; drizzle with the butter mixture and toss to coat. **Yield:** 2 servings.

VEAL SCALOPPINI

Mrs. Ruth Lee, Troy, Ontario

I found the original version of this dish in a magazine and adjusted it to suit my taste. The delicate veal requires only a short cooking time, something that makes this simple entree even more appealing.

    2 veal cutlets (about 4 ounces *each*)
    2 tablespoons all-purpose flour
Salt and pepper to taste
    3 tablespoons butter, *divided*
    1 tablespoon olive oil
  1/4 pound fresh mushrooms, thinly sliced
  1/3 cup chicken broth
    2 teaspoons minced fresh parsley

Flatten cutlets to 1/8-in. thickness. In a resealable plastic bag, combine the flour, salt and pepper. Add veal; seal bag and shake to coat evenly. In a skillet, heat 2 tablespoons butter and oil. Add veal; cook over medium heat for about 1 minute on each side or until juices run clear. Remove and keep warm.

Add mushrooms to skillet; cook and stir for 2-3 minutes or until tender. Spoon over veal. Stir broth into skillet, stirring up any browned bits. Add parsley and remaining butter; cook and stir 2 minutes longer or until slightly thickened. Pour over veal and mushrooms. **Yield:** 2 servings.

BROCCOLI CHICKEN STIR-FRY
(Pictured below)

Marie Curry, Granbury, Texas

Few things are faster than a stir-fry. This savory dish feeds a pair on busy nights.

- 1/2 pound boneless skinless chicken breasts, cut into 1/2-inch strips
- 1 tablespoon olive oil
- 2 celery ribs, sliced
- 1 small onion, cut into thin wedges
- 2 cups fresh broccoli florets
- 1 garlic clove, minced
- 2 to 3 teaspoons minced fresh cilantro
- 1/2 teaspoon salt
- 1/8 teaspoon pepper
- Hot cooked rice
- 2 teaspoons soy sauce

In a nonstick skillet or wok, stir-fry chicken in oil for 2 minutes or until no longer pink. Remove and keep warm. In the same pan, stir-fry celery and onion for 2 minutes. Add broccoli and garlic; stir-fry for 2-3 minutes or until vegetables are crisp-tender.

Return chicken to the pan; sprinkle with cilantro, salt and pepper. Cook and stir until heated through. Serve over rice; sprinkle with soy sauce. **Yield:** 2 servings.

PORK TENDERLOIN WITH FRUIT SAUCE

Linda Brown, Columbus, North Carolina

Since my husband usually dislikes leftovers and there are just the two of us to cook for, I'm always trying to pare down recipes. This sweet-and-sour pork dish that serves two is one I turn to regularly.

- 1 cup chicken broth
- 1/4 cup uncooked brown rice
- 4-1/2 teaspoons cornstarch
- 2 tablespoons water
- 1 can (8 ounces) unsweetened pineapple chunks, undrained
- 1/2 cup 100% raspberry spreadable fruit
- 2 tablespoons reduced-sodium soy sauce
- 1/2 teaspoon garlic powder
- 1/4 teaspoon ground ginger
- 1 pork tenderloin (3/4 pound)

In a small saucepan, bring broth and rice to a boil. Reduce heat; cover and simmer for 30 minutes or until rice is tender.

Meanwhile, in a small bowl, combine cornstarch and water until smooth; set aside. In a saucepan, combine the pineapple and spreadable fruit; cook and stir until spreadable fruit is dissolved. Stir in the soy sauce, garlic powder and ginger. Bring to a boil. Stir cornstarch mixture and stir into pineapple mixture; cook and stir for 2 minutes or until thickened. Keep warm.

Cut pork into 3/4-in.-thick slices. In a nonstick skillet coated with nonstick cooking spray, cook pork for 2-3 minutes on each side or until browned. Pour fruit sauce over meat. Reduce heat; cover and simmer for 10-12 minutes or until a meat thermometer reads 160°. Serve with rice. **Yield:** 2 servings.

PEACH PIE BUNDLES

Janet Barnard, Toronto, Ontario

With only six ingredients, this dessert is simple yet so satisfying. The sweetness of the peaches is the perfect follow-up to grilled foods.

- 2 cups frozen unsweetened sliced peaches, thawed
- 4 teaspoons all-purpose flour
- 4 teaspoons sugar
- 1/2 cup graham cracker crumbs
- 1/4 cup packed brown sugar
- 4 teaspoons cold butter

Place the peaches in a bowl. Combine the flour and sugar; sprinkle over the peaches and toss to

In a saucepan, saute celery and onion in butter until tender. Add the peas, water and tomatoes. Bring to a boil. Stir in the ham, Italian seasoning, pepper and salt. Reduce heat; simmer, uncovered, for 20 minutes or until heated through. **Yield:** 2 servings.

BLUE CHEESE TURKEY ROLLS
(Pictured below)

Candace Wiley, Lolo, Montana

I first prepared these rolls for my mother's retirement party, and they were snatched up so quickly that I had to make another batch! I've since scaled down the recipe so it's ideal for two.

    3 to 4 tablespoons crumbled blue cheese
    2 tablespoons cream cheese, softened
1-1/2 teaspoons sour cream
    1/4 teaspoon Worcestershire sauce
Dash garlic powder
    2 thin slices deli turkey
    1 tablespoon minced fresh parsley

In a bowl, combine the first five ingredients. Spread over each slice of turkey; roll up each from a long side. Wrap in plastic wrap and refrigerate for 30 minutes or until chilled. Cut into 1-in. slices. Dip one cut end into parsley. Serve immediately. **Yield:** 2 servings.

coat. In a small bowl, combine the graham cracker crumbs and brown sugar; cut in the butter until the mixture is crumbly.

For each bundle, place half of the peach mixture on a double thickness of heavy-duty foil (about 18 in. x 12 in.). Sprinkle the crumb mixture over the peaches. Fold the foil around the mixture and seal tightly. Grill, covered, over medium heat for 5-10 minutes or until the peaches are tender. **Yield:** 2 servings.

BLACK-EYED PEA SOUP
(Pictured above)

Yvonne Peterson, Mountain View, Missouri

Thanks to this recipe, I can enjoy down-home soup without having to deal with lots of leftovers. It's also a great way to use up any extra cooked ham you may have in the fridge.

    1/4 cup sliced celery
    1/4 cup chopped onion
1-1/2 teaspoons butter
    1 can (15-1/2 ounces) black-eyed peas,
        rinsed and drained
    1 cup water
    3/4 cup Italian stewed tomatoes, cut up
    1/2 cup cubed fully cooked ham
    1/2 teaspoon Italian seasoning
    1/8 teaspoon pepper
Pinch salt

Pork Chops with Red Cabbage

(Pictured at left)

Doris Heath, Franklin, North Carolina

My mother was of German heritage, and she frequently served pork dishes like this for supper. When you have a little leftover cranberry sauce from your Thanksgiving or Christmas dinner, this recipe is a great way to use it up. The sauce gives this entree a flavorful surprise.

  2 boneless pork loin chops (3/4 inch thick)
  1 tablespoon vegetable oil
1/4 cup water
  1 teaspoon cider vinegar
  3 cups shredded red cabbage
1/2 cup applesauce
1/4 cup jellied cranberry sauce
1/4 teaspoon caraway seeds

In a skillet, brown the chops in oil; remove and set aside. Add the water, vinegar and cabbage to the drippings; cover and cook over medium-low heat for 10 minutes.

Remove the skillet from the heat; stir in the applesauce, cranberry sauce and caraway seeds. Pour into a greased 11-in. x 7-in. x 2-in. baking dish; top with the browned pork chops. Cover and bake at 350° for 50-60 minutes or until the pork is tender. **Yield:** 2 servings.

Black 'n' White Pistachio Bark

Louise Delozier, Albuquerque, New Mexico

You need only four basic ingredients to whip up this sweet and nutty treat. Sized right for two, it's an easy way to satisfy a sweet tooth. You could also double or triple the recipe if you want to have more candy on hand for the holiday season.

  1 cup (6 ounces) semisweet chocolate chips
1/2 cup coarsely chopped pistachios, toasted, *divided*
1/3 cup dried cranberries
2/3 cup vanilla *or* white chips

Line a baking sheet with foil; set aside. In a small microwave-safe bowl, melt chocolate chips; stir until smooth. Stir in 1/4 cup pistachios and cranberries. Spread in a thin layer on prepared baking sheet.

Melt vanilla chips; drop by teaspoonfuls over chocolate layer. Cut through with a knife to swirl. Sprinkle with the remaining pistachios. Chill until firm. Break into pieces. **Yield:** 3/4 pound.

Cottage Cheese Waffles

(Pictured above)

Lisabeth Hess, Chambersburg, Pennsylvania

Cottage cheese and extra eggs make these from-scratch waffles soft and moist, with a different texture than most. Topped with plenty of maple syrup, it's a favorite Sunday breakfast at our house.

  1 cup cream-style cottage cheese, undrained
  6 eggs
1/4 cup vegetable oil
1/2 teaspoon vanilla extract
1/2 cup all-purpose flour
1/4 teaspoon salt
Maple syrup

In a blender, combine the cottage cheese, eggs, oil and vanilla. Cover and process until well combined. Add flour and salt; process until smooth. Bake in a preheated waffle iron according to manufacturer's directions until golden brown. Serve with syrup. **Yield:** 4 waffles (6-1/2 inches).

Creative Candy

Feel free to try different add-ins when making Black 'n' White Pistachio Bark. For example, use crushed candy canes or pretzels instead of the nuts and dried cranberries.

▰▰▰▰▰▰▰▰▰▰▰

BREAKFAST CASSEROLE

(Pictured above)

Sorrel Pickle, Arcadia, Florida

This is a good breakfast dish when you're short on time. It's simple to prepare and can be made early... or even frozen until needed.

    2 slices bread
  1/2 pound bulk pork sausage
  1/2 cup shredded cheddar cheese
    3 eggs
    1 cup milk
  1/2 teaspoon ground mustard
  1/4 teaspoon salt
  1/8 teaspoon pepper

Remove the crust from the bread and cut into 1-in. cubes. Place in a greased 8-in. square baking dish. In a skillet, brown the sausage over medium heat until no longer pink; drain. Sprinkle the sausage and cheese over bread cubes.

In a bowl, whisk the eggs, milk, mustard, salt and pepper. Pour over the sausage and cheese. Bake at 350° for 30 minutes or until puffed and golden. **Yield:** 2-4 servings.

SAVORY SUBSTITUTION

I like to vary the flavor and cut calories in my main-dish casseroles by using finely chopped, low-fat ham or cooked and crumbled turkey bacon when the recipe calls for sausage.

—*Ruth Rigoni, Hurley, Wisconsin*

▰▰▰▰▰▰▰▰▰▰▰

PAN-BARBECUED PORK

Robyn Limberg-Child, St. Clair, Michigan

You'll want to have sliced bread on hand to soak up the yummy sauce on these barbecued pork chops. The down-home dinner for two is sure to get smiles.

  1/2 teaspoon garlic powder
  1/4 teaspoon ground ginger
  1/4 teaspoon pepper
  1/8 teaspoon cayenne pepper, optional
    2 pork loin chops (1 inch thick)
    1 tablespoon vegetable oil
  1/4 cup ketchup
    2 tablespoons reduced-sodium soy sauce
    2 tablespoons honey

In a small bowl, combine the garlic powder, ginger, pepper and cayenne if desired; rub over pork chops. In a skillet, brown pork chops in oil over medium heat.

Combine the ketchup, soy sauce and honey; pour over the chops. Reduce the heat; cover and simmer until meat is tender and juices run clear. **Yield:** 2 servings.

▰▰▰▰▰▰▰▰▰▰▰

JIFFY CINNAMON ROLLS

Heather Maldaner, Rolling Hills, Alberta

The recipe for these mouth-watering treats came from my mom. I refrigerate the dough overnight so I can quickly shape and bake the rolls in the morning.

1-1/4 cups all-purpose flour
    1 tablespoon sugar
    1 teaspoon baking powder
  1/2 teaspoon salt
    2 tablespoons cold butter
    7 to 8 tablespoons milk
FILLING:
    2 tablespoons plus 2 teaspoons butter, softened, *divided*
  1/3 cup packed brown sugar
    1 teaspoon ground cinnamon

In a bowl, combine the flour, sugar, baking powder and salt. Cut in butter until crumbly. Stir in milk, a tablespoon at a time, and toss with a fork until mixture forms a ball. Turn dough onto a lightly floured surface; roll into a 7-in. square. Spread with 2 tablespoons butter.

Combine the brown sugar and cinnamon; sprinkle over butter. Roll up jelly-roll style. Cut into six even slices. Place cut side up in greased muffin cups. Bake at 400° for 18-20 minutes or until golden brown. Melt remaining butter; brush over rolls. Serve warm. **Yield:** 6 rolls.

CHINESE PEPPER STEAK
(Pictured below)

Shirley Claggett, Melfort, Saskatchewan

My husband is a big fan of Chinese food, and he's my personal test-kitchen judge for the recipes I try. Thus far, there haven't been many dishes he doesn't care for. This beefy specialty is a favorite.

1-1/2 cups julienned green pepper
3/4 cup chopped onion
2 tablespoons vegetable oil, *divided*
2 cups sliced fresh mushrooms
3/4 pound boneless beef sirloin steak, cut into thin strips
1/2 teaspoon salt
1/4 teaspoon pepper
1 garlic clove, minced
1 tablespoon cornstarch
1 cup apple juice
1/4 cup cold water
Hot cooked rice

In a wok or skillet, stir-fry green peppers and onion in 1 tablespoon oil for 2-3 minutes. Add mushrooms; stir-fry 1 minute longer. Remove and keep warm.

Season the beef with salt and pepper. In the same skillet, stir-fry the beef and garlic in remaining oil for 6-8 minutes or until no longer pink; drain.

Combine the cornstarch, apple juice and water until smooth; stir into the beef mixture. Bring to a boil; cook and stir for 1 minute or until thickened. Return the green peppers, onion and mushrooms to the pan; heat through. Serve over the rice. **Yield:** 2 servings.

BREADED BUFFALO CHICKEN SANDWICHES

Tracy Boleware, Covington, Louisiana

Topped with melted mozzarella cheese and a spicy sauce, these breaded chicken breasts make fantastic sandwiches. Try them whenever you're short on time but need a satisfying dinner.

  2 boneless skinless chicken breast halves
     (4 ounces *each*)
1/4 teaspoon salt
1/8 teaspoon garlic powder
1/8 teaspoon pepper
1/4 cup seasoned bread crumbs
  2 tablespoons all-purpose flour
  1 tablespoon vegetable oil
  2 slices part-skim mozzarella cheese
  3 tablespoons butter
  1 teaspoon cornstarch
1/4 to 1/2 teaspoon hot pepper sauce
  2 sandwich buns, split
Blue cheese *or* ranch salad dressing

Sprinkle the chicken with salt, garlic powder and pepper. In a shallow bowl, combine the bread crumbs and flour; dredge the chicken. In a skillet over medium heat, brown chicken in oil. Reduce the heat; cover and cook for 10 minutes or until the juices run clear.

Place cheese over chicken; cover and cook for 1 minute or until cheese is melted. In a small saucepan over medium heat, melt the butter; whisk in cornstarch and hot pepper sauce until smooth. Bring to a gentle boil, whisking constantly for 1 minute or until thickened. Drizzle over chicken. Serve on buns with blue cheese or ranch dressing. **Yield:** 2 servings.

CREAM OF POTATO SOUP

Nancy Mosher, Sun City, California

This recipe proves you don't have to make a big batch in order to enjoy home-style soup. It's the perfect way to warm up on chilly nights...just add your favorite fresh-baked biscuits or rolls.

  1 medium potato, peeled and cubed
1/2 cup water
  1 celery rib, diced
  2 tablespoons finely chopped onion
  2 tablespoons butter
3/4 cup evaporated milk
  1 teaspoon dried parsley flakes
1/4 teaspoon salt
Dash pepper

In a small saucepan, bring the potato and water to a boil. Reduce heat; cover and cook for 10-15 minutes or until tender.

In a small skillet, saute celery and onion in butter until tender. Add to potato mixture. Stir in the milk, parsley, salt and pepper; heat through. **Yield:** 2 servings.

CRANBERRY WALDORF SALAD

Barbara McFeters, Wilsonville, Oregon

A touch of honey gives this simple salad a bit of sweetness while chopped apple and celery provide crunch. Best of all, it takes mere minutes to toss together for a quick lunch or side dish.

  1 large apple, chopped
2/3 cup dried cranberries
  1 celery rib, diced
  2 tablespoons mayonnaise
  1 tablespoon honey

In a small bowl, combine the apple, cranberries and celery. Combine the mayonnaise and honey; pour over the apple mixture and toss to coat. Cover and refrigerate for 30 minutes or until serving. **Yield:** 2 servings.

SOFT LEMON-GINGER COOKIES

Sharon Bretz, Havre de Grace, Maryland

Loaded with old-fashioned flavor, this yummy cookie is hard to beat. You'll love munching a few with coffee, tea or a glass of cold milk.

1/2 cup butter, softened
  1 cup packed brown sugar
  1 egg
  3 tablespoons sour cream
1/2 teaspoon lemon extract
1/2 teaspoon vanilla extract
1-3/4 cups all-purpose flour
  1 teaspoon baking soda
  1 teaspoon cream of tartar
  1 teaspoon ground ginger
1/4 teaspoon salt

In a small mixing bowl, cream the butter and brown sugar. Beat in the egg, sour cream and extracts. Combine the flour, baking soda, cream of tartar, ginger and salt; gradually beat into the creamed mixture.

Drop by rounded teaspoonfuls 2 in. apart onto ungreased baking sheets. Bake at 350° for 10-12 minutes or until lightly browned. Immediately remove from pans to wire racks. **Yield:** 2 dozen.

BLUEBERRY BUCKLE
(Pictured below)

Carol Dolan, Mt. Lauel, New Jersey

My sister and I have fond memories of going to Pennsylvania for blueberry picking when we were children. Mother taught us to pick only perfect berries, and those juicy gems went into this wonderful recipe. It came from our grandmother.

> 1/4 cup butter, softened
> 3/4 cup sugar
> 1 egg
> 2 cups all-purpose flour
> 2 teaspoons baking powder
> 1/4 teaspoon salt
> 1/2 cup milk
> 2 cups fresh blueberries

TOPPING:

> 2/3 cup sugar
> 1/2 cup all-purpose flour
> 1/2 teaspoon ground cinnamon
> 1/3 cup cold butter

In a small mixing bowl, cream butter and sugar. Beat in the egg. Combine the flour, baking powder and salt; add to creamed mixture alternately with milk. Fold in the blueberries. Pour into greased 9-in. square baking pan.

For topping, combine the sugar, flour and cinnamon in a bowl; cut in butter until crumbly. Sprinkle over blueberry mixture. Bake at 375° for 40-45 minutes or until a toothpick inserted near the center comes out clean. Cool on a wire rack. **Yield:** 4-6 servings.

PEANUT BUTTER SURPRISE MUFFINS

Joan Dobry, Hardy, Arkansas

Miniature peanut butter cups are the hidden surprise inside these yummy little muffins. They are especially good warm from the oven, when the chocolaty center is smooth and creamy. People who try one say they taste like a dessert.

> 3/4 cup all-purpose flour
> 1/4 cup sugar
> 1-1/2 teaspoons baking powder
> 1/8 teaspoon salt
> 1 egg
> 1/3 cup milk
> 1/4 cup creamy peanut butter
> 1 tablespoon butter, softened
> 6 miniature peanut butter cups

In a large bowl, combine the flour, sugar, baking powder and salt. In a small bowl, whisk the egg and milk. Stir into dry ingredients just until moistened. Combine peanut butter and butter; fold into batter.

Fill greased or paper-lined muffin cups one-fourth full; place a miniature peanut butter cup in each. Cover with the remaining batter. Bake at 400° for 18-20 minutes or until a toothpick inserted into muffin comes out clean. Cool for 5 minutes before removing from pan to a wire rack. **Yield:** 6 muffins.

SPLASH-OF-COLOR SKILLET

Laurie Diggins, West Chester, Pennsylvania

My husband frequently volunteers to take meals to folks who are just home from the hospital or going through family emergencies. Because so many people like carrots, I often prepare recipes like this flavorful and colorful side dish.

> 1 medium onion, cut into thin wedges
> 1 medium green pepper, julienned
> 1 small carrot, julienned
> 1 tablespoon vegetable oil
> 1/4 teaspoon salt

Dash pepper

> 1 teaspoon Dijon mustard
> 1/4 teaspoon Worcestershire sauce
> 1/4 teaspoon lemon juice

In a skillet, saute the onion, green pepper and carrot in oil until tender. Sprinkle with the salt and pepper. Remove from the heat. In a small bowl, whisk the mustard, Worcestershire sauce and lemon juice. Drizzle over vegetables and toss to coat. **Yield:** 2 servings.

▪▪▪▪▪▪▪▪▪▪▪▪▪

SALMON WITH SPINACH SAUCE
(Pictured above)

You won't have to fish for compliments with this delicious recipe created by the Taste of Home Test Kitchen. Cooked in a pressure cooker, the salmon stays moist and tender. Top it with the spinach sauce for a pretty, tasty accent.

  1 package (10 ounces) frozen chopped
     spinach, thawed and squeezed dry
3/4 cup mayonnaise
  1 tablespoon Dijon mustard
  2 teaspoons lemon juice
1/4 teaspoon garlic salt
1-1/2 cups water
  2 salmon fillets (6 ounces *each*)
1/2 teaspoon lemon-pepper seasoning
  4 slices lemon

In a small bowl, combine the spinach, mayonnaise, mustard, lemon juice and garlic salt; cover and refrigerate until serving.

Pour water into a pressure cooker. Place salmon on rack; sprinkle with lemon-pepper and top with lemon slices. Close cover securely; place pressure regulator on vent pipe. Bring cooker to full pressure over high heat. Reduce heat to medium-high and cook for 2 minutes. (Pressure regulator should maintain a slow steady rocking motion; adjust heat if needed.)

Remove from the heat. Immediately cool according to manufacturer's directions until pressure is completely reduced. Discard lemon slices. Serve salmon with spinach sauce. **Yield:** 2 servings.

Editor's Note: This recipe was tested at 15 pounds of pressure (psi).

▪▪▪▪▪▪▪▪▪▪▪▪▪

SAVORY GRILLED POTATOES
(Pictured above)

Darlene Brenden, Salem, Oregon

These well-seasoned potato packets are easy to make ahead of time and toss on the grill when needed.

1/4 cup mayonnaise
  1 tablespoon grated Parmesan cheese
  1 garlic clove, minced
1/2 teaspoon minced fresh parsley
1/4 to 1/2 teaspoon salt
1/4 teaspoon paprika
1/4 teaspoon pepper
  2 medium baking potatoes, cut into
     1/4-inch slices
  1 small onion, sliced and separated into
     rings
  2 tablespoons butter

In a large bowl, combine the first seven ingredients. Add potatoes and onion; toss gently to coat. Spoon onto a double thickness of greased heavy-duty foil (about 18 in. square). Dot with butter. Fold foil around potato mixture and seal tightly. Grill, covered, over medium heat for 30-35 minutes or until potatoes are tender, turning once. **Yield:** 2 servings.

FLUFFY SAUSAGE OMELET

Jean Tyner, Darlington, South Carolina

At Christmastime, we always get family members together for a special breakfast. I serve this hearty microwaved omelet with a fruit salad, hash brown casserole and oven-fresh biscuits.

- 1/4 pound bulk pork sausage
- 2 tablespoons chopped onion
- 2 tablespoons chopped sweet red pepper
- 1/4 cup sour cream
- 3 eggs, *separated*
- 3 tablespoons milk
- 1/4 teaspoon salt
- 1/4 teaspoon baking powder
- 1/8 teaspoon pepper
- 1 tablespoon butter

Crumble the sausage into a small microwave-safe dish; add onion and red pepper. Cover and microwave on high for 2 minutes; drain. Stir in sour cream; set aside.

In a bowl, whisk the egg yolks, milk, salt, baking powder and pepper. In a mixing bowl, beat egg whites until stiff peaks form. Gently fold into egg yolk mixture. Place the butter in a greased 9-in. microwave-safe pie plate. Microwave on high for 30 seconds.

Pour egg mixture into plate. Microwave, uncovered, at 50% power for 3-5 minutes or until partially set. Lift edges, letting uncooked portion flow underneath. Cook at 50% power 2-3 minutes longer or until eggs are set. Spoon sausage mixture over one side; fold omelet over the filling. **Yield:** 2 servings.

Editor's Note: This recipe was tested in a 1,100-watt microwave.

CREAMY CURRY SHRIMP
(Pictured above)

Collette Conlan, Burleson, Texas

We really like the spicy flavor of this seafood dish. You can give it even more zip by increasing the amount of hot pepper sauce. If you're not a big fan of curry, try substituting paprika.

- 1/2 cup finely chopped onion
- 2 teaspoons butter
- 1/4 teaspoon curry powder
- 1 tablespoon all-purpose flour
- 1 tablespoon tomato paste
- 1/4 cup water
- 1/2 cup heavy whipping cream
- 1/4 teaspoon salt
- Dash pepper
- Dash hot pepper sauce
- 3/4 pound uncooked medium shrimp, peeled and deveined
- Hot cooked pasta *or* rice
- 1 tablespoon minced fresh parsley

In a skillet, saute onion in butter until tender. Sprinkle with curry powder; cook for 1 minute. Sprinkle with flour; stir until blended. Stir in tomato paste. Gradually stir in water; then cream. Bring to a boil over medium heat; cook and stir for 2 minutes or until thickened.

Add the salt, pepper and hot pepper sauce. Add shrimp; cook until shrimp turn pink, about 3 minutes. Serve over pasta. Sprinkle with parsley. **Yield:** 2 servings.

SESAME PORK

Stephanie Gillett, Ann Arbor, Michigan

When my opera-singing husband has to get out the door fast for an evening rehearsal, I reach for recipes like this stir-fried pork tenderloin. It's delicious and a cinch to put together.

- 2 teaspoons cornstarch
- 3/4 cup chicken broth
- 4 teaspoons soy sauce
- 2 tablespoons vegetable oil
- 1 pork tenderloin (3/4 pound), cut into 1-inch cubes
- 1 garlic clove, minced
- 3 cups broccoli coleslaw mix
- 1-1/2 teaspoons sesame seeds, toasted
- Hot cooked rice, optional

In a small bowl, combine the cornstarch, broth and soy sauce until smooth; set aside. In a skillet or wok, heat oil; stir-fry the pork and garlic for 5 minutes. Add broccoli coleslaw mix; stir-fry 3-4 minutes longer or until meat is no longer pink and broccoli is crisp-tender.

Stir cornstarch mixture and add to the pan. Bring to a boil; cook and stir for 1 minute or until thickened. Sprinkle with sesame seeds. Serve with rice if desired. **Yield:** 2 servings.

Editor's Note: Broccoli coleslaw mix may be found in the produce section of most grocery stores.

CUBE STEAK STROGANOFF
(Pictured below)

Margery Bryan, Royal City, Washington

This "comfort food" dish is a favorite main course in our house. I've shared the recipe many times.

       2 tablespoons all-purpose flour
    1/4 teaspoon salt
       2 beef cube steaks
       1 to 2 tablespoons vegetable oil
       1 can (4 ounces) mushroom stems and
         pieces, drained
       3 green onions, thinly sliced
    2/3 cup water
       1 teaspoon beef bouillon granules
    1/8 teaspoon pepper
       7 to 8 tablespoons sour cream
    Hot cooked egg noodles

In a resealable plastic bag, combine the flour and salt. Add the cube steaks, one at a time, and shake to coat. In a skillet, cook the steaks in oil over medium heat for 4-5 minutes on each side or until browned and tender. Remove and keep warm.

In the same skillet, saute the mushrooms and onions until tender. Add the water, beef bouillon and green pepper; cook and stir until the mixture comes to a boil, scraping up browned bits from the bottom of pan. Reduce heat; stir in the sour cream and heat through (do not boil). Return the cube steaks to pan; heat through. Serve over noodles. **Yield:** 2 servings.

CORN BREAD SALAD
(Pictured above)

Marge Price, Dothan, Alabama

Looking for a tasty way to use up extra corn bread? Give this change-of-pace salad with vegetables and bacon a try. Perfect for two, it's guaranteed to shake up the dinner doldrums.

    1-1/2 cups coarsely crumbled corn bread
       1/4 cup diced tomato
       1/4 cup diced green pepper
       1/4 cup chopped green onions
       1/4 cup chopped celery
          3 tablespoons mayonnaise
          2 bacon strips, cooked and crumbled

In a small bowl, combine the corn bread, tomato, green pepper, onions and celery. Add mayonnaise; toss to coat. Sprinkle with bacon. Serve immediately. **Yield:** 2 servings.

GREEK-STYLE GREEN BEANS
(Pictured at right)

Michele Scharf, Lindenhurst, New York

I was captivated by this recipe since I'm both Italian and Greek. The colorful medley of beans, tomato and onion has a decidedly Mediterranean flair.

    2 cups fresh green beans, cut into 2-inch
      pieces
  1/2 small sweet onion, cut into thin wedges
    1 tablespoon olive oil
    1 small tomato, cut into eighths
  1/2 teaspoon dried oregano
  1/4 teaspoon salt
Dash pepper

Place the beans in a saucepan and cover with water; bring to a boil. Cook for 3-4 minutes or until crisp-tender; drain.

In a small skillet, saute onion in oil for 3 minutes. Add the beans; saute for 5 minutes or until tender. Reduce heat. Add the tomato, oregano, salt and pepper; cool 1 minute longer or until heated through. **Yield:** 2 servings.

TOMATO-BASIL BAKED FISH
(Pictured below)

Annie Hicks, Zephyrhills, Florida

This tasty dish looks impressive yet is simple to fix. The recipe works well with several kinds of fish—try orange roughy, red snapper, cod or haddock.

    1 tablespoon lemon juice
    1 teaspoon olive oil
    8 ounces orange roughy, red snapper, cod
      or haddock fillets
  1/4 teaspoon dried basil
  1/8 teaspoon salt
  1/8 teaspoon pepper
    2 plum tomatoes, thinly sliced
    2 teaspoons grated Parmesan cheese

In a shallow dish, combine the lemon juice and oil. Add fish fillets; turn to coat. Place in a greased 9-in. square baking dish. Sprinkle with basil, salt and pepper. Arrange tomatoes on top; sprinkle with Parmesan cheese. Cover and bake at 400° for 10-12 minutes or until fish flakes easily with a fork. **Yield:** 2 servings.

CARAMEL PUDDING

Loretta Fisher, Dayton, Virginia

Combining most of the ingredients in a blender makes quick work of preparing this smooth pudding. It's a comforting, yummy dessert for two. I like to add a garnish of whipped topping and toffee bits.

    3/4 cup milk
    1/2 cup water
      2 egg yolks
    1/2 cup packed brown sugar
    1/4 cup all-purpose flour
    1/4 teaspoon salt
  1-1/2 teaspoons butter
      1 teaspoon vanilla extract
      2 tablespoons whipped topping
      2 teaspoons English toffee bits or almond
        brickle chips

In a blender, combine the first six ingredients; cover and process until smooth. Pour into a small saucepan. Bring to a boil over medium heat, stirring constantly. Cook and stir 1 minute longer or until thickened.

Remove from the heat; stir in butter and vanilla. Pour into two dessert dishes. Serve warm or chilled. Garnish with whipped topping and toffee bits. **Yield:** 2 servings.

chocolate chip mixture down the center of tortillas; fold top and bottom of tortilla over filling and roll up.

In a skillet over medium heat, cook burritos in oil for 1-2 minutes or until lightly browned, turning once. In a microwave-safe bowl, melt shortening and remaining chocolate chips; stir until smooth. Drizzle over burritos. Serve immediately. **Yield:** 2 servings.

▪▪▪▪▪▪▪▪▪▪▪▪
WALNUT CHOCOLATE BURRITOS

Kay Martin, Greenville, South Carolina

Inspired by my love of Mexican food, I experimented with tortillas, chocolate, nuts and cinnamon to create a sweet treat that's fun and different. I serve the burritos warm with chocolate drizzled on top.

- 1/2 cup plus 1 tablespoon semisweet chocolate chips, *divided*
- 2 tablespoons chopped walnuts
- 1/8 teaspoon ground cinnamon
- 2 flour tortillas (8 inches)
- 2 teaspoons vegetable oil
- 1/2 teaspoon shortening

In a small bowl, combine 1/2 cup chocolate chips, walnuts and cinnamon. Place tortillas on a microwave-safe plate; microwave, uncovered, on high for 10-15 seconds or until pliable. Spoon

▪▪▪▪▪▪▪▪▪▪▪▪
GARLIC-ROASTED SWEET POTATOES
(Pictured below)

Carol Ferranti, Esmond, Rhode Island

This unexpected combination is so good and makes a wonderful fall or winter side dish with any meat. You can easily double or triple the recipe for a holiday meal or when guests stop by.

- 2 cups cubed peeled sweet potatoes
- 1 garlic clove, minced
- 1 tablespoon olive oil
- 1/8 teaspoon salt
- Pinch pepper

In a small baking dish, combine the sweet potatoes and garlic. Drizzle with oil; sprinkle with salt and pepper. Bake, uncovered, at 425° for 30 minutes or until tender, stirring every 10 minutes. **Yield:** 2 servings.

BLUEBERRY MUFFINS

Virginia Sollitt, Redmond, Washington

These treats are a variation of a recipe passed down by my mother-in-law. I made the muffins lighter and used half whole wheat flour to add fiber. They're a great, nutritious way to start your day. Best of all, you don't end up with a large batch.

- 1/2 cup all-purpose flour
- 1/2 cup whole wheat flour
- 1/3 cup sugar
- 1-1/2 teaspoons baking powder
- 1/4 teaspoon salt
- 1/4 teaspoon ground nutmeg
- 1 egg
- 1/3 cup milk
- 3 tablespoons vegetable oil
- 1/2 teaspoon vanilla extract
- 1 cup fresh blueberries

In a bowl, combine the all-purpose flour, whole wheat flour, sugar, baking powder, salt and nutmeg. Combine the egg, milk, oil and vanilla extract; add to the dry ingredients just until moistened. Gently fold in the blueberries.

Fill greased or paper-lined muffin cups two-thirds full. Bake at 375° for 25-27 minutes or until a toothpick comes out clean. Cool for 5 minutes before removing from pan to a wire rack. **Yield:** 6 muffins.

PEANUT BUTTER CANDY

Deloris Morrow, Lake City, Iowa

During the holiday season, I make a lot of candy for friends, and this simple recipe is requested often. The white candy coating and chunky peanut butter go together wonderfully.

- 1/2 teaspoon butter
- 1-1/4 pounds white candy coating, cut into chunks
- 1-1/2 cups chunky peanut butter

Line a 9-in. square pan with foil; butter the foil with 1/2 teaspoon butter and set aside. In a microwave-safe bowl, microwave candy coating, uncovered, on high for 45 seconds; stir.

Microwave candy coating 1 to 1-1/2 minutes longer, stirring every 30 seconds, or until candy coating is melted and mixture is smooth. Stir in peanut butter until melted. Transfer to prepared pan. Cool to room temperature. Cut into squares. **Yield:** about 1-1/2 pounds.

Editor's Note: This recipe was tested in a 1,100-watt microwave.

FRUITY STRAWBERRY SHAKE

Carol Ann Davis, Steelville, Missouri

My husband and I created this yummy shake through trial and error. You can easily customize the flavor by changing the ingredients. For example, try a different kind of ice cream or ice cream topping.

- 2 cups Neapolitan ice cream
- 1 small firm banana, cut into chunks
- 1/2 cup milk
- 1 tablespoon strawberry preserves
- 1 tablespoon pineapple ice cream topping

In a blender, combine the Neapolitan ice cream, banana and milk; cover and process until smooth. Add the strawberry preserves and pineapple ice cream topping; cover and process until well combined. Pour into chilled glasses; serve immediately. **Yield:** 2 servings.

TURKEY WALDORF PITA

Rita Miller, Huntingdon, Pennsylvania

We like to roast turkey throughout the year because we enjoy the leftovers. Several years ago, while nibbling on a fresh Waldorf salad and some cold turkey separately, I decided to combine the two. The results were an instant hit.

- 1 cup cubed cooked turkey
- 2 celery ribs, chopped
- 1/2 cup chopped tart apple
- 1/2 cup halved seedless grapes
- 1/4 cup chopped walnuts
- 1/4 cup mayonnaise
- 4 lettuce leaves
- 2 pita breads (6 inches), halved

In a bowl, combine the turkey, celery, apple, grapes, walnuts and mayonnaise. Place a lettuce leaf in each pita half; fill with turkey salad. **Yield:** 2 servings.

CANDY COATING CLUES

Candy coating is available in dark, milk or white chocolate varieties and is often used for dipping candies and fruits. Package labels sometimes refer to it as confectionery coating or almond bark.

It is commonly sold in bulk in large individual blocks, in bags of flat disks or in packages of individual 1-ounce squares.

■■■■■■■■■■■■

GREEN BEAN AND BLUE CHEESE SALAD
(Pictured above)

Donna Cline, Pensacola, Florida

Fresh green beans and ripe olives make a delicious pairing when combined with some blue cheese. Try this unique recipe and see!

1-1/2 cups cut fresh green beans
1/2 cup crumbled blue cheese
1/2 cup pitted ripe olives, halved lengthwise
2 tablespoons olive oil
1/4 teaspoon salt
1/8 teaspoon pepper

Place green beans in a small saucepan and cover with water. Bring to a boil. Cook, uncovered, for 8-10 minutes or until crisp-tender; drain. Place the beans in a bowl; refrigerate until chilled.

Add the blue cheese, olives, oil, salt and pepper; toss gently to coat. Refrigerate until serving. **Yield:** 2 servings.

■■■■■■■■■■■■

COCONUT PEAR BARS

Cora Dunlop, Boston Bar, British Columbia

When you're in the mood for bars that are a little bit different, bake these spiced goodies featuring mellow pears and tender coconut. The small-size batch will disappear before you know it.

1-1/4 cups all-purpose flour
1/2 cup sugar
1/2 cup cold butter
FILLING:
2 eggs
1/2 cup packed brown sugar
1/2 teaspoon vanilla extract
1/3 cup all-purpose flour
1/4 teaspoon baking powder
1/4 teaspoon salt
1/4 teaspoon ground ginger
2 medium pears, peeled and diced
1/2 cup flaked coconut

In a small bowl, combine the flour and sugar. Cut in butter until mixture resembles coarse crumbs. Press into a greased 9-in. square baking pan. Bake at 350° for 25-28 minutes or until golden brown.

In a small mixing bowl, beat the eggs, brown sugar and vanilla. Combine the flour, baking powder, salt and ginger; stir into egg mixture just until moistened. Gently stir in pears and coconut. Spread over warm crust. Bake 20-23 minutes longer or until golden brown. Cool on a wire rack. Cut into bars. **Yield:** 16 bars.

■■■■■■■■■■■■

ASPARAGUS CREPES

Carol Hemker, Phenix City, Alabama

I love serving these tender crepes with a light lemony sauce in spring, but my husband would happily eat them any time of year at all. In fact, it's the only way he'll eat asparagus!

1/2 cup milk
1 egg
1/3 cup plus 2 teaspoons all-purpose flour
24 asparagus spears, cooked and drained
SAUCE:
2 egg yolks
1/4 cup water
1 tablespoon butter, melted
1 tablespoon lemon juice
1/8 teaspoon salt
Dash cayenne pepper
Paprika

For batter, combine milk and egg in a blender; cover and process until blended. Add flour; cover and process until blended. Cover and refrigerate for 1 hour.

Heat a lightly greased 8-in. skillet over medium heat. Pour 1/4 cup batter into center of skillet; lift and tilt pan to coat evenly. Cook until top appears dry; turn and cook 15-20 seconds longer. Remove and keep warm. Repeat with remaining batter, greasing skillet as needed.

Place six asparagus spears on one side of each crepe; roll up. Place seam side down in a greased 11-in. x 7-in. x 2-in. baking dish. Bake, uncovered, at 350° for 10-15 minutes or until heated through.

In a saucepan, whisk egg yolks and water. Cook over low heat, stirring constantly, until mixture is thickened and coats the back of a metal spoon or until the temperature reaches 160°. Whisk in the butter, lemon juice, salt and cayenne. Pour over warm crepes; sprinkle with paprika. Serve immediately. **Yield:** 2 servings.

HERBED CHICKEN STRIPS
(Pictured below)

Barbara Wall, Yucalpa, California

A mild mixture of herbs and spices adds sensational flavor to these chicken breasts. They don't take long to prepare, so it's a recipe I pull out of my file often.

- 1/2 **pound boneless skinless chicken breast, cut into thin strips**
- 1 **small onion, halved and sliced**
- 2 **garlic cloves, minced**
- 1/4 **cup butter**
- 1 **tablespoon minced fresh parsley**
- 1 **teaspoon minced fresh dill**
- 1/2 **teaspoon dried oregano**
- 1/4 **teaspoon salt**
- 1/8 **teaspoon pepper**

Hot cooked rice, optional

Place chicken strips in a greased 1-qt. baking dish. In a skillet, saute onion and garlic in butter until tender. Stir in the parsley, dill, oregano, salt and pepper. Pour over chicken.

Bake, uncovered, at 350° for 15 minutes. Stir; bake 5-10 minutes longer or until the chicken juices run clear. Serve the chicken over rice if desired. **Yield:** 2 servings.

WHITE CHOCOLATE PRETZEL SNACK
(Pictured above)

Estelle Cummings, Cambridge, Maryland

I like to make these sweet, crunchy treats for holidays. The snacks are nice to have on hand to serve guests or to take as a hostess gift. Plus, they're so easy to fix that my children want to help.

- 1/2 **cup pretzel sticks**
- 1/2 **cup salted peanuts**
- 1/2 **cup crisp rice cereal**
- 4 **squares (1 ounce *each*) white baking chocolate**
- 1 **teaspoon shortening**

In a bowl, combine the pretzels, peanuts and cereal. In a microwave or heavy saucepan, melt chocolate and shortening; stir until smooth. Pour over pretzel mixture; toss to coat evenly. Drop by heaping tablespoonfuls onto waxed paper; cool. **Yield:** 1 dozen.

TANGY APRICOT PORK CHOPS
(Pictured at right)

Phyllis Flint, San Antonio, Texas

For a stovetop supper that's guaranteed to please, try this pork chop specialty. Apricot preserves jazz it up without much effort.

        2 bone-in pork loin chops (1 inch thick)
    1/2 teaspoon salt
    1/8 teaspoon pepper
        2 teaspoons vegetable oil
    1/4 cup apricot preserves
    1-1/2 teaspoons cider vinegar
    1-1/2 teaspoons prepared mustard

Sprinkle pork chops with salt and pepper. In a skillet, brown chops in oil for 3 minutes on each side. In a small bowl, combine the preserves, vinegar and mustard. Spoon half of the mixture over pork. Reduce heat; cover and simmer for 3 minutes. Turn chops; top with remaining preserves mixture. Cover and simmer 4-5 minutes longer or until meat is no longer pink. **Yield:** 2 servings.

SAUERBRATEN STEW
(Pictured below)

Margaret Ashcraft, Piqua, Ohio

With this recipe, I was one of 10 finalists in a beef cooking contest. Serve the spicy dish with parsley potatoes, German spaetzles or noodles if you'd like.

    1/2 cup water
    1/4 cup red wine vinegar
        1 tablespoon sugar
        1 boneless beef chuck roast (3/4 pound),
            cut into 1-inch cubes
    3/4 teaspoon salt
Dash pepper
Dash ground nutmeg
        1 small onion, sliced
        2 teaspoons minced fresh parsley
        1 bay leaf
        3 tablespoons raisins
        2 teaspoons cornstarch
        2 tablespoons half-and-half cream
Hot cooked egg noodles

In a small saucepan, combine the water, vinegar and sugar. Cook and stir over medium heat until sugar is dissolved; cool. Sprinkle beef with salt, pepper and nutmeg; place in a large resealable plastic bag. Add onion, parsley, bay leaf and cooled marinade. Seal bag and turn to coat; refrigerate overnight.

Drain, reserving 1/2 cup marinade. Discard bay leaf. Place the beef and reserved marinade in a saucepan; bring to a boil. Reduce heat; cover and simmer for 2 hours or until meat is tender.

Stir in raisins. Combine cornstarch and cream; stir into beef mixture. Bring to a boil; cook and stir for 2 minutes or until slightly thickened. Serve over noodles. **Yield:** 2 servings.

Stuffed Iceberg Salad

Della Biddiscombe, Lewiston, Idaho

Looking for a refreshing side dish to really dress up a summer meal? Consider this iceberg lettuce stuffed with ham salad. It's hearty enough to enjoy as a light lunch on a hot day, and it can be made ahead of time for added convenience.

- 1 medium head iceberg lettuce
- 2 tablespoons mayonnaise
- 1/8 teaspoon curry powder
- 1/2 cup shredded cheddar cheese
- 1/4 cup julienned sliced deli ham
- 2 tablespoons finely chopped celery
- 2 tablespoons minced fresh parsley
- 1 tablespoon diced pimientos
- 1/4 cup salad dressing of your choice

Remove and discard core from lettuce. Place lettuce core side down and cut in half with a plastic lettuce knife from top to bottom (save one half for another use). With knife, remove enough leaves from the center of the cut side of lettuce to create a 2-in. circle, about 1-1/4 in. deep.

In a bowl, combine mayonnaise and curry powder. Stir in the cheese, ham, celery, parsley and pimientos. Spoon into center of lettuce. Wrap tightly in plastic wrap; refrigerate for 30 minutes or until serving. Cut in half, forming two wedges. Serve with salad dressing. **Yield:** 2 servings.

Lemon Scallop Linguine
(Pictured below)

Elizabeth Kudriavetz, Carver, Massachusetts

I love how this recipe turns out delicious and satisfying every time. With guests, I double the recipe and serve it with bright mixed vegetables and dinner rolls.

- 4 ounces uncooked linguine
- 1 teaspoon dried minced onion
- 3 tablespoons butter
- 3/4 pound bay scallops
- 1/8 teaspoon lemon-pepper seasoning
- Pinch pepper
- 2 tablespoons lemon juice
- Minced fresh parsley

Cook linguine according to package directions. Meanwhile, in a skillet, saute onion in butter over medium heat for 2-3 minutes or until golden. Add scallops, seasoning and pepper. Cook and stir for 4-5 minutes or until scallops are firm and opaque.

Add the lemon juice; cook 1 minute longer. Drain the linguine; toss with the scallop mixture. Sprinkle with parsley. **Yield:** 2 servings.

Meals in Minutes

*These time-saving recipes make mealtime
a snap—all in 30 minutes or less!*

Chicken Dinner Is Fast to Fix

RUNNING THE RANGE keeps Tanya McKay so busy, she can't afford to be corralled in her Wells, Nevada kitchen for very long.

"My husband, Rye, works on a cattle and horse ranch where we live with our two children, Zion and Quaid," Tanya notes. "Rye's schedule changes from day to day and hour to hour, so our meals need to be flexible."

By necessity, Tanya has become among the fastest cooks in the West. She relies on recipes like the three speedy ones here, which all can be prepared in just 30 minutes or less.

"On days I help Rye and the crew with the cows, I need a no-fuss supper like my apricot chicken," Tanya writes. "Often I make the sauce ahead of time and use precooked chicken.

"My granny came up with the recipe for my broccoli side dish as a tricky way to get us kids to eat our greens," Tanya laughs. "Daughter Zion likes the thick mustard sauce so much, she's willing to dip all kinds of vegetables in it."

A fast finale to any meal is as close as the freezer, Tanya adds. "Everyone has room for some light, refreshing Fruit Fluff."

SAUCY APRICOT CHICKEN

    8 boneless skinless chicken breast halves
      (4 ounces *each*)
    1 tablespoon butter
    1 tablespoon vegetable oil
    1 cup apricot jam
    1 cup Catalina salad dressing
    2 to 3 tablespoons onion soup mix

In a large skillet, brown chicken in butter and oil over medium heat for 3 minutes on each side or until lightly browned. Combine the jam, salad dressing and soup mix; pour over chicken. Cover and simmer for 10 minutes or until juices run clear. **Yield:** 8 servings.

BROCCOLI WITH MUSTARD SAUCE

    8 cups fresh broccoli florets
    1 cup mayonnaise
    4-1/2 teaspoons Dijon mustard
    1 teaspoon dill pickle juice

Place broccoli in a steamer basket; place in a saucepan over 1 in. of water. Bring to a boil; cover and steam for 6-8 minutes or until crisp-tender. Meanwhile, in a small bowl, combine the mayonnaise, mustard and pickle juice. Serve over broccoli. **Yield:** 8 servings.

FRUIT FLUFF

    1 carton (8 ounces) frozen whipped
      topping, thawed
    1 can (14 ounces) sweetened condensed
      milk
    1 package (16 ounces) frozen
      unsweetened raspberries
    3 cups frozen unsweetened blackberries

In a large bowl, combine whipped topping and milk; fold in berries. Serve immediately or refrigerate until serving. Freeze leftovers; remove from freezer 30 minutes before serving. **Yield:** 8 servings.

SAUCY SUBSTITUTIONS

"It's simple to change the sauce for the chicken by replacing the apricot jam with peach or plum," notes Tanya. "You could also substitute French dressing for the Catalina."

Hearty Soup And Salad Are Satisfying

WHENEVER Carole Holder of Norman, Oklahoma needs to warm up winter in a hurry, she "soups up" her kitchen routine.

During that time of year, the avid gardener looks in her refrigerator and sighs at the lack of summer-fresh garden veggies. "Luckily," Carole points out, "it's possible to make great meals fast with staples straight from my pantry."

Comforting, flavorful foods don't have to be time-consuming to prepare, as Carole proves with the quick-to-fix menu here.

"Both husband Richard and I work full-time. So it's nice to have a winter pick-me-up like Taco Minestrone to call on when I need a speedy and filling entree for supper," Carole notes. "Almost as fast as I can open a few cans, I'm ladling out steaming bowlfuls.

"On nights when we get drop-in company, I make a more substantial batch of soup by adding green beans or corn."

Carole's snappy Tossed Green Salad is served with a light vinegar and oil dressing. "I never clutter the table with different bottles of dressing," she says. "Everyone who tastes my quick and easy herbed version loves it.

"For a refreshing dessert, a simple fruit medley is perfect," she adds. "Whether I use canned fruit or in-season varieties for my Fruit with Whipped Topping, I can count on an empty bowl when dinner is finished."

The seconds Carole saves on cooking never go to waste. She enjoys making handcrafts when she's not busy with church activities and her favorite pastime of all—spending quality time with grandchildren Dalton and Makayla.

✦✦✦✦✦✦✦✦✦✦
TACO MINESTRONE

1/2 pound ground beef
2 cans (15 ounces *each*) ranch-style beans
2 cans (10-3/4 ounces *each*) condensed minestrone soup, undiluted
2 cans (10 ounces *each*) diced tomatoes and green chilies, undrained

In a saucepan, cook beef over medium heat until no longer pink; drain. Stir in the beans, soup and tomatoes. Bring to a boil. Reduce heat; simmer, uncovered, for 15-20 minutes. **Yield:** 8 servings.

✦✦✦✦✦✦✦✦✦✦
TOSSED GREEN SALAD

8 cups torn mixed salad greens
1 small cucumber, thinly sliced
3/4 cup frozen peas, thawed
2 green onions, sliced
1 celery rib, sliced
DRESSING:
1/4 cup vegetable oil
3 tablespoons white wine vinegar
1 tablespoon sugar
1 tablespoon dried parsley flakes
1/2 teaspoon salt
1/4 teaspoon dried oregano
1/8 teaspoon pepper

In a large bowl, combine the mixed greens, cucumber, peas, onions and celery. In a jar with a tight-fitting lid, combine the dressing ingredients; shake well. Pour the dressing over the salad and toss to coat. **Yield:** 8 servings.

✦✦✦✦✦✦✦✦✦✦
FRUIT WITH WHIPPED TOPPING

1 can (20 ounces) pineapple tidbits, undrained
2 medium firm bananas, sliced
2 cups sliced fresh strawberries
1 can (15-1/4 ounces) sliced peaches, drained
1 cup seedless grapes
Whipped topping, chopped nuts and toasted coconut

In a large bowl, combine the fruit. Top each serving with whipped topping, nuts and coconut. **Yield:** 8 servings.

EXTRA, EXTRA!

"Taco Minestrone is just as good made with leftover cooked chicken instead of ground beef," Carole suggests.

"Just dice it and toss it in. If you like, adjust the spiciness by adding your favorite herbs. Warm corn bread is great on the side."

Easy Meal Has Fun and Flavor

A BALANCING ACT takes place in Ruth Lee's Troy, Ontario kitchen daily as she juggles her cooking routine with a bustling schedule.

"Between babysitting my grandchildren and making meals for students at the school my daughter runs, I do keep busy," Ruth admits. "I also manage a home-based electric farm fence business."

Compliments come quickly whenever Ruth prepares the fast-moving menu that follows. The main course, side salad and dessert are all ready to serve in only 30 minutes or less.

"Smoked Sausage Kabobs are a convenient entree since the ingredients can be cut, marinated and threaded ahead of time," Ruth says. "Then they go immediately from the fridge to the grill or broiler. I often make extras for my husband Doug's lunch. They're simple to reheat at work.

"It takes no time to toss together the corn, lettuce and red peppers in my Corny Lettuce Salad," she assures. "People love the sweet and tangy homemade dressing and the nutty crunch of poppy seeds. I've taken it to potlucks and picnics, and it's gone in no time!"

For dessert, few things dress up a family meal or special occasion faster than Ruth's spiced Banana Pineapple Sundaes. "I served them at a shower," she shares. "No sooner did I pass out the spoons than the room was filled with oohs and aahs."

SMOKED SAUSAGE KABOBS

- 1/3 cup honey
- 1/4 cup spicy brown mustard
- 2 tablespoons vegetable oil
- 1 tablespoon soy sauce
- 2 garlic cloves, minced
- 1/2 teaspoon minced fresh gingerroot
- 1-1/4 pounds fully cooked smoked sausage, cut into 1-inch pieces
- 16 cherry tomatoes
- 8 medium fresh mushrooms
- 1 large green pepper, cut into 1-inch pieces
- 1 medium onion, cut into eight wedges
- 1 small zucchini, cut into 1-inch pieces

In a large bowl, combine the first six ingredients. Add the sausage and vegetables; toss to coat.

Drain and reserve marinade.

On eight metal or soaked wooden skewers, alternately thread sausage and vegetables. Broil 3-4 in. from the heat for 3-4 minutes on each side or until vegetables are tender and sausage is heated through, basting occasionally with the reserved marinade. **Yield:** 4 servings.

CORNY LETTUCE SALAD

- 3 cups shredded lettuce
- 3/4 cup fresh *or* frozen corn, thawed
- 2 tablespoons sugar
- 2 tablespoons cider vinegar
- 1-1/2 teaspoons poppy seeds
- 1/2 teaspoon grated onion
- 1/4 teaspoon salt
- 1/4 teaspoon ground mustard
- 1/4 cup vegetable oil
- 1/4 cup finely chopped sweet red pepper

In a salad bowl, toss the lettuce and corn. In a small bowl, combine the sugar, vinegar, poppy seeds, onion, salt and mustard; gradually whisk in oil. Pour over salad and toss to coat. Sprinkle with red pepper. **Yield:** 4 servings.

BANANA PINEAPPLE SUNDAES

- 6 tablespoons brown sugar
- 1/4 cup orange juice
- 1-1/2 teaspoons butter
- 1/8 teaspoon ground cinnamon
- 2 small firm bananas, sliced
- 1 cup cubed fresh pineapple
- 1/2 teaspoon rum extract
- 2 cups vanilla ice cream

In a large saucepan, combine the brown sugar, orange juice, butter and cinnamon. Bring to a boil. Reduce heat to medium; cook and stir for 2 minutes. Add the bananas and pineapple; cook and stir 1-2 minutes longer. Remove from the heat; stir in extract. Serve over ice cream. **Yield:** 4 servings.

IRRESISTIBLE OPTION

"The topping for Banana Pineapple Sundaes is also yummy over pound cake or plain yellow cake," says Ruth. "If you don't have rum extract, simply use vanilla instead."

Summery Menu Is a Breeze

THOSE fabled lazy days of summer are anything but for Flori Christensen of Bloomington, Indiana...particularly at mealtime.

"I love to cook healthy meals for my husband, Rob, and our young daughters," Flori relates. But being a stay-at-home mom to Madeline, Eloise and Sarah Jane means she doesn't stay in any one place for long, including the kitchen.

Flori's recipe box is chock-full of quick-and-easy dishes. Here, she's shared three of her fast favorites for dinnertime.

"People say that the sweet potatoes in my quesadillas make them think of Thanksgiving," Flori says. "I like to mix and refrigerate the filling in advance, so it takes me no time at all to layer all the tortillas.

"I usually have the ingredients for the melon salad on hand. It's a light, refreshing side dish for any meal, and it's a nice contribution to a potluck or brunch, too."

Flori always has time to squeeze in a cool lemon pie as a frosty finish. With a graham cracker crust and instant pudding, it makes a tangy dessert. "Kids have fun helping make it," she adds.

CARIBBEAN QUESADILLAS

- 1 large sweet potato, peeled and diced
- 1 medium onion, chopped
- 2 garlic cloves, minced
- 1/2 to 1 teaspoon pumpkin pie spice
- 2 teaspoons vegetable oil
- 2 cans (15 ounces *each*) black beans, rinsed and drained
- 1/2 cup chicken broth
- 12 flour tortillas (8 inches)
- 1-1/2 cups (6 ounces) shredded Monterey Jack cheese
- 1 can (4 ounces) chopped green chilies
Sour cream and salsa

Place the sweet potato in a microwave-safe dish. Cover and microwave on high for 5 minutes or until tender.

Meanwhile, in a large skillet, saute the onion, garlic and pumpkin pie spice in oil until onion is tender. Stir in beans and broth. Bring to a boil. Reduce heat; simmer, uncovered, for 3 minutes or until thickened. Mash beans slightly with a fork. Stir in sweet potato. Cook until heated through.

Layer six tortillas with 3/4 cup bean mixture, 1/4 cup cheese and a rounded tablespoonful of chilies. Top each with another tortilla. Cook quesadillas on a greased griddle or in two large greased skillets over medium heat for 3-4 minutes on each side or until browned. Cut into wedges; serve with sour cream and salsa. **Yield:** 6 servings.

Editor's Note: This recipe was tested in a 1,100-watt microwave.

HONEY-LIME MELON SALAD

- 3 cups cubed honeydew
- 2 cups cubed watermelon
- 2 cups cubed cantaloupe
- 1/2 cup seedless red grapes
DRESSING:
- 2 tablespoons vegetable oil
- 2 tablespoons lime juice
- 1 tablespoon honey
- 1/4 teaspoon grated lime peel

In a serving bowl, combine the fruits. Whisk together dressing ingredients; toss with fruit before serving. **Yield:** 6-8 servings.

FROZEN LEMON PIE

- 1-3/4 cups cold milk
- 2 packages (3.4 ounces *each*) instant vanilla pudding mix
- 1 can (6 ounces) frozen lemonade concentrate, thawed
- 1 carton (8 ounces) frozen whipped topping, thawed
- 1 graham cracker crust (9 inches)

In a large bowl, whisk milk and pudding mixes for 2 minutes. Let stand for 2 minutes or until soft-set. Add lemonade concentrate; whisk for 30 seconds. Immediately fold in whipped topping. Spoon into crust. Freeze until set, about 25 minutes. **Yield:** 6-8 servings.

SUREFIRE SHORTCUT

"Caribbean Quesadillas are even faster to fix if you use canned sweet potatoes," says Flori. "Sometimes I serve the filling in taco shells, adding shredded lettuce and tomatoes."

Roast Dinner Has Home-Style Taste

▰▰▰▰▰▰▰▰▰▰▰

DILLED POT ROAST

Judy Poor, Overland Park, Kansas

This pot roast is a top choice of mine when I'm having guests. Sometimes I serve it with noodles or rice.

1 bone-in beef arm pot roast *or* chuck
  roast (about 3-1/2 pounds)
2 tablespoons vegetable oil
1 tablespoon dill seed
1 teaspoon salt
1/4 teaspoon pepper
1 cup water
2 tablespoons white wine vinegar
3 tablespoons all-purpose flour
1-1/4 cups sour cream
2 teaspoons dill weed

In a Dutch oven, brown roast in oil on all sides; drain. Sprinkle with dill seed, salt and pepper. Add water and vinegar to the pan. Cover and bake at 325° for 3 hours or until meat is tender.

Remove roast and keep warm. Pour drippings into a measuring cup. Strain and skim fat, reserving 3 tablespoons fat and all of the drippings. In a saucepan, heat reserved fat and drippings; stir in flour until blended. Bring to a boil; cook and stir for 1 minute or until thickened.

Reduce heat to low. Stir in the sour cream and dill weed; heat through (do not boil). Serve with the roast. **Yield:** 10-12 servings.

▰▰▰▰▰▰▰▰▰▰▰

CARROT BROCCOLI CASSEROLE

Ann Janis, Tucson, Arizona

Even folks who claim they don't like broccoli end up enjoying this veggie bake. With cheddar cheese, the casserole makes a colorful and tasty side dish.

1 cup diced carrots
1 cup diced celery
1 cup chopped onion
4 teaspoons butter, *divided*
1-1/2 cups (6 ounces) shredded cheddar
  cheese, *divided*
2 cups fresh broccoli florets
1/4 cup chicken broth
Salt and pepper to taste

In a large skillet, saute the carrots, celery and onion in 3 teaspoons butter until tender. Transfer to a greased 1-1/2-qt. baking dish. Top with 3/4 cup cheese. In the same skillet, saute broccoli in the remaining butter for 1 minute. Place over cheese; pour broth over all.

Cover and bake at 350° for 25 minutes. Uncover; sprinkle with remaining cheese. Bake 5 minutes longer or until cheese is melted and vegetables are tender. Season with salt and pepper. Serve with a slotted spoon. **Yield:** 6-8 servings.

▰▰▰▰▰▰▰▰▰▰▰

STUFFED SWEET POTATOES

Shirley Petry, Cherry Log, Georgia

These are the best twice-baked potatoes I've ever had. Pineapple and walnuts add an interesting texture.

6 medium sweet potatoes
1/4 cup orange juice
3 tablespoons butter, melted, *divided*
1 teaspoon salt
1 can (8 ounces) crushed pineapple,
  drained
1/2 cup chopped walnuts
1/2 cup miniature marshmallows
1/2 cup crushed cornflakes

Bake sweet potatoes at 350° for 65-75 minutes or until tender. When cool enough to handle, cut potatoes in half lengthwise; scoop out pulp and place in a bowl. Add orange juice, 2 tablespoons butter and salt; mash. Stir in the pineapple and walnuts. Spoon into potato shells.

Place in two greased 11-in. x 7-in. x 2-in. baking dishes. Sprinkle with marshmallows and cornflakes. Drizzle with remaining butter. Bake, uncovered, at 400° for 15 minutes or until heated through. **Yield:** 12 servings.

▰▰▰▰▰▰▰▰▰▰▰

BLACK WALNUT CAKE

Elisabeth Garrison, Elmer, New Jersey

A family favorite for generations, this old-fashioned cake was always expected at our holiday dinners.

1 cup chopped black *or* English walnuts
3 cups all-purpose flour, *divided*
1 cup butter, softened
2 cups sugar
4 eggs
1 teaspoon vanilla extract
2 teaspoons baking powder
1/4 teaspoon salt
1 cup milk

FROSTING:
1-3/4 cups sugar
4 egg whites
1/2 cup water
1/2 teaspoon cream of tartar
1 teaspoon vanilla extract

In a bowl, toss walnuts with 1/4 cup flour; set aside. In a mixing bowl, cream butter and sugar. Add eggs, one at a time, beating well after each addition. Add vanilla; mix well. Combine the baking powder, salt and remaining flour; add to the creamed mixture alternately with milk. Stir in the reserved nut mixture.

Transfer to a greased and floured 10-in. tube pan. Bake at 350° for 50-55 minutes or until a toothpick inserted near the center comes out

clean. Cool for 10 minutes before removing from pan to a wire rack to cool completely.

In a heavy saucepan, combine sugar, egg whites, water and cream of tartar. With a portable mixer, beat on low speed for 1 minute. Continue beating on low speed over low heat until frosting reaches 160°, about 9 minutes.

Pour into a large mixing bowl; add vanilla. Beat on high speed until frosting forms stiff peaks, about 7 minutes. Frost cake. **Yield:** 12-16 servings.

Editor's Note: A stand mixer is recommended for beating the frosting after it reaches 160°. We recommend that you test your candy thermometer before each use by bringing water to a boil; the thermometer should read 212°. Adjust your recipe temperature up or down based on your test.

Flavors of Italy Are Irresistible

▰▰▰▰▰▰▰▰▰

SPAGHETTI SAUCE WITH MEATBALLS

Anne Eynon, Rockville, Maryland

This recipe was my first adventure into serious cooking when I was a newlywed. It makes enough for several meals, and the leftovers taste just as good.

   1 cup chopped onion
   1 large green pepper, chopped
   2 celery ribs, chopped
   4 garlic cloves, minced
   2 tablespoons olive oil
   2 cans (28 ounces *each*) diced tomatoes, undrained
   1 can (6 ounces) tomato paste
3/4 cup water
   3 bay leaves
   1 tablespoon sugar
   1 tablespoon dried oregano
1/4 teaspoon ground cloves
1/4 teaspoon crushed red pepper flakes
1/4 teaspoon pepper
MEATBALLS:
   1 egg
   1 cup chopped onion
   2 slices bread, cubed
1/4 cup milk
   2 tablespoons chopped fresh parsley
   1 garlic clove, minced
   1 teaspoon salt
   1 pound ground beef
1/4 pound ground veal
1/4 pound ground pork
   2 tablespoons vegetable oil
Hot cooked spaghetti

In a large saucepan or Dutch oven, saute the onion, green pepper, celery and garlic in oil until tender. Stir in the tomatoes, tomato paste, water, bay leaves, sugar, oregano, cloves, pepper flakes and pepper; bring to a boil. Reduce heat; cover and simmer for 2 hours, stirring occasionally.

Meanwhile, in a bowl, combine the egg, onion, bread cubes, milk, parsley, garlic and salt. Crumble meat over mixture and mix well. Shape into 1-1/2-in. balls. In a skillet, brown the meatballs in batches in oil; drain.

Add meatballs to sauce. Cover and simmer for 30 minutes. Discard bay leaves. Serve meatballs and sauce over spaghetti. **Yield:** 12 servings.

▰▰▰▰▰▰▰▰▰

CUCUMBER TOMATO SALAD

Jan Peterson, Mesa, Arizona

I tried out this dish on my future husband when we were dating. I discovered later that he didn't care for vinegar, but he came to enjoy this simple, colorful salad and called it piccalilli.

   2 medium tomatoes, sliced and quartered
   1 large cucumber, peeled and sliced
   4 green onions, chopped
   1 tablespoon sugar
   1 teaspoon salt
1/4 teaspoon pepper
1/3 cup cider vinegar
   1 cup water

In a bowl, combine the tomatoes, cucumber and onions. In a small bowl, combine the sugar, salt and pepper. Whisk in the vinegar and water. Pour over vegetables and toss to coat. Cover and refrigerate for 4 hours or overnight. Serve with a slotted spoon. **Yield:** 8 servings.

▰▰▰▰▰▰▰▰▰

ITALIAN DROP BISCUITS

LaDonna Reed, Ponca City, Oklahoma

I'd been baking garlic cheese biscuits for years before I tried spicing them up with green chilies. These bites go well with Mexican as well as Italian foods.

   2 cups biscuit/baking mix
   1 cup (4 ounces) shredded cheddar cheese
1/2 cup cold water
   2 tablespoons chopped green chilies
1/4 cup butter, melted
   1 teaspoon dried parsley flakes
1/2 teaspoon Italian seasoning
1/4 teaspoon garlic powder

In a bowl, combine biscuit mix, cheese, water and chilies just until moistened. Drop by heaping tablespoonfuls onto a greased baking sheet. Bake at 450° for 8-10 minutes or until golden brown. In a small bowl, combine the butter, parsley, Italian seasoning and garlic powder; brush over warm biscuits. **Yield:** 1-1/2 dozen.

▰▰▰▰▰▰▰▰▰

BANANA CHOCOLATE COCONUT PIE

Carol Gaus, Elk Grove Village, Illinois

A friend gave me the recipe for a chocolate-coconut pie crust, and it goes wonderfully with the smooth banana filling in this irresistible pie.

1-1/2 teaspoons plus 2 tablespoons butter,
       divided
  1/3 cup plus 1-1/2 cups flaked coconut,
       divided
    2 squares (1 ounce *each*) unsweetened
       chocolate
  2/3 cup confectioners' sugar
    2 tablespoons milk
FILLING:
    2 medium bananas, cut into 1/4-inch
       slices
1-3/4 cups cold milk
    1 package (3.9 ounces) instant chocolate
       pudding mix

Coat a 9-in. pie plate with 1-1/2 teaspoons butter. Sprinkle 1/3 cup coconut over pie plate; set aside. In a microwave or heavy saucepan, melt chocolate and remaining butter; stir until smooth.

Combine confectioners' sugar and milk. Stir into chocolate mixture. Stir in remaining coconut. Carefully press onto the bottom and up the sides of prepared pie plate. Refrigerate for 1 hour or until firm.

Arrange bananas in crust. In a bowl, whisk cold milk and pudding mix for 2 minutes; let stand for 2 minutes or until soft-set.

Spoon over bananas. Chill for 3 hours before serving. Refrigerate leftovers. **Yield:** 6-8 servings.

Fresh Fare Brings Variety to Meals

◤◥◤◥◤◥◤◥

SESAME-CRUSTED PORK LOIN

Ray Moe, Pelican Rapids, Minnesota

This recipe was a winner at our state fair. The Asian flavors give the pork a tongue-tingling twist.

- 1/2 cup soy sauce
- 3 tablespoons sugar
- 3 tablespoons finely chopped onion
- 2 tablespoons vegetable oil
- 2 teaspoons ground ginger
- 1 garlic clove, minced
- 3/4 cup sesame seeds
- 1 boneless rolled pork loin roast (about 5 pounds)
- 2 cups water

In a large resealable bag, combine the first seven ingredients. Add the roast; seal bag and turn to coat. Refrigerate overnight.

Drain and discard marinade. Place roast on a rack in a shallow roasting pan; pour water into pan. Bake at 350° for 1-3/4 to 2 hours or until a meat thermometer reads 160°. Let stand for 10-15 minutes before carving. **Yield:** 14-16 servings.

◤◥◤◥◤◥◤◥

TWO-POTATO SWIRLS

Ruth Plaushin, Swiftwater, Pennsylvania

Here's a fancy way to serve sweet potatoes. I like to make this ahead of time and reheat it before dinner.

- 3 large russet potatoes, peeled and quartered
- 3 medium sweet potatoes, peeled and quartered
- 1 package (3 ounces) cream cheese, softened
- 2 to 8 tablespoons milk
- 2 tablespoons butter, *divided*
- 2 tablespoons orange juice
- 1 tablespoon honey

Place the russet potatoes in a large saucepan and cover with water. Bring to a boil. Reduce heat; cover and cook for 20-25 minutes or until tender. Place sweet potatoes in another saucepan and cover with water. Bring to a boil. Reduce heat; cover and cook for 20-25 minutes until tender.

Drain russet potatoes. Place in a large mixing bowl; mash until smooth. Add cream cheese, 2 tablespoons milk and 1 tablespoon butter; beat until light and fluffy, adding milk as needed. Drain sweet potatoes. Place in another bowl; mash until smooth. Add juice, honey and remaining butter.

Insert tip #409 into a pastry bag. Spoon russet potatoes into one side of bag; spoon sweet potatoes into the other side. Pipe 3-in. swirls, forming rosettes, onto a greased baking sheet. Bake at 350° for 25-30 minutes or until heated through and tops are lightly browned. **Yield:** 7-8 servings.

◤◥◤◥◤◥◤◥

SQUASH MEDLEY

Dolores Wolff, Roseberg, Texas

I finally got my family to eat squash when I served this well seasoned, bacon-topped side dish.

- 1 medium summer squash, halved and sliced
- 1 medium zucchini, halved and sliced
- 4 bacon strips, diced
- 3/4 cup chopped onion
- 2 tablespoons brown sugar
- 1/2 teaspoon salt
- 1/2 teaspoon dried basil
- 1/2 teaspoon dried oregano
- 1/2 teaspoon chili powder
- 1/2 teaspoon garlic powder
- 1/4 teaspoon pepper
- 1-1/2 cups diced, seeded and peeled fresh tomatoes

Place 1 in. of water in a saucepan. Add squash and zucchini. Bring to a boil; cook for 4-5 minutes or until crisp-tender. Drain and set aside. In a large skillet, cook bacon over medium heat until crisp. Using a slotted spoon, remove to paper towels. Drain, reserving 1 tablespoon drippings.

In the drippings, saute onion until tender. Add the squash, brown sugar and seasonings. Stir in tomatoes. Bring to a boil over medium heat. Reduce heat; simmer, uncovered, for 10 minutes or until heated through. Sprinkle with bacon. Serve with a slotted spoon. **Yield:** 4-6 servings.

◤◥◤◥◤◥◤◥

STRAWBERRY CREAM CAKE

Frankie Allen Mann, Warrior, Alabama

I made this one day for my daughter and her friends. They now call this "Amber's Dad's Good Stuff."

- 1/2 cup butter, softened
- 1 cup sugar, *divided*
- 2 egg yolks
- 1 teaspoon vanilla extract
- 2 teaspoons grated orange peel

2 cups cake flour
2 teaspoons baking powder
1/4 teaspoon salt
1/3 cup milk
1/3 cup orange juice
4 egg whites
FILLING:
2-1/4 cups chopped fresh strawberries
2 tablespoons sugar
2 cups heavy whipping cream
1 teaspoon vanilla extract
1/3 cup confectioners' sugar
1/4 cup sour cream
Whole strawberries for garnish

Line two greased 9-in. round baking pans with waxed paper and grease the paper; set aside. In a large mixing bowl, cream butter and 3/4 cup sugar. Add egg yolks, vanilla and peel; mix well. Combine flour, baking powder and salt; add to creamed mixture alternately with milk and juice.

In a mixing bowl, beat egg whites on medium speed until soft peaks form. Gradually beat in remaining sugar, 1 tablespoon at a time, on high until stiff glossy peaks form. Fold into batter.

Pour into prepared pans. Bake at 350° for 18-22 minutes or until a toothpick comes out clean. Cool for 10 minutes before removing from pans to wire racks. Gently peel off waxed paper and discard. Cool cakes completely.

In a bowl, combine chopped berries and sugar; let stand for 30 minutes. In a mixing bowl, beat cream and vanilla until cream begins to thicken. Gradually beat in confectioners' sugar on high until stiff peaks form. Fold in sour cream.

Place one cake layer on a serving plate; top with chopped berries and half of cream mixture. Top with remaining cake and cream mixture. Garnish with whole berries. **Yield:** 10-12 servings.

Savor a Supper Like Mom Made

MOM'S POT ROAST

Dorothy Duder, North Hollywood, California

My mother taught me how to cook for a crowd. This entree always pleases everyone at the table.

- 3 tablespoons all-purpose flour, *divided*
- 1 teaspoon salt
- 1/4 teaspoon *each* dried chives, parsley flakes and tarragon
- 1/4 teaspoon pepper
- 1 boneless beef chuck roast (3 to 3-1/2 pounds)
- 2 tablespoons vegetable oil
- 8 cups water
- 2 tablespoons beef bouillon granules
- 2 tablespoons Worcestershire sauce
- 1 large onion, chopped
- 3 celery ribs, cut into chunks
- 3 garlic cloves, minced
- 2 bay leaves
- 4 medium potatoes, peeled and quartered
- 4 medium carrots, cut into chunks
- 2 tablespoons butter

Combine 1 tablespoon flour and seasonings; rub over roast. In a Dutch oven, brown roast on all sides in oil over medium-high heat. Add water, bouillon, Worcestershire, onion, celery, garlic and bay leaves. Bring to a boil. Reduce heat; cover and simmer for 2 hours, turning roast after 1 hour.

Turn roast again. Add potatoes and carrots. Cover and simmer 1 hour longer or until meat and vegetables are tender.

Discard leaves. Remove meat and vegetables to a platter and keep warm. Pour 2 cups cooking juices and loosened browned bits into a 2-cup measuring cup; skim fat. (Save remaining juices for another use.) For gravy, in a saucepan, melt butter; stir in remaining flour until smooth. Gradually stir in cooking juices. Bring to a boil; cook and stir for 2 minutes or until thickened. Serve with roast and vegetables. **Yield:** 8 servings.

CHIVE BISCUITS

Norma Erne, Albuquerque, New Mexico

I serve these light, moist biscuits with roasts, soups and stews during the fall and winter. Sometimes I substitute different herbs for a change of pace.

- 2 cups all-purpose flour
- 3 teaspoons baking powder
- 1/2 teaspoon salt
- 1/4 teaspoon baking soda
- 1/3 cup butter-flavored shortening
- 1 cup buttermilk
- 2 tablespoons minced chives

In a small bowl, combine the flour, baking powder, salt and baking soda. Cut in shortening until mixture resembles coarse crumbs. Stir in buttermilk and chives just until moistened.

Drop by tablespoonfuls 2 in. apart onto a greased baking sheet. Bake at 450° for 10-12 minutes or until lightly browned. Serve warm. **Yield:** 1 dozen.

COOKED SALAD DRESSING

Doreen Martin, Kitimat, British Columbia

My mom used this for potato salad, green salad and even pasta salad. If you like, add up to 2 teaspoons of Dijon mustard, honey or garlic to the basic recipe.

- 1/4 cup sugar
- 1 teaspoon all-purpose flour
- 1 teaspoon ground mustard
- 1/2 teaspoon salt
- 1 egg, lightly beaten
- 1/3 cup white vinegar
- 2 tablespoons water
- 1 teaspoon butter
- 1/2 cup mayonnaise

Torn mixed salad greens

In a small saucepan, combine sugar, flour, mustard and salt. Stir in egg until smooth. Gradually add vinegar and water. Cook and stir over medium heat for 3 minutes or until mixture reaches at least 160° and coats the back of a metal spoon.

Remove from the heat; stir in butter. Let stand for 5 minutes. Stir in mayonnaise until smooth. Cover and refrigerate until chilled. Serve with salad greens. **Yield:** 1-1/4 cups.

PEANUT BUTTER BANANA CAKE

Lee Deneau, Lansing, Michigan

I've had this well-worn recipe for as long as I've been married. The cake has been a scrumptious staple for potluck suppers and other get-togethers.

- 1/2 cup butter, softened
- 1-1/2 cups sugar

2 eggs
1 cup mashed ripe bananas (2 to 3 medium)
1 teaspoon vanilla extract
2 cups all-purpose flour
2 teaspoons baking powder
1 teaspoon baking soda
1/2 cup milk

FROSTING:
1/3 cup creamy peanut butter
1/3 cup milk
1-1/2 teaspoons vanilla extract
3 cups confectioners' sugar

In a large mixing bowl, cream the butter and sugar. Add eggs, one at a time, beating well after each addition. Add bananas and vanilla; mix well. Combine the flour, baking powder and baking soda; add to creamed mixture alternately with milk.

Transfer to a greased 13-in. x 9-in. x 2-in. baking pan. Bake at 350° for 30-35 minutes or until a toothpick inserted near the center comes out clean. Cool on a wire rack.

For frosting, in a mixing bowl, beat the peanut butter, milk and vanilla until blended; beat in confectioners' sugar until smooth. Spread over cake. **Yield:** 12-15 servings.

Comfort Foods Can't Miss

▛▚▞▙▞▚▞▙▞▚▞▙

WARM BROCCOLI CHEESE DIP

Barbara Maiol, Conyers, Georgia

This creamy dip is a "must" for family parties. Everyone loves the zippy jalapeno and crunchy broccoli.

2 jars (8 ounces *each*) process cheese sauce
1 can (10-3/4 ounces) condensed cream of chicken soup, undiluted
1 package (10 ounces) frozen chopped broccoli, thawed and drained
1/2 pound fresh mushrooms, chopped
2 tablespoons chopped seeded jalapeno pepper
Assorted fresh vegetables

In a 1-1/2-qt. slow cooker, combine cheese sauce and soup. Cover; cook on low for 30 minutes or until cheese is melted, stirring occasionally. Stir in broccoli, mushrooms and jalapeno. Cover; cook on low for 2 hours or until heated through. Serve with vegetables. **Yield:** 5-1/2 cups.

Editor's Note: When cutting or seeding hot peppers, use rubber or plastic gloves to protect your hands. Avoid touching your face.

▛▚▞▙▞▚▞▙▞▚▞▙

VEGETABLE CHICKEN POTPIE

Debbie Chilton, Franklin, Ohio

We briefly relocated to New Hampshire after 50 years in Ohio. One way we kept "close" to loved ones in the Midwest was by fixing family favorites like this.

1 unbaked deep-dish pastry shell (9 inches)
3/4 cup *each* chopped carrot, celery and onion
1 garlic clove, minced
1 tablespoon vegetable oil
1/2 pound boneless skinless chicken breasts, cut into 1-inch cubes
1 cup chicken broth
3/4 cup cubed peeled potatoes
3/4 cup frozen peas
2 tablespoons minced fresh parsley
2 tablespoons butter
2 tablespoons all-purpose flour
1 cup milk

1/2 cup condensed cream of chicken soup, undiluted
1/4 teaspoon hot pepper sauce
TOPPING:
2 cups all-purpose flour
3 teaspoons baking powder
1/2 teaspoon baking soda
1/4 teaspoon salt
1 cup buttermilk
1/3 cup unsweetened applesauce
2 tablespoons butter, melted

Line unpricked pastry shell with a double thickness of heavy-duty foil. Bake at 425° for 8 minutes. Remove foil; bake 5 minutes longer.

In a large skillet, saute vegetables and garlic in oil for 5 minutes or until crisp-tender. Add chicken; cook until lightly browned. Add broth; bring to a boil. Add the potatoes, peas and parsley. Reduce heat; simmer, uncovered, for 10 minutes.

In a small saucepan, melt butter over medium heat. Stir in flour; gradually stir in milk. Bring to a boil; cook and stir for 2 minutes or until thickened. Reduce heat; stir in soup until smooth. Add hot pepper sauce. Stir into vegetable mixture. Transfer to pastry shell.

In a bowl, combine flour, baking powder, baking soda and salt. Combine buttermilk, applesauce and butter; stir into dry ingredients just until moistened. Drop by spoonfuls over filling. Bake at 425° for 20-25 minutes or until puffed and golden brown (if necessary, cover edges loosely with foil to prevent overbrowning). **Yield:** 6 servings.

▛▚▞▙▞▚▞▙▞▚▞▙

CRAN-RASPBERRY SAUCE

Madeline Farina, Leola, Pennsylvania

When I was asked to bring a cranberry dish to a holiday party, I created this recipe. The not-too-sweet sauce is also nice as a condiment or dessert topping.

1 package (12 ounces) fresh *or* frozen cranberries
1 cup cranberry juice
1/2 cup water
1/4 cup sugar
1 package (3 ounces) raspberry gelatin
1 cup ice cubes
2 cups fresh *or* frozen raspberries

In a large saucepan, combine cranberries, cranberry juice, water and sugar. Bring to a boil. Reduce heat; simmer, uncovered, for 10 minutes or until cranberries pop. Stir in gelatin until dissolved.

Remove from heat. Add ice cubes; stir until melted. Gently fold in raspberries. Cool to room temperature. Cover and refrigerate overnight. **Yield:** 4 cups.

■■■■■■■■■■■■

DATE OAT BARS

Joyce Eastman, Garden Grove, California

My mother found this recipe in 1936. The citrusy treats taste just as good today as they did back then.

1-3/4 cups chopped dates
 1/2 cup water
   2 tablespoons brown sugar
   1 teaspoon grated orange peel
   2 tablespoons orange juice
   1 teaspoon lemon juice
CRUST:
1-1/2 cups all-purpose flour
   1 teaspoon baking powder
 1/2 teaspoon baking soda
 1/4 teaspoon salt
   1 cup cold butter

1-1/2 cups old-fashioned oats
   1 cup packed brown sugar

In a small saucepan, combine dates, water, brown sugar and orange peel. Cook and stir over medium heat until mixture comes to a boil, about 4 minutes. Cook and stir 3 minutes longer or until liquid is absorbed. Remove from heat. Stir in orange and lemon juices. Cool to room temperature.

In a large bowl, combine flour, baking powder, baking soda and salt. Cut in butter until crumbly. Add oats and brown sugar; mix well. Set aside half for topping. Press remaining crumb mixture into a greased 13-in. x 9-in. x 2-in. baking pan.

Drop date mixture by small spoonfuls onto crust. Sprinkle with reserved crumb mixture; press down gently. Bake at 325° for 30-35 minutes or until golden brown. Cool on a wire rack. Cut into bars. **Yield:** 3 dozen.

General Recipe Index

A

APPETIZERS & SNACKS

Cold Appetizers & Snacks
Blue Cheese Turkey Rolls, 133
Egg Penguins, 7
✓Smoked Salmon New
   Potatoes, 6
White Chocolate Pretzel
   Snack, 149

Dips & Spreads
Chocolate Fruit Dip, 10
Creamy Shrimp Spread, 11
Hot Artichoke-Spinach Dip, 6
Layered Cheese Spread, 11
Mango Salsa, 5
✓Roasted Pepper Bean Dip, 5
Swiss Walnut Cracker Snack, 8
10-Minute Zesty Salsa, 10
Warm Broccoli Cheese Dip, 170

Hot Appetizers
Asparagus Appeteaser, 10
Bacon-Wrapped Stuffed
   Jalapenos, 7
Crab Puffs, 9
Hearty Ham Balls, 9

APPLES
Apple Butterscotch Cake, 125
Apple Cheddar Cheesecake, 106
Baked Sweet Potatoes and
   Apples, 84
Cran-Apple Raisin Pie, 107
Cranberry Waldorf Salad, 138
Grilled Apple Crisp, 102
New York State Apple Muffins, 89
Raisin-Apple Bread Pudding, 128
Swiss Apple Pie, 103
Turkey Waldorf Pita, 146
Upside-Down Apple Pie, 120

APRICOTS
Apricot Chip Cookies, 107
Apricot Chip Triangles, 129

Fruited Gelatin Salad, 24
Harvest Stuffing, 80
Mashed Potato Kolachkes, 97
Saucy Apricot Chicken, 152
Tangy Apricot Pork Chops, 150

ARTICHOKES
Artichoke Ravioli, 57
Hot Artichoke-Spinach Dip, 6

ASPARAGUS
Asparagus Appeteaser, 10
Asparagus Crepes, 148
Flavorful Oniony Asparagus, 160
Parmesan Asparagus, 126
Stir-Fried Asparagus, 83

AVOCADOS
Frozen Grapefruit-Avocado
   Salad, 32
Grapefruit Avocado Salad, 40
Green Bean Tossed Salad, 41
Zesty Garlic-Avocado
   Sandwiches, 40

B

BACON
Asparagus Appeteaser, 10
Bacon 'n' Egg Salad
   Sandwiches, 13
Bacon-Wrapped Stuffed
   Jalapenos, 7
Triple Pork with Rice, 57

BANANAS
Banana Chocolate Coconut
   Pie, 164
Banana Pineapple Sundaes, 156
Bumblebee Banana Cupcakes, 118
Fruit Compote, 124
Honey Banana Sundaes, 127
Peanut Butter Banana Bread, 92
Peanut Butter Banana Cake, 168
Three-Fruit Slushies, 5

BARS & BROWNIES
Black Forest Brownies, 116
Coconut Pear Bars, 148
Date Oat Bars, 171
Pecan Caramel Bars, 120
Raisin Pumpkin Bars, 108

BEANS
Bean and Pork Chop Bake, 55
✓Beef 'n' Chili Beans, 43
Cajun Red Beans, 56
Chili with Barley, 31
Greek-Style Green Beans, 144
Green Bean and Blue Cheese
   Salad, 148
Green Bean Tossed Salad, 41
Green Beans with Almond
   Butter, 75
Pasta Bean Soup, 129
Quick 'n' Easy Bean Pot, 83
✓Roasted Pepper Bean Dip, 5
Spicy Slow-Cooked Chili, 16
Tangy Green Beans, 130

BEEF *(also see Ground Beef)*

Main Dishes
✓Beef 'n' Chili Beans, 43
Beef Cassoulet, 66
Chinese Pepper Steak, 137
Cube Steak Stroganoff, 143
Dilled Pot Roast, 162
Louisiana Barbecue Brisket, 44
Marinated Chuck Roast, 47
Mom's Pot Roast, 168
Mustard-Herb Grilled
   Tenderloin, 53
Sauerbraten Stew, 150
Steak Potpie, 48
Veal Scaloppini, 130

Salads & Sandwiches
Beef Gyros, 25
✓Grilled Steak Salad, 18
Hearty Stir-Fry Salad, 19
Open-Faced Reubens, 34

*✓Recipe includes Nutrition Facts
and Diabetic Exchanges*

✓*Recipe includes Nutrition Facts
and Diabetic Exchanges*

*✓Recipe includes Nutrition Facts
and Diabetic Exchanges*

*✓Recipe includes Nutrition Facts
and Diabetic Exchanges*

*✓Recipe includes Nutrition Facts
and Diabetic Exchanges*

Alphabetical Recipe Index

*✓Recipe includes Nutrition Facts
and Diabetic Exchanges*

✓*Recipe includes Nutrition Facts
and Diabetic Exchanges*